Collaborators for Emancipation

Collaborators for Emancipation

Abraham Lincoln and Owen Lovejoy

WILLIAM F. MOORE AND
JANE ANN MOORE

University of Illinois Press
URBANA, CHICAGO, AND SPRINGFIELD

First Illinois paperback, 2019
© 2014 by the Board of Trustees
of the University of Illinois
All rights reserved
1 2 3 4 5 C P 5 4 3 2 1
∞ This book is printed on acid-free paper.

Library of Congress Control Number: 2014940418
ISBN 978-0-252-03846-4 (hardcover)
ISBN 978-0-252-09634-1 (e-book)
ISBN 978-0-252-08355-6 (paperback)

Contents

Acknowledgments   vii

Lincoln's Words of Remembrance   xi

Introduction   1

PART 1. ATTAINING POLITICAL POWER, 1854–1860

1. Hating the Zeal to Spread Slavery, 1854   11

2. Traversing Uneven Political Ground, 1855   19

3. Standing Together Nobly, 1856   38

4. Disputing the Supreme Court Decision, 1857   51

5. Trusting Those Who Care for the Results, 1858   64

6. Remaining Steadfast to the Right, 1859   78

7. Disenchanting the Nation of Slavery, 1860   90

PART 2. MAINTAINING POLITICAL POWER, 1861

8. Holding Firmly to Their Promises, 1861   107

PART 3. APPLYING POLITICAL POWER, 1862–1864

9. Restoring the Founding Purposes, 1862   125

10. Assuring That the Nation Would Long Endure, 1863   143

11. Binding Up the Nation's Wounds, 1864   154

Appendix   159

Notes   163

Index   189

Acknowledgments

We gratefully knowledge those who prepared the ground, planted the seeds, watered the crop, and cultivated the field now ready to harvest. We begin with those professors who in the 1950s grounded our religious and philosophical thinking: Joseph D'Alfonso of Bates College; Dean Walter Muelder, Paul Johnson, and Dean of the Chapel Howard Thurman of Boston University School of Theology; Richard Niebuhr, Hal Luccock, and Kenneth Underwood of Yale Divinity School; and William O. Brown of Boston University African Studies Program. All these scholars considered love, power, and justice, individual and social, as part of the same fertile field.

In the 1990s, the seeds were planted when we read Edward Magdol's book on Owen Lovejoy and met Dr. Clifton Johnson of the Amistad Research Center. Next we became acquainted with Lincoln scholars, including Michael Burlingame, Rodney Davis, Allen Guelzo, Matthew Pinsker, and Illinois historian Thomas Schwartz, and antislavery and political abolitionist scholars, including Frederick Blue, Merton Dillon, George R. Price, Stacey M. Robertson, Mitchell Snay, James Brewer Stewart, and Hans Trefousse.

Then we encountered and became deeply indebted to two scholars who know how to teach by asking perceptive questions and pointing in new directions. They are the thorough and challenging reviewers of our manuscript, Stewart Winger of Illinois State University at Bloomington and Ed Crowther of Adams State College, Alamosa, Colorado.

Many able and cooperative librarians and archivists located new seeds. Special among them are John Hoffman of the Illinois Historical Survey; Kathryn Harris, director of the Abraham Lincoln Presidential Library, and her staff; Pam Lange of the Bureau County Historical Society; Lee Hampton of the Amistad Research Center; the always helpful librarians at Northern Illinois University in DeKalb; and all the staffs at the historical depositories listed in the notes.

viii   *Acknowledgments*

Some of those who encouraged us to plant the seeds we had discovered were politically invested. The many prophetic pastor-preachers of the civil rights era and our own parishioner, the Honorable Idamae Garrott of Montgomery County, Maryland, gave us experience and insight into campaigning, legislating, and governing as they baptized us in realpolitik. We also were greatly influenced by the Reverend Harry Applewhite, George Haley, and the Reverend Theodore Ledbetter of Washington, D.C.

Friends and acquaintances watered the crop as they graciously listened and creatively responded to the multiple variations of "How was Owen Lovejoy Lincoln's best friend?" Friends include William Furry and the Illinois State Historical Society Symposiums; Thomas Schwartz and the Illinois Historical Preservation Society Conferences; James B. Stewart and the young academicians at annual gatherings of the Society for Historians of the Early American Republic; and those who shared books, articles, and newspaper clippings about Lovejoy and Lincoln.

Descendants of the churches that Owen Lovejoy nurtured in Illinois have shared their commitment. The community of Princeton preserves the Lovejoy Homestead. Ezby Collins has been one of its docents. The Reverend Gordon Grant, former pastor of Hampshire Colony Church, has hosted Lovejoy Society symposia, and the Reverend Mary Gay McKinney, pastor of Open Prairie United Church of Christ, continues Lovejoy's congregation. The Reverend Richard Taylor of the Historical Council of the UCC has clarified the denominational connections.

Our efforts have been sustained by the Lovejoy Society of the Illinois Conference of the UCC, which studies the lives of Elizabeth, Elijah, and Owen Lovejoy. Members of its board of directors have added greatly to our work, especially Marlene Meeter, the Reverend Robert Meissner, and Lorna Vogt. We have also been supported by the children of First Congregational Church, DeKalb, with the help of Barbara Meisenheimer Mitchell. Northern Illinois University English professor Glenn Meeter has read many portions of our manuscripts over the years, leading to their improvement. Other supportive friends and members of the Lovejoy Board include Tim Blickhan, the Reverend Robert and Joyce Dell, the Reverend Joseph Gastiger, Clinton Jesser, Robert and Pat Suchner, and Lolly Voss.

Colleagues and other groups who provided intellectual stimulation were Sarah Cooper, Sarah Criner, the Reverend Mary Gay McKinney, the Reverend Robert Sandman, and the Reverend Bennie Whiten; the Adult Study group at Pilgrim Church, Oak Park; and the DeKalb Writers' Group, led by Dan and Maylan Kenney.

Our family contributors include Jane Ann's brothers, Tony Stoneburner, professor of English at Denison University, Granville, Ohio, and John Stoneburner, professor of religion at Guilford College, Greensboro, North Carolina, and the supportive and patient family of our daughter, Deborah: her husband, Bill, and their children, Kyle and Kaitlin Kent.

Most important, this field would not be ready for harvest without the cultivation by able and disciplined professionals and consultants at the University of Illinois Press. They perceived its potential, weeded out the excesses, and shined enough new light to let the crop grow. We thank insightful editor in chief Laurie Matheson, skilled copyeditor Ellen Goldlust, assistant acquisitions editor Dawn Durante, EDP manager Jennifer Comeau, art director Dustin Hubbart, and catalog and copywriting coordinator Kevin Cunningham.

Executive Mansion, Washington

May 30, 1864

Hon. John H Bryant

My Dear Sir,

Yours of the 14th. Inst. inclosing a card of invitation to a preliminary meeting contemplating the erection of a monument to the memory of Hon. Owen Lovejoy, was duly received. As you anticipate, it will be out of my power to attend. . . .

My personal acquaintance with him commenced only about ten years ago, since when it has been quite intimate, and every step in it has been one of increasing respect and esteem, ending, with his life, in no less than affection on my part. It can be truly said of him that while he was personally ambitious, he bravely endured the obscurity which the unpopularity of his principles imposed, and never accepted official honors, until those honors were ready to admit his principles with him. Throughout my heavy and perplexing responsibilities here to the day of his death, it would scarcely wrong any other to say, he was my most generous friend. Let him have the marble monument, along with the well assured and more enduring one in the hearts of those who love liberty, unselfishly, for all men.

Yours truly

A. Lincoln

Bureau County Republican, June 9, 1864

Introduction

In human history, it is the relation that matters. Owen Lovejoy and Abraham Lincoln were remarkable men with a remarkable relationship. Lincoln confirmed that "every step in it has been one of increasing respect and esteem." Their mutual trust grew as they saw things as they were while holding a radical vision of what could be. This approach provided them the pragmatic ability to better know what to do and how to do it. Collaborating, they made a major contribution to moving the nation toward emancipation. For more than five decades, historians Edward Magdol, Hans Trefousse, Frederick Blue, Richard Carwardine, Matthew Pinsker, and Eric Foner have been keeping alive the study of the positive relation between Lincoln and Radical Republicans. This book follows their leads, fills in some gaps, and provides a new perspective on the role of Lincoln and the radicals in the process of ending slavery. It proposes the existence of an inherent relation between radical ends and pragmatic means in the realm of governance. In this context, the term *radical* indicates a firm moral commitment to the goal of ending slavery, while the term *pragmatic* indicates the flexible, realistic means applied to achieve that goal. Lincoln was not only a pragmatist but also a radical, while Lovejoy was not only a radical but also a pragmatist.

An Unlikely Friendship

Abraham Lincoln was a leader of a fading Whig Party. On October 4, 1854, he shunned an invitation from Owen Lovejoy to attend a convention to form a Republican Party in Illinois. Convinced that abolitionists complicated the question of slavery, Lincoln was leery of Lovejoy's reputation as a fanatical abolitionist. However, four months later, Lincoln became aware that Lovejoy was a leader in

Illinois's rising religious and political antislavery movement. Approximately ten years later, Lincoln attested that Lovejoy was a bosom friend whom the president regarded with affection and appreciation.[1] The differences they overcame were huge; when they met, few thought they ever could be friends.

By the time they met at the Springfield State Fair in October 1854, Lovejoy had been a successful Congregational minister in Princeton, Illinois, for seventeen years. He had a spontaneous temperament, was dedicated to the higher law of God, and served as a captain on the Underground Railroad, defying the nation's fugitive slave laws. He had run unsuccessfully for Congress with the Liberty Party in 1846 and with the Free Soil Party in 1848. He had helped form the Illinois State Liberty Party in 1842 and the Free Democratic Party in 1852. Committed primarily to the Declaration of Independence and the Bible, with respect for the Constitution, he had helped form a vibrant antislavery organization. He would be elected to the Illinois General Assembly later in 1854 and to the U.S. Congress in 1856. For seven years, he would serve as the leading antislavery voice in the U.S. House of Representatives.

Lincoln had been a successful Whig lawyer for twenty years in the Springfield area. He had served in the General Assembly from 1834 to 1842. He had a cautious temperament and was dedicated to the rule of law; he abhorred abolitionists' defiance of the fugitive slave laws. His temperament and his logical mind made him skeptical of biblical miracles and inconsistencies, yet the Bible reinforced his compassionate sympathies. Committed primarily to the Constitution, the Declaration of Independence, and the Bible, he was a Whig political organizer and leader. Elected to the U.S. Congress in 1846, he served one term. He returned to an expanded law practice and continued his interest in politics. In 1860, he would become the sixteenth president of the United States.

Different as they were in 1854, they shared some experiences. Lovejoy evidenced a comprehensive mind and a reputation for saying what he meant and doing what he said. He was beloved by his congregation and respected in the community. He had experienced the senseless deaths of his brother, Daniel, by alcohol; his father, Daniel, by suicide; and his brother, Elijah, at the hands of an angry pro-slavery mob in Alton, Illinois. Lincoln was an honest lawyer with integrity. He gained much respect from both the public and his associates during his time on the Eighth Judicial Circuit. He had experienced the senseless deaths of his mother after she drank milk from cows that had grazed on poisonous plants, of his sister during childbirth, of his boyhood chum by suicide, and of his dear friend, Ann Rutledge.

Both Lincoln and Lovejoy were geniuses in the sense that they had high intellectual capacity as well as the power to influence others. Lovejoy's tribute to Lincoln applied equally well to Lovejoy himself: "Come what will, unseduced by ambition and unterrified by power, he will remain loyal to the principles of

Introduction 3

the Republican Party."[2] Each appreciated that the other was not governed by self-interest or by the self-deceiving forces of domination. Historian Carl Sandburg appreciated their journey together, writing in 1927 that "amid inscrutable political labyrinths," they would come to "understand and cling to each other."[3]

Lincoln and the Radicals

Since the 1941 publication by T. Harry Williams of *Lincoln and the Radicals*, the debate among historians on who did more to effectively free the slaves has waxed and waned. Were the radicals heroes or villains? Was Lincoln the emancipator or the puppet? Since the end of World War II, the argument has been formulated in several basic configurations.

Williams saw the radicals as effective heroes and Lincoln the ineffective puppet, a position that has had enduring influence: Williams's book has been reprinted four times, most recently in 2005.[4] Williams framed the issue in a confrontational manner, arguing that Radical Republicans—with the "revolutionary ardor" of the Jacobins, the "fanaticism that was inherent in the abolitionists," and "hasty plans to bring about immediate abolition"—constantly contested a weak and inexperienced president who supported the sketchy conservative approach of "gradual extinction of slavery, compensated emancipation, and colonization of Negroes."[5] Williams claimed that the radicals scorned Lincoln because he had no appreciation of moral theory and considered them true revolutionaries and that "Lincoln, the supreme American Pragmatist, [was] their main obstacle."[6]

Williams described Lovejoy as belonging to the radical faith, a zealous, fiery, Calvinist minister in politics who hated slavery because his brother had been murdered by a pro-slavery mob. Williams began his book by using Lovejoy as the symbol of the radical cause, following the well-known image in the crisis of 1862 of Lincoln in the Republican political buggy led by the radical steed, with a hobbling conservative horse tied behind, slowing down progress.[7] In contrast, this volume sees Lovejoy as placing Lincoln in the driver's seat, warning the radicals not to pull too fast downhill and throw him out of the buggy.[8]

In 1945, James G. Randall began publishing his four volumes of *Lincoln the President*.[9] His work established the revisionist theory that Lincoln and the radicals were part of the social and political leadership that blundered into an unnecessary civil war, and this approach subsequently became the standard interpretation. Lincoln was seen as a conservative man hampered as much by the radicals in his own party as by the Democratic fire-eaters, and the two factions were depicted as equally responsible for causing the war. Such a framework does not provide any reason to explore the positive role of the radical Owen Lovejoy.

Another early vibrant theory with lingering influence came from Charles and Mary Beard's *The Rise of American Civilization* (1927).[10] They "tended to see economic interests as the motor of history" and moral and religious concerns regarding slavery as primarily a veil for material interests.[11] According to Merton Dillon, when it came to abolitionism, the Beards' "interpretative genius faltered."[12] Such an analysis reduces Lincoln and the radicals to irrelevancy.

Kenneth M. Stampp's *And the War Came: The North and the Secession Crisis, 1860–1861* (1950) was a significant transitional work.[13] It rejected the revisionist argument that extremists on both sides caused the war and affirmed that the cooperation of Lincoln and the radicals to foil the attempts for compromise was significant but claimed that economic factors were more crucial. Stampp presented an analysis of the political factors with concern for slavery as a causal issue.

With the celebration of the sesquicentennial of Lincoln's birth, the centennial of the Emancipation Proclamation, and the rise of the civil rights movement, new ways of interpreting racial freedom became prominent. First published in 1947, John Hope Franklin's *From Slavery to Freedom* recognized that during the Civil War years, African Americans "had moved significantly in the direction of freedom," though that freedom "had not been achieved."[14] Franklin described the major role that black troops and slave resistance played in helping the North win the war, and his account spawned a surge in the production of black history, which accompanied and affected the growth of the civil rights movement.

White historians subsequently recognized that slavery was the essential moral issue of the 1860 Republican victory. They researched the rise of the Republican Party and the influence of abolitionist and radical commitments to equality. Edward Magdol's political biography, *Owen Lovejoy: Abolitionist in Congress* (1967) led the way, claiming that the seldom-mentioned "friendship between the radical abolitionist and the former Whig" called into question the thesis that Lincoln had faced off against the radicals in the Civil War Congress.[15]

Other significant books of this period relating to the role of radical antislavery leadership included James M. McPherson's *Struggle for Equality: Abolitionists and the Negro in the Civil War and Reconstruction* (1964), Hans Trefousse's *Radical Republicans: Lincoln's Vanguard for Social Justice* (1969), Eric Foner's *Free Soil, Free Labor, Free Men: The Ideology of the Republican Party before the Civil War* (1970), Frederick Blue's *The Free Soilers: Third Party Politics, 1848–54* (1973), and James Brewer Stewart's *Holy Warriors: The Abolitionists and American Slavery* (1976).[16]

With the backlash against President Lyndon Johnson's signing of the Voting Rights Act in 1965 and the resurgence of the Republican Party in the late 1960s came a revision of the revisionists. The radicals were still considered blunderers, impetuously getting in the way of practical governance, but Lincoln was seen as a pragmatic, prudent, great leader. Seasoned scholarly researchers made their contributions. Mark Neely's *The Last Best Hope of Earth: Abraham Lincoln and the Promise of America* (1993) revised the revisionism more boldly by emphasizing Lincoln's radical qualities. Neely saw "Lincoln's political ambitions yoked to a fierce nationalism and a keen sense of moral purpose—the preservation of the Union and the demise of slavery."[17] But he did not mention the radicals.

Allen C. Guelzo's *Abraham Lincoln: Redeemer President* (1999) highlighted Lincoln's intellectual grasp of the Enlightenment and his prudent wisdom as a Whig leader. However, he took a step beyond Neely's neglect of the radicals by deriding them as problematic at best. Guelzo appreciated Lincoln as having redeemed the nation from the guilt of slavery but could not accept that he could have done so without being a confessing Christian. Guelzo claimed that Lincoln's religious thoughts provided him only "the lonely murmur of abandonment, deathlike in the leafless trees."[18] In contrast, this volume sees Lincoln as a responsible man faithfully negotiating the tensions of life without yielding to the absolutes of finite minds. His religious thoughts provided him a walk with a friend through any woods, enabling him to perceive both the trees and the forest.

The magnum opus of this period came from Randall's most distinguished student, Harvard professor of history David Herbert Donald, whose *Lincoln* (1995) deserved the widespread acclaim it received for a time. Donald revised the revisionist perception of Lincoln as a blunderer, agreeing with many other scholars that Lincoln was "a master of ambiguity and expediency." In one sense, Donald observed the radical aspect of Lincoln as a "great moral leader, inflexibly opposed to slavery and absolutely committed to preserving the Union." And in another sense, Donald questioned Lincoln's pragmatic ability by asserting the "essential passivity of his nature."[19]

Conversely, Donald joined the revisionist chorus in believing that Lincoln saw a basic "incompatibility between himself and" the radicals and that the radicals were irrelevant.[20] Within a decade, this consensus was slowly fading, though Donald tenaciously resisted recognizing the radicals' significance in *"We Are Lincoln Men": Abraham Lincoln and His Friends* (2003). Donald mentioned thirteen friends, describing six in detail, but did not even acknowledge the radical Lovejoy as a close associate of the president.[21]

With the coming of the bicentennial of Lincoln's birth and the sesquicentennial of the Emancipation Proclamation and an increasing awareness of the concentration of power and wealth in a few, an outpouring of cogent books examined the moral dimensions of Lincoln and the radicals. Matthew Pinsker saw "Guelzo's dissection of Lincoln's fatalism" in *Abraham Lincoln: Redeemer President* as sparking much discussion and Stewart Winger's *Lincoln, Religion, and Romantic Cultural Politics* (2002) as "recognizing Lincoln as a nineteenth-century moralist with religious sensibilities."[22] Lincoln differed from the evangelicals in using romantic religious language to make sense of and change a mixed-up world.[23] Winger claimed that Lincoln's appreciation of "the bold strokes of the poet's pen" and "his underlying piety" allowed him "to reconstruct a usable form of Christianity."[24] Pinsker saw William Lee Miller's *Lincoln's Virtues: An Ethical Biography* (2002) as recognizing Lincoln as "a natural-born moral statesman who reject[ed] perfectionism and fatalism from his earliest days."[25] Miller went further by seeing Lincoln's later years as a struggle between Max Weber's "ethic of unconditional absolutes" and an "ethic of calculating responsibility."[26] Richard J. Carwardine's *Lincoln* claimed that his "effective channeling of the forces of mainstream Protestant orthodoxy" "provided the foundation for his greatest political achievements as president."[27]

The historians' long debate about whether the prudent Lincoln was more effective than the radical members of Congress has been revived in the twenty-first century, reflecting an essential conflict regarding the relative efficacies of pragmatically maintaining and conserving the best of governance and radically reforming and improving governance to higher standards. The two leading proponents in the debate are Guelzo and Foner.

In *Lincoln's Emancipation Proclamation: The End of Slavery in America* (2004), Guelzo claimed that Lincoln distanced himself from the radicals, singing the praises of Lincoln's "prudential politics."[28] In contrast, Foner's *The Fiery Trial: Abraham Lincoln and American Slavery* (2010) distanced Lincoln from the radicals but sang the latter's praises. In Foner's view, although Lincoln was neither an abolitionist nor a radical Republican, he "came to occupy positions first staked out by them."[29] Both authors ignored the extent of the political agreement and cooperation between Lincoln and the radicals in obtaining political power in Illinois, in maintaining political power by refusing to compromise with southerners in Congress during the winter of 1860–61, and in applying legislative and political power during the Civil War period.

Foner recognized that the Illinois Republican Party "needed to harness the intense commitment that Lovejoy's supporters would bring to the [1856] campaign" and stated that he was particularly interested "in Lincoln's complex relationship with abolitionists."[30] Yet he did not mention their continuous cooperation over the next eight years, especially during the Thirty-Seventh Congress. And Guelzo claimed that in 1856, Lincoln "was anxious to keep Owen Lovejoy and the abolitionists out of the Republican vanguard."[31]

There are some points on which Guelzo and Foner agreed, however. According to Guelzo, "prudence demanded that [Lincoln] balance the integrity of *ends* (the elimination of slavery) with the integrity of *means* (his oath to uphold the Constitution)."[32] Likewise, Foner wrote, "Much of Lincoln's career can fruitfully be seen as a search for a reconciliation of means and ends."[33] Describing how they brought a balance between legal constitutional means and moral authoritative ends is common ground for understanding Lincoln and the radicals.

But there were many more points of difference. Guelzo insisted on Lincoln's lifelong hatred of slavery and his desire to do something about it.[34] Guelzo contended that from the time of Lincoln's election to the presidency, he believed that his administration would end slavery and that a good deal of the radicals' failure and frustration "was vented upon Lincoln."[35] Moreover, Guelzo argued that the war led Lincoln to shift his religious determinism, coming to believe that Providence intervenes in history but does so in mysterious ways.[36] Yet Guelzo remained adamant that Lincoln's moral commitment to ending slavery did not change or waver.

Foner claimed the opposite: "The hallmark of Lincoln's greatness was his capacity for growth."[37] Neither Lincoln nor anyone else had any "real idea how to rid the United States of slavery," but the Radicals took the lead in the effort, and "Lincoln came to occupy positions first staked out by abolitionists and Radical Republicans."[38] For Foner, Lincoln "had more in common with the deism of the Enlightenment," believing in a divine Creator who does not intervene in history.[39]

Other historians have championed the roles of other constituencies in ending slavery in America, widening the context beyond the radicals-versus-Lincoln debate. Garrisonian immediate abolitionists used only moral suasion in seeking to create the righteous Kingdom of God on earth. Free and fugitive blacks in the North, resistant blacks in the South, and the many blacks who served in the military made their voices heard through Frederick Douglass. Union soldiers not only fought but came to accept the goal of freeing the enslaved, a perspective embodied in the words and deeds of General Ulysses S. Grant. All of these groups had an impact, but we concentrate here on the relative influence of Lincoln and the political radicals in the process of emancipation.

Our Interpretative Perspective

The second decade of the twenty-first century brought a catastrophic worldwide fiscal crisis that had been brewing for years. With it came a political struggle between negotiating practical regulations and demanding a radical commitment to ideology. This context has given rise to a different framework for interpreting Lincoln and Lovejoy. The question is not whether radicalism or pragmatism is better; rather, the question is how both viewpoints interact in a person and an organization. Both Lincoln and Lovejoy exemplify that kind of collaboration, which has been dramatically presented in Tony Kushner's script for Steven Spielberg's *Lincoln*. The filmmakers chose to include an authentic quotation from their Thaddeus Stevens character about the passage of the Thirteenth Amendment—"The greatest measure of the nineteenth century was passed by corruption, aided and abetted by the purest man in America."[40] In governance, purity and practicality go together.

8 *Introduction*

This book revives Magdol's key thesis that mutual trust and respect enabled Lincoln and Lovejoy to influence and collaborate with each other to make significant contributions for emancipation.[41] It elaborates the nature of their collaboration in the context of the ongoing debate over Lincoln and the radicals, proposing that Lincoln was a radical pragmatist and Lovejoy was a pragmatic radical. They took risks to develop a shared vision that helped mold (practical) public opinion to accept the (radical) objective of freeing the slaves and shrewdly attained (practical) political power and appropriated it for their (radical) goal.

This book assumes that history relates the past to the future in a present that depends on the history of the interpreters. Our history has brought us to the perspective that the trusting relationship between Lincoln and Lovejoy enabled them to maintain their radical commitment while shifting their tactics when events had made previous approaches obsolete. The trust between the two men was grounded in the clear evidence of their integrity and wisdom and persisted despite the inconclusive evidence regarding the success of their differing tactics. Their mutual trust was strengthened by a realistic perception of the untrustworthy—those governed more by self-interest, self-deception, and domination. What mattered was their gradual, cautious discerning and communicating with the public about who could be trusted and who could not be trusted.

The details of their collaborative relationship can be gleaned from their writings and actions, public and private, as well as their backgrounds and personal qualities. At key moments, the prudent Lincoln performed the role of radical, and the radical Lovejoy shrewdly and practically performed the role of a pragmatist. Spielberg's film has affirmed that both roles were necessary for success, but *Lincoln* merely depicted Act 4 of the drama. Here, we present the first three acts, all of them just as dramatic and decisive. From 1856 to 1860, Lincoln and Lovejoy gained political power by holding together divergent factions that developed a winning political coalition in Illinois. During the chaotic and critical 1860–61 interregnum between Lincoln's election and his inauguration, they maintained power by using heavy political pressure to hold together the divergent wings of the Republican Party. From 1861 to 1864, they applied political power to pull together the divergent elements of Congress to win passage of legislation preparing for the freedom of the enslaved. As they came to rely on and sustain each other while making these essential contributions, they indeed became "Collaborators for Emancipation."

PART 1

Attaining Political Power, 1854–1860

1 Hating the Zeal to Spread Slavery, 1854

> "This . . . *real* zeal for the spread of slavery, I cannot but hate. I hate it because of the monstrous injustice of slavery itself. I hate it because it deprives our republican example of its just influence in the world."
>
> —Abraham Lincoln, Speech at Springfield, October 16, 1854

Springfield lawyer Abraham Lincoln and Princeton pastor Owen Lovejoy met for the first time on a muddy afternoon at the Springfield State Fair on October 4, 1854.[1] The speeches of the day were moved inside to the stately Hall of Representatives in the newly constructed State Capitol. At that time, both Lincoln and Lovejoy were fuming over a new federal law that Illinois Democratic senator Stephen A. Douglas had championed through Congress during the preceding May, the Kansas-Nebraska Act. In 1820, after protracted and contentious negotiations, Missouri had been allowed to enter the Union as a slave state on condition that all territories in the Louisiana Purchase north of the Missouri's southern border would be considered free. This compromise had been respected for thirty-four years but was repealed in conjunction with the Kansas-Nebraska Act, allowing slavery to spread into those territories.

Lincoln wanted the Whigs and Lovejoy wanted the emerging Republican Party to lead the "fusion" movement uniting all those opposed to Douglas's Kansas-Nebraska Act and advocating the restoration of the Missouri Compromise. Both men were working to unite various political elements into a new organization that would defeat the pro-slavery Democratic Party's domination of Illinois politics since 1818. Since July, they had been campaigning for seats in the Illinois House of Representatives.

In 1850, after the end of his only term in Congress, Lincoln had returned to Springfield to resume his law career, but the Kansas-Nebraska Act reenergized his political instincts. According to Eric Foner, "Virtually every major speech of Lincoln's between 1854 and 1860 originated as a response to some action or statement by Douglas."[2] Lincoln's speech at the State Fair in Springfield on October 4, 1854, is a prime example.

When Douglas returned to Illinois after the act's passage, he was excoriated and harangued. Speaking at the State Fair on October 3, he defended himself against the charges that he had betrayed a long-standing agreement among the American people. The next day, the forty-five-year-old Lincoln strode into the Hall of Representatives, tall and lanky, and earnestly told the audience, "This . . . real zeal for the spread of slavery, I cannot but hate."[3]

The forty-three-year-old Lovejoy was among those in attendance, with his thatch of black hair framing his forehead and his athletic body no doubt sitting upright as he identified with Lincoln's emotion and conviction. After the murder of his brother, Elijah, an abolitionist newspaperman, by a pro-slavery mob, Owen Lovejoy had not sought revenge on the four men who pulled the triggers but instead "swore by the everlasting God eternal hostility to African slavery."[4]

Lincoln had opened his speech with an emphatic declaration about the conditions under which the opposition to the Douglas Democrats could unite. "I wish to MAKE and to KEEP the distinction between the existing institution [of slavery], and the EXTENSION of it, so broad, and so clear, that no honest man can misunderstand me, and no dishonest one, successfully misrepresent me."[5] He was advocating not an end to slavery but an end to its spread. Lovejoy had held that political position since 1842, but Lincoln initially did not fully comprehend and accept the significance of Lovejoy's commitment to nonextension.

The primary purpose of Lincoln's speech was to reach out to northern and southern Whigs. He hoped to make the Whig Party the instrument for fusing various political factions against Douglas. He also made it clear that he had "no prejudice against the Southern people. They are just what we would be in their situation. If slavery did not now exist amongst them, they would not introduce it."[6] Then, speaking from his experience as a southerner, he publicly admitted that he did not know what to do to end slavery: "When southern people tell us they are no more responsible for the origin of slavery than we; I acknowledge the fact. . . . I surely would not blame them for not doing what I should not know how to do myself. If all earthly power were given me, I should not know what to do, as to the existing institution."[7]

He explained both his and the Southern Whigs' position on slavery, declaring, "We can not, then make [African Americans] equals," and thereby distinguishing himself from the Garrisonian abolitionists who advocated full equality. But he continued, "It does seem to me that systems of gradual emancipation might be adopted,"[8] demonstrating some agreement with the political abolitionists. Inviting the South to join him in restoring the Missouri Compromise, he declared his convictions of prudence while presenting a unifying vision: "We thereby restore the national faith, the national confidence, the national feeling of brotherhood, we therefore reinstate the spirit of concession and compromise—that spirit which has never failed us in the past perils, and may be safely trusted for all the future."[9]

Lincoln appealed to the human compassion in all peoples. "The great majority, south as well as north, have human sympathies, of which they can no more divest themselves than they can of their sensibilities to physical pain. These sympathies in the bosoms of the southern people manifest in many ways their sense of the wrong of slavery, and their consciousness that, after all, there is humanity in the Negro."[10] This assurance of the humanity of southern citizens was based in his radical belief in the "better angels of our nature," to which he appealed persistently.[11] He also sought to stir the sympathies of northerners when he warned the South of the dangers ahead: "Let no one be deceived. The spirit of seventy-six and the spirit of Nebraska are utter antagonisms; and the former is being rapidly displaced by the latter."[12] In so doing, he exhibited his understanding that self-deception is a root problem in all people. His most risky statement was to give lukewarm support to the "abolitionists." He "good humoredly" called his Whig friends rather silly for refusing to advocate restoring the Missouri Compromise line just because the abolitionists did the same.[13]

After the speech, Lovejoy and antislavery political organizer Ichabod Codding invited Lincoln to attend a meeting the next day for citizens opposed to "the further extension and consolidation of the Slave Power."[14] Lincoln politely declined, finding necessary business outside the county. Lincoln clearly was not interested in a permanent alliance led by abolitionists at this time, preferring to rejuvenate the Whig Party as the leader of the fusion process.[15]

The Beginning of the Republican Party in Illinois

Lovejoy helped to organize the first meeting of the statewide Illinois Republican Party. Alvan Bovay had led a February 28, 1854, meeting in Ripon, Wisconsin, at which attendees discussed forming a political party based on the principle of nonextension of slavery. On May 28, 1854, a day after the passage of the Kansas-Nebraska Act, Congressman Israel Washburn of Maine called a meeting of members of Congress to respond to the crisis and suggested the name *Republican* for the group. By the following October, parties had been organized in five midwestern and four eastern states.[16]

On the evening of Lincoln's speech, ten antislavery leaders from different Illinois counties met in the dingy candlelit office of abolitionist Erastus Wright to draft resolutions to be presented the next day at the Republican Convention.[17] Lincoln was not in attendance, possibly because he had had a significant legal misunderstanding with Wright that had caused some tension.[18]

The next day, the men who had met in Wright's office presented a more moderate platform to the convention than the ones passed previously at Republican congressional district conventions in the northern Illinois cities of Rockford and Aurora and the central Illinois city of Bloomington. The resolutions reflected conciliatory language and emphasized the nonextension of slavery. They called not for the repeal of the Fugitive Slave Act but for a key modification. They bore the imprint of the representatives from Morgan and Adams Counties in the central part of the state. The convention was intended to attract moderate Whigs such as Lincoln as well as Democrats such as Congressman Lyman Trumbull from Alton, who had spoken out against Douglas's act.[19]

The proposed platform for the new party resolved to "prohibit and preclude the extension, establishment and perpetuation of human slavery in any and every Territory of the United States." According to the organizers, "the Nebraska Bill was an attempt totally to reverse" that doctrine by allowing slavery to now expand into the Nebraska Territory.[20] This platform of nonextension was the position taken by the Liberty Party, which had been organized in 1840 in Upper New York State by Myron Holly and Alvan Stewart to promote the end of slavery through political and constitutional means. Lovejoy had been active in that movement since its inception, helping to form the first Liberty Party organization in the Midwest at a July 4, 1840, meeting in Princeton.[21] Whereas the Liberty Party called for a repeal of the fugitive slave laws, the Republican Springfield platform did not. However, it advocated the legal right for African Americans to testify on their own behalf on the grounds that "trial by jury and the writ of habeas corpus [are] safeguards of personal liberty so necessary . . . that no citizens of other States can fairly ask us to consent to their abrogation."[22]

The Republicans also reached out to southern citizens, saying, "We recognize no antagonism of national interests between us and the citizens of Southern States. . . . [W]e recognize them as kindred and brethren of the same national family." But, the platform concluded, "We heartily approve the course of freemen of Connecticut, Vermont, Iowa, Ohio, Indiana, Wisconsin, New York, Michigan, and Maine, postponing or disregarding their minor differences of opinion or preferences, on acting together cordially and trustingly in the sacred cause of freedom, of free labor, and free soil."[23]

Paul Selby, the editor of the *Morgan Journal* and an opponent of the Kansas-Nebraska Act, reported years later, "The conservative character of the platform adopted is a conclusive rebuttal to the charge of fanaticism. This went no farther than a distinct declaration of opposition to the extension of slavery in free territory, which became the essence of Republicanism two years later."[24] Selby believed "that Lincoln could easily have agreed with these resolutions."[25] They resembled Lincoln's core statements that he stood with the abolitionists in advocating the restoration of the Missouri Compromise but broke from them when they called for the repeal of fugitive slave laws. Lincoln, too, bore no antagonism toward the citizens of the South. However, Illinois Whig and Democratic newspapers were suspicious of the growing threat of the rise of a Republican Party, not only discouraging readers and supporters from participat-

Hating the Zeal to Spread Slavery

ing but also refusing to allow their presses to be used to print flyers supporting the Republican effort.[26]

Lincoln's failure to participate in the 1854 Republican Convention did not deter Lovejoy from reaching out again to include him. Selby had "a distinct recollection that Owen Lovejoy, *in emphatic terms*, vouched for [Lincoln's] fidelity to the principles enunciated in our platform."[27] This statement implies that Lovejoy probably had information about Lincoln's background from others, including leading antislavery congressman Joshua Giddings, who had resided in the same Washington boardinghouse as Lincoln did in 1849.

After the convention, both progress for the fusion movement and Lincoln's participation were delayed by newspapers' distortions of the substance of the meeting. The Whig *Illinois State Journal* underestimated the number of participants and claimed that since Lincoln had refused to attend, other responsible Whigs had also stayed away, leaving the meeting to disgruntled and discredited abolitionists from northern Illinois.[28] The Democratic *Illinois State Register* was even more caustic, declaring, "Ichabod [Codding] raved, and Lovejoy swelled."[29] On October 8, the paper substituted the "radical" platform of the Kane County Convention held in Aurora on August 19, 1854, for the more moderate one adopted by the Republican Springfield Convention.[30] The *Register* also sought to embarrass Lincoln by exaggerating his speech in the Hall of Representatives, which the paper described as "a glorious abolition speech, and worthy of Ichabod himself."[31] Lincoln had been worried about precisely this sort of misrepresentation, which he feared would alienate him from his conservative Whig and Know-Nothing friends.[32] As Lovejoy had already recognized, Lincoln's abilities and his political network were essential for the cause in the long run: "Only Lincoln could hold this rag-tag coalition together."[33]

Victor B. Howard has noted that "early historians did not present an accurate account of the origin of the Republican party in Illinois."[34] Writing in 1922, Arthur C. Cole, for example, claimed that after 1854, "party loyalty deterred all except discredited 'abolitionists' from participating in the movement," leading to "the prompt death of this 'republican' state organization."[35] Similarly, according to Don E. Fehrenbacher, "In any case, this abortive 'Republican' movement of 1854 had no connection with the party organized two years later."[36] Echoed William E. Gienapp, Lincoln's refusal to join the Republicans in 1854 "symbolized the failure of the fusion movement to enlist the support of downstate Whigs, a development that doomed it to ineffectiveness."[37] Relying on both Fehrenbacher and Gienapp, David H. Donald contended that "the abolitionist Republican party of Codding and Lovejoy was too extreme to attract a wide following"; Lincoln, however, "was ready to take the lead."[38] Allen C. Guelzo, too, followed suit, declaring that Lovejoy and Codding had an "anti-slavery passion" that "made them too hot for either Whigs or Democrats to handle."[39]

Foner grasped that by 1856, the new party "needed to harness the intense commitment that Lovejoy's supporters would bring to the campaign."[40] Yet it is not clear that even Foner recognized the growing influence of the Illinois antislavery political parties led by Codding; Zebina Eastman, editor of the *Free West*; and Lovejoy. Foner and other historians also neglected to recognize that the well-organized Illinois Free Democratic Party formed the three northern congressional districts of the early Republican conventions in the spring and summer of 1854, leading antislavery Republicans to account for a quarter of the Illinois General Assembly in 1855.

All of these historians also failed to note the assets claimed by these Illinois radicals in 1855 and 1856—their ongoing ad hoc steering committee in Chicago; their strong religious basis; their ability to negotiate as a swing bloc of votes; their command of a daily statewide newspaper, the *Chicago Tribune*; and their full appreciation of Lincoln's strengths. The pragmatic in Lincoln knew well enough not to ignore them; the radical in Lincoln could tolerate and appreciate some of their radical tactics and slowly came to accept and embrace them by 1862.[41]

Lincoln had taken a radical step toward Lovejoy by chiding his conservative Whig friends not to be afraid to stand with antislavery leaders when they were right. It was now Lovejoy's turn to demonstrate his pragmatism, shrewdness, and political effectiveness.

Lovejoy and Lincoln Elected

On November 7, 1854, both Lincoln and Lovejoy were elected to the Illinois House of Representatives. Whigs had suffered enough election losses nationally to be declared dead as an effective party. The Democratic Party in Illinois had lost the majority of its congressional seats as well as the majority in the state legislature for the first time since statehood in 1818. Opponents of the Kansas-Nebraska Act won majorities in both the Senate and House of Representatives. And twenty-six of the one hundred members of the legislature officially listed themselves as Republicans, though not all of them were active in the emerging party.[42]

Delighted, Lovejoy, a Republican, immediately wrote to his political mentor, Giddings, the leading antislavery member of Congress, who had campaigned in Illinois on behalf of the anti-Nebraska candidates.[43] Lovejoy recognized that Giddings's skill and status had made a difference in the campaign, good-naturedly telling his friend, "By the way I heard of at least one vote you made for me at Henry in Marshall County." More seriously, Lovejoy found the victory satisfying in light of the fact that he had been "cursed & abused & vilified for a long series of years. I was drawn into politics on the antislavery principle apparently from the necessity of the case, & in consequence brought down upon me a great deal of wrath."[44]

Lovejoy soon realized that he would be a leading voice in the new state legislature. He was among a significant minority who were learning the practical advantages of being a swing bloc on critical votes, such as a bill for public education that had previously failed and the selection of the next U.S. senator.

Lincoln, however, was elected as a Whig. He and his wife, Mary Todd Lincoln, "plotted strategy" for him to become the U.S. senator by filling several notebooks "with the name and the anticipated partisan position of each legislator."[45] He set to work writing letters to friends and acquaintances indicating his interest in the position and asking for their support.

On November 27, Lincoln turned down Codding's invitation to join the Illinois Republican Central Committee. Over the preceding year, Codding had made ninety-four speeches across the state in support of a unified opposition to the Kansas-Nebraska Act, making him the leader in laying the foundation for the emerging Republican Party.[46] Lincoln began his letter with the rather radical assertion that his opposition to "the principle of slavery [was] strong as that of any member of the Republican Party." But he was perplexed that he had been asked to serve on the committee because he believed that the extent to which he felt "authorized to carry that opposition, practically, was not at all satisfactory to that party." He then shrewdly pondered whether the leading Republican men misunderstood him or whether he misunderstood them. Lincoln appears to have been misled by the *Register*'s false report that the convention had passed a resolution asking for the repeal of the Fugitive Slave Law. When Lincoln learned of the falsehoods and inaccuracies three years later, he was furious and unforgiving. Charles Lanphier, editor of the *Register*, maintained for years that Lincoln's charges of intentional falsehood were an "unwarranted public defamation" of character.[47]

Lincoln also declined to join the Republicans at that point because he prudently recognized that this was a confusing transitional period in which to take a position. He was not a supporter of the secretive and strongly anti-immigrant Know-Nothings, but openly stating that position would alienate many of the close friends who had encouraged him to run for the state legislature, including Simeon Francis, editor of the *Illinois State Journal*. But Lincoln was unsure about whether he was still a Whig.[48] He had been conciliatory to the southern citizens, recognizing their basic humanity, and he had vague hopes that the national Whig Party could be reenergized on the moral grounds of the Missouri Compromise, devised by his political idol, Henry Clay. Though he had taken a risk in reaching out to ask the antislavery Republicans to join his cause, he was completely unwilling to be part of their organization, with its odium of abolitionism. Lincoln would wait to make his next move.

For his part, Lovejoy was convinced that Lincoln's full participation in the antislavery cause was necessary for political victory. He understood the reasons for Lincoln's timidity, a reluctance based in part on the fanatical labels placed on Lovejoy by his opponents. Lovejoy waited for opportunities in the Illinois House of Representatives to make his views clear to Lincoln. Lovejoy consulted with his Chicago and General Assembly colleagues to devise a plan to win Lincoln's respect while still maintaining their principles.

2 Traversing Uneven Political Ground, 1855

"We could hitch our short bob sleds to suit the inequalities of the political surface."
—Owen Lovejoy

In the winter of 1855, the Democrats, though the largest minority party, were unable to negotiate a deal to maintain control of the Illinois General Assembly, leaving a power vacuum. The work of Ichabod Codding, Zebina Eastman, and Owen Lovejoy in creating a fusion of the factions opposed to the Kansas-Nebraska Act created a storm of political maneuvering. As the Democrats floundered, the Whigs ebbed, and the antislavery Republicans rose, Abraham Lincoln and Owen Lovejoy found a new wave that within eighteen months would push them together into the future.

Over the preceding seventeen years, both men had built up considerable political constituencies. Lincoln did so mainly in central Illinois, around Springfield, traveling the Eighth Judicial Circuit with fellow lawyers and judges, winning cases and friends with his logical mind. Lovejoy did so mainly in northern Illinois, from as far away as Chicago to the counties around his parish in Princeton, helping his associates in the Congregational tradition establish antislavery congregations and seeking political power as a congressional candidate to further his antislavery cause.[1]

Lincoln's Political Grounding

Since the beginning of his political career, Lincoln had sought to be worthy of respect and admiration. During his first campaign for political office in 1832, he stated, "Every man is said to have his peculiar ambition. Whether it be true or not, I can say for one that I have no other so great as that of being truly esteemed of my fellow men, by rendering myself worthy of their esteem."[2] He lost, but he had clearly won the high regard of his neighbors, receiving 277 out of 300 votes in New Salem, where he had lived for only a year.[3]

20   CHAPTER 2

In 1834, he ran again for the legislature. Since the top four candidates would be elected, some Democrats suggested a deal: they would withdraw two candidates against him if he would not support their chief rival, incumbent member of the legislature John T. Stuart. In what would become a typically shrewd maneuver, Lincoln neither rejected nor accepted the deal. Instead, he waited and consulted with Stuart. Stuart, confident of his own election, suggested that Lincoln accept it, for it could help him get elected. Lincoln garnered the most votes, another Whig took second, a Democrat finished third, and Stuart won the final seat.[4]

In the 1842 congressional campaign, Lincoln again demonstrated his political cleverness, ambition, and patience. Stuart; a close legal associate of Lincoln's, Jacksonville lawyer John J. Hardin; and Lincoln all wanted to run for Congress in the Seventh Congressional District, the state's only Whig district. Lincoln, like Lovejoy, believed that local organization was essential for political victory and had worked extensively to build up Whig county nominating conventions that advised their representatives whom they should vote for in congressional district nominating conventions.[5]

Nevertheless, Lincoln lost the nomination to Hardin. However, he seized a critical moment and negotiated an agreement in which all of the candidates agreed that they would serve only one two-year term and would support each other's candidacies. Lincoln's turn came in 1846, and he was a member of the Thirtieth Congress.[6]

While Lincoln was campaigning successfully as a Whig in the Seventh Congressional District, Lovejoy was campaigning unsuccessfully as a member of the Liberty Party in the neighboring Fourth District. Both men were unintimidated by presidential power, and both highlighted the questionable circumstances of the beginning of the Mexican War. Lovejoy called President James K. Polk's explanation for the war "a plain, plumb lie," while Lincoln demanded that Polk name the spot where Mexican troops had invaded the United States.[7]

In 1854, Lincoln still sought to renew the Whig Party's fortunes rather than join the new Republican Party. Fifty-three Whigs in Congress had voted against Stephen A. Douglas's Kansas-Nebraska Act, and only twelve southern Whigs had voted for it.[8] Lincoln decided to stay with his Whig strategy and not venture into an unknown group with abolitionist footprints.

Lincoln had learned how to work behind the scenes, writing confidential letters, making deals, winning elections, gaining respect, and taking some risky political positions. He soon began to apply those strategies in his bids for senator and president.

Lovejoy's Political Grounding

The first pastor-politician Owen Lovejoy encountered was one of his father's Congregational colleagues, the Reverend Joshua Cushman, who was a member of the U.S. House of Representatives and who lived ten miles away from the Lovejoys in the town of Winslow, Maine. In 1819, the South demanded that Maine statehood be coupled with the admission of Missouri as a slave state. Cushman protested, calling for "national sectional unity" to prohibit slavery in Missouri.[9] The independent frontier people in Maine were outraged. Few people in Maine had expected that another slave state would be added to the Union, and they were not prepared for such intrigue. After a long and contentious political process, the U.S. Congress admitted both states under the Missouri Compromise, which ultimately played a decisive role in the political life of Lovejoy, a Maine native.[10]

Lovejoy had been politicized by the events leading up to the death of his brother, Elijah, in 1837. However, he had not sought revenge, and he had ignored the trial of the murderers and their release by the court. Instead, Lovejoy directed his energy toward exposing the lies and distortions of the leading men of Alton who were doing the slaveholders' bidding. In 1838, Owen and another brother, Joseph, published *The Memoir of the Rev. Elijah P. Lovejoy Who Was Murdered in Defence of the Liberty of the Press, at Alton, Illinois, Nov. 7, 1837*, helping to spread word of their brother's martyrdom. His death became a clear symbol of southern slaveholding interests' encroachment on northerners' civil right of free speech. The book exposed the duplicity of supposedly good men, especially public officials and ministers, who deceived themselves and others. The *Memoir* chastised Alton's citizens for failing to abide by the rule of law and the Bill of Rights, which should have protected Elijah Lovejoy and his right to publish: "Resolutions to this very effect were brought before you. How could you have done otherwise than adopt them? . . . What spirit of delusion, what smooth-lipped Belial could have induced you to swallow such logic? One would have thought your understandings, if not your consciences would have retched at it."[11] Among the "smooth-lipped" devils were state's attorney Usher Linder, a friend of Lincoln's; the Reverend John Hogan, a former member of the Illinois legislature; and State Senator Cyrus Edwards, a relative of Mary Todd Lincoln. In September, October, and November 1837, prior to the murder, Linder made inflammatory statements against Lovejoy's paper, alleging that it had been "brought here to teach rebellion and insurrection to the slave to excite servile war, to preach murder in the name of religion, to strike dismay to the hearts of the people, and to spread desolation over the face of the land."[12] Linder and Hogan also organized a local meeting of the American Colonization Society. They invited Edwards, who was running for governor; the Reverend John Mason Peck, a former editor and Baptist minister who disapproved of Elijah's work; and a biblical defender of slavery, the Reverend Joel Parker. The speakers denounced Elijah Lovejoy's friends as "fanatics," and the meeting "cordially adopted" a resolution urging Elijah to "discontinue his incendiary publications." Then Linder exhorted the crowd to disrupt the Alton convention to organize the

Illinois State Antislavery Society. Elijah had published the call for the convention in his newspaper, the *Observer*, including the signatures of 255 Illinois "Friends of Freedom." When about 75 opponents of slavery arrived in Alton, they found their numbers dwarfed by those of Linder's followers. The convention ended in chaos, unable to take any action. After the meeting adjourned, Linder took to the stump outside and labeled the antislavery men fanatical, meddlesome, foreign reformers from New England. He then left Alton. However, the mob that he incited attacked the warehouse where Elijah Lovejoy had hidden his printing press, and Lovejoy was killed in the ensuing exchange of gunfire.[13]

Lincoln, at the time a member of the state legislature, was one of the few to condemn the violent incident in Alton, declaring, "Let every man remember that to violate the law, is to trample on the blood of his father, and to tear the charter of his own, and his children's liberty. Let reverence for the laws be breathed by every American mother to the lisping babe that prattles on her lap."[14]

Lincoln's friendship with Linder as well as Linder's career soon began precipitous declines as a consequence of "his heavy drinking and bad reputation" caused by the Lovejoy tragedy, though for the remainder of his life, Linder stressed "that he was out of town when a mob killed Lovejoy." Linder became a Whig in 1838, but his hatred for abolitionism brought him back into the Democratic Party in 1850, supporting Douglas. In 1863, Lincoln arranged for Linder's son, a captured Confederate, to be released and sent home. A year later, citing poverty, Linder asked Lincoln for a government position. The president turned down the request, noting that after four years of "diligent and prudent" work, "no prosperous wind has filled my sail."[15]

In 1838, Lovejoy sought not only to expose Linder but also to counteract the rumors and innuendos about Elijah that were circulating nationally as part of an effort to minimize the tragedy of his death. The rumormongers argued that Elijah's friends had illegally taken up arms to defend the warehouse and had instigated the riot; they also made derogatory comments about Elijah's character. Owen wrote full accounts of the proceedings and sent them to the national newspaper of the American Anti-Slavery Society, the *Emancipator*, edited by the Reverend Joshua Leavitt, which published a full extra edition lauding Elijah's martyrdom.[16]

Owen Lovejoy saved his sharpest rebukes for the duplicitous clergy. In a letter to the *Emancipator*, Lovejoy described Hogan as "intimidated, seduced, or deluded, he presents the darkest and saddest of enigmas."[17] Parker visited Illinois and distributed pamphlets from Mississippi that were "full of gross perversions, gilded over with a smirking cant of Christian sincerity. This tract with a specious sophistry well calculated to deceive, endeavours to prove that the Holy Bible sanctions the system of American Slavery."[18] Lovejoy also challenged William Lloyd Garrison's pacifist remark in the *Liberator* that while Elijah was a martyr, he was not a Christian martyr because he resorted to the use of what nonresistant abolitionists called "carnal weapons."[19] According to Owen, "All the weapons used for this purpose [were for] self-defense, and [for] the maintenance of civil government, of order and law. . . . If ever physical resistance is justified, I am persuaded it was in this case."[20] Lovejoy had established a pattern of responding specifically, persuasively, and quickly to his opponents' accusations.

In 1842, he demonstrated his ability to organize people around a clear vision for action when he helped write the call for the convention establishing the Illinois Liberty Party. He became the party's congressional candidate four years later, receiving one-third of the vote. The Liberty Party's New England leaders then invited the "Orator of the West" to come east, where he delivered fifty-five addresses in forty-one days on behalf of the party.[21] Through the mid-1840s, he attended all the critical national and state Liberty Party conventions. He joined the Free Soil Party in 1848 and ran enthusiastically on its ticket but was disappointed with the results. He waited a year and then was one of the first national leaders to call for renewal of an antislavery party. Along with Ohio congressman Joshua Giddings, a leader in the Free Soil Party, Lovejoy was one of the founders of the National Free Democratic Party in Pittsburgh in August 1853.[22] In the spring and summer of 1854, Lovejoy helped Codding and Eastman form the three fusion/Republican nominating conventions in Rockford, Aurora, and Bloomington. In November 1854, Lovejoy was elected a member of the Illinois House of Representatives, and by January 1855, he was ready to negotiate from a basis of political strength.

Political Agreement

The stage was set for Lincoln to work behind the scenes and make a deal to advance his candidacy and for Lovejoy to find a venue to correct some intentional mischaracterizations of the early Republican Party in Illinois. Three informative letters to Lincoln from Elihu Washburne, a former Whig and now a Republican congressman from Galena, indicate that Lincoln recognized he needed the votes of Lovejoy and the early Republicans to win the Senate seat. On December 26, 1854, Washburne wrote that he had "had a long talk with Giddings and he is your strongest possible friend and says he would walk clear to Illinois to elect you." Moreover, Washburne said that he would write to "Lovejoy to advise them most strongly to go for you en masse."[23]

On January 6, 1855, Lincoln sent Washburne a detailed analysis of the situation. He figured that he had twenty-six committed votes and that no one else had more than ten. But he needed fifty-one to win. Though "there were more than 22 anti-Nebraska members who are not committed to me," even if he received all of those votes, they would not put him over the top. Lincoln closed by telling

Washburne that Giddings's "letter to L[ovejoy] I think has not been received. Ask him if he sent it."[24] Eleven days later, Washburne answered, "As soon as Giddings returns from N.Y. I shall try and get him to write again to Lovejoy."[25] On January 20, Washburne again wrote to Lincoln, reporting that "Giddings has written another letter to Lovejoy, which he gave to me to read and send off which I have done. . . . I think his letter to L. will do you much good."[26]

Lincoln had also written to several of his fellow lawyers on the Eighth Circuit, including Judge T. Lyle Dickey, Leonard Swett, and Ward Lamon, all of whom were conservative Whigs with antiabolitionist leanings.[27] They too were lobbying on Lincoln's behalf, and Dickey, an old friend of Lincoln's who had served with him in the Illinois legislature, heard that there was some hope that Lovejoy would back Lincoln.[28] Jesse Norton, a former Whig who had just been elected to Congress from Lovejoy's Fourth Congressional District, was not sure which candidate Lovejoy would support for senator and encouraged Lincoln to reach out to some "first rate fellows" in the legislature whom Norton knew. Norton had already written to two members of the legislature on Lincoln's behalf.[29]

In December, Norton urged Lincoln to make whatever concessions "could be made by you without sacrifice to principle," a change that Norton believed would persuade all of the Free Soilers to support Lincoln. Norton asked, "Are you bound to stand by *every thing* in the compromise measures of 1850? Couldn't you concede to them a modification of the Fugitive Slave Act?"[30] Lincoln subsequently told some legislators that he would not vote to repeal the Fugitive Slave Act, "but he would vote to strip one obnoxious feature," since granting accused runaways due process according to the Constitution could help prevent a free man from being carried into slavery.[31]

Lincoln's position thus moved into almost perfect alignment with that of Lovejoy. Presenting his antislavery resolutions to the Illinois House on February 6, 1855, Lovejoy advocated the repeal of the Fugitive Slave Law, but if that goal could not be achieved, he would support "such a modification of it as shall secure the right of habeas corpus and the trial by jury before the regularly constituted authorities of the state to all persons claimed as owing service of labor."[32]

Lincoln had become a firm supporter of black civil rights, a radical commitment that he made known to his close associates—but only to his close associates. Lincoln worked to build a coalition without compromising his integrity. He could gain support among conservatives by arguing for the constitutionality of the Fugitive Slave Law while appealing to radicals by supporting the constitutionality of due process for blacks.

As early as December 10, a close associate of Washburne's, Thomas J. Turner of Freeport, one of the few legislators who had served during the legislature's previous January–February 1853 term, had written Lincoln a straight-on, single-sentence letter: "I am not committed to any one for the office of U.S. Senator, nor do I intend to be until I know where I can exert my influence the most successfully against those who are seeking to extend the *era* of slavery."[33] Lincoln thus believed that he could win over Turner "when I can make it appear to be in his interest to go for me."[34] Similarly, Anson Miller of Rockford reported that the legislative delegates from his area were not committed to Lincoln because he was not antislavery enough. Miller encouraged Lincoln "to take the ground of 'no further extension of slavery'—'no more slave territory.'" Miller stressed "the absolute importance of taking high ground in the slavery question. Without this [Lincoln] cannot get the vote of the Northern members."[35]

While some legislators seemed open to persuasion, some powerful and more radical antislavery political organizers actively resisted Lincoln's candidacy, believing that he remained committed to the Whigs and desired to become a U.S. senator "to revive the Whig Party as the appropriate vehicle for mobilizing Free Soil sentiment." Wrote one such antislavery editor, "God help us, if . . . we have all to admit that the Whig Party is the party of freedom."[36]

Eastman, the editor of the *Free West*, was another vocal critic, declaring Lincoln "only a Whig, and the people's movement is no Whig triumph. All of whiggery has been crushed out in the recent Congressional election."[37] Eastman was leery of the Whigs' previous lack of support for the Republican cause and was especially upset that Lincoln and other conservatives had ignored the efforts by leaders of the Springfield Convention to moderate their previous platforms. For Eastman, the Whigs lacked the imperatives of the Free Democratic Party, which he had worked so hard to include. He claimed that Lincoln was a Compromise Whig, "having a full attachment to that mummy of a party, which has done us no good in this state, but has brought upon us all the calamities and defeats of the Republican movement." Eastman was holding out for Lincoln's support on three issues that would become Lovejoy's resolutions in the Illinois House of Representatives—no extension of slavery into the territories, no admission of new slave states, and the repeal of the Fugitive Slave Act. "If these can not be gotten from him, of what service would he be in the Senate, when the Slavery question comes up?"[38] Eastman preferred stronger antislavery men—Lovejoy, Codding, Democrat William Bissell, or Whig Richard Yates.[39]

Washburne was aware of Eastman's distrust of Lincoln and wrote to Eastman on December 19 that Lincoln was "a man of splendid talents, of great probity of character," deserving of support "because he threw himself into the late fight on the republican platform and made the greatest speech in reply to Douglas ever heard in the State. . . . He will not carry out our views fully in the Senate, but he will be with us in our views and feelings."[40]

Charles H. Ray, the former editor of the *Galena Jeffersonian*, attended the 1854 Republican Springfield Convention and shared Lovejoy's antislavery commitment. He echoed Eastman's skepticism about Lincoln's antislavery commitments.

According to Ray, in an interview about the Senate seat, "Lincoln procrastinated, refused to declare himself, and was reminded of a funny story."[41] Consequently, Ray told Washburne in mid-December, he could not back Lincoln but would insist on "someone whose opposition to the institution admits of no question." He did not think Lincoln could stand up "in a hand to hand fight with Southern influence and dictation." He wanted to help "check-mate the rascals who are making our government the convenient tool of the slave power."[42] But within a month, Ray had changed his tune, writing to Washburne, "I have made up my mind—this private—that our best course is to go in strong for Lincoln when the day comes, and I shall so advise our friends of the Anti-Nebraska Party, and shall labor to that end."[43]

For his part, Lincoln was slowly revising his estimation of the antislavery Republicans. He came to realize that the Republicans had formed a competent, well-motivated organization with a strategy to unite the factions, but he continued to consider their leadership abolitionist, and that label concerned him. However, two of his closest political associates, Judge David Davis and Stephen T. Logan, Lincoln's former law partner, began working to secure a political deal. Davis suggested to Lincoln an agreement under which "the Republicans, as they call themselves, [would] have all the offices of the House, if they would agree to let the Whigs have the Senator without the troublesome platform."[44] Lincoln then turned to Logan, an experienced member of the state legislature and now the floor manager for Lincoln's candidacy. Logan recalled, "Lincoln was in a fix. Lovejoy and others in the legislature wanted him to say that he would go for the doctrine that there should be no Slavery in the Territories: Lincoln came to me and asked me about the matter, Saying to me 'Knowing my politics, will it tramp your toes'—I said 'No—whatever you do, though I don't agree to the doctrine it won't tread on my toes.' Lincoln made the pledge. Lincoln and I had supported the Wilmot Proviso, but this pledge was broader—more radical."[45]

Under the deal, the speakership of the Illinois House went to Turner, a member of the antislavery wing of the anti-Nebraska faction. He, in turn, granted Lovejoy the privilege of speaking about his resolutions to the full legislature in front of a large public audience in the Hall of Representatives on February 6, 1855, two days before the senatorial election. On February 7, the House voted on whether to table Lovejoy's resolutions. In keeping with his pledge to Lincoln, Logan forwent the opportunity to deliver a rebuke to Lovejoy and the emerging Republican Party, and the measure to table failed by a single vote.[46]

The legislature then took up the three resolutions, which were recommendations to the Illinois congressional delegation for consideration in national legislation. The vote on the resolution for the nonextension of slavery into the territories passed the House by a forty-one to thirty-two vote, a major victory for the fledgling Republicans. However, the resolutions on the prohibition of new slave states and on the repeal of the Fugitive Slave Act failed by substantial margins.[47]

On February 8, the legislature voted on the next U.S. senator from Illinois. Thirty-nine of the forty-one members who voted in favor of the resolution for the nonextension of slavery voted for Lincoln on the first three ballots.[48] On the tenth ballot, however, Lincoln saw that his own victory was not possible and encouraged his supporters to elect Democrat Lyman Trumbull, an opponent of the Kansas-Nebraska Act.[49] The pattern of the votes showed the Democrats "that the radicals had proposed a deal with Lincoln," and party members encouraged *Illinois State Register* editor Charles H. Lanphier to find proof of the agreement. None was found, and as late as 1967, Lovejoy biographer Edward Magdol remained convinced that there was "no evidence that Lincoln made a deal with Lovejoy and the radicals."[50] However, Logan's statement, which was not published until 1998, provides evidence of just such a deal.

Lincoln and Lovejoy had taken steps toward increasing their mutual esteem. More important, a precedent had been set that a major legislative body, even in a state bordered by two slave states, could pass a resolution to prohibit the extension of slavery into the territories. The close vote may well have reflected some support for free labor and antiblack sentiment, but it was clearly initiated and supported by antislavery political forces.

Speeches on Restoring the Missouri Compromise

Lovejoy's February 6, 1855, speech was titled "Joint Resolutions of Instruction to the Illinois Delegation in Congress to Restore the Missouri Compromise Line."[51] Lincoln's speech at the Springfield Fair on October 4, 1854, and presented again in Peoria on October 16, 1854, was titled "The Repeal of the Missouri Compromise, and the Propriety of Its Restoration."[52] Both speeches were delivered in the Hall of Representatives in the State Capitol.

Both Lovejoy and Lincoln regarded the repeal of the Missouri Compromise as a big mistake. Lincoln recognized that the compromise forbade slavery in the northern territories and that the Kansas-Nebraska Act had "opened the door for slavery to enter where before it could not go." He considered the change "practically legislating for slavery, recognizing it, endorsing it, propagating it, extending it . . . a woeful coming down from the early faith of the republic."[53]

Speaking in a different cadence, Lovejoy queried the audience, "Was this government organized in any way to extend and propagate slavery! Never, Never, Sir." After explaining the bargain contained in the Missouri Compromise, Lovejoy indignantly asserted, "They still hold their part of the bargain"—Missouri as slave state—"and with brazen effrontery, seek to deprive us of the equivalent they were to give; that is the whole of it."[54]

Both men denounced the way Douglas and the southern Democrats abused the concept of popular sovereignty. After reminding his audience that governments derive their just powers from the consent of the governed, Lincoln declared that slavery was a total violation of this principle: "The master not only governs the slave without his consent; but he governs him by a set of rules altogether different from those which he prescribes for himself. Allow ALL the governed an equal voice in the government. . . . [T]hat only is self-government."[55] Lovejoy said, "I do not admit that these 'sovereigns' or any other sovereigns have any right to convert man into a chattel, into goods, into four-footed beasts. I tell you gentlemen, they have no authority to do it." And, he continued, "I am not fighting Senator Douglas particularly; he is a mere item or instrument that the Slave Power has used in the fraud."[56]

Both Lincoln and Lovejoy valued compromise and cooperation, with Lincoln asking whether the United States had not "discarded from the councils of the Nation—the SPIRIT OF COMPROMISE: for who after this will ever trust in a national compromise?"[57] For his part, Lovejoy maintained the major compromise he had made back in the early 1840s, when he left the Garrisonian immediate abolitionists in favor of the Liberty Party's position of an eventual end to slavery but within constitutional limits: "I have no more power to enter the state of South Carolina and abolish slavery there by an act of Congress than I have to go into Brazil and abolish it there. But we have the power to do it in the territories as they are under the exclusive jurisdiction of the people of the United States."[58]

Both men also went to the root of the problem when they made it clear that it was wrong to reduce persons to property as southern laws did. Said Lincoln, "It is said that the slaveholder has the same political right to take his negroes to Kansas that a freeman has to take his hogs or his horses. . . . Now, I admit this is perfectly logical, if there is no difference between hogs and negroes. . . . But is this the case? It is notoriously not so."[59] Lovejoy similarly proclaimed, "No power on earth has the right to make a man a slave. In doing so, you trample upon the principles of the Declaration of Independence. They have no right to blot out his humanity and convert him into a thing and carry him to market, as they would a mere brute."[60] This argument provided the foundation stone for their radical pragmatic agenda.

In 1854–55, Lincoln and Lovejoy differed in their approach to their use of religious language. When Douglas claimed that the Kansas-Nebraska Act resembled the biblical injunction from God to choose between good and evil, Lincoln responded that this argument sounded like the justification for the divine right of kings: "The King is to do just as he pleases with his white subjects, being responsible to God alone. . . . [T]he white man is to do just as he pleases with black slaves, being responsible to God alone."[61] Lovejoy, conversely, expressed his resistance to slavery in basic religious terms: "I deny in the name of the great principles of the Revolution—in the name of a common God, and a common father, I deny this right to anybody and everybody. God made that man as he made you and me in his own image, and the sanction of his authority is around him. Sir, you had better take your foot from his neck, you might as well trample the Son of God."[62]

By 1858, however, Lincoln had modified his position so that he was reading from the same biblical page as Lovejoy. Speaking in Lewistown, Lincoln said, "Nothing stamped with the Divine image and likeness was sent into the world to be trodden on, and degraded, and imbruted by its fellows."[63] According to Richard Carwardine, "Lincoln's use of the Bible in the struggle over slavery was driven by conviction not expediency." However, Lincoln had a growing appreciation of the effectiveness of Lovejoy and other antislavery leaders' use of the Bible, and that tactic in part resulted in what Carwardine calls Lincoln's "remarkable success in reaching out to what was the most powerful of all the era's subcultures, evangelical Protestantism."[64]

Different Perspectives on Abolitionists

The major complication to a political alliance between Lincoln and Lovejoy was their contradictory perceptions of the abolitionists. The word *abolitionist* could tilt an election. Lincoln's perception came from his awareness of prejudiced folk in Kentucky, from reading partisan newspapers, and from listening to slavery-sympathizing politicians. Lovejoy's perception came from his abolitionist friends in Maine, from his experiences with his brother in Alton, and from the leaders of American Anti-Slavery Society in the New York office in 1838.

During Lovejoy's 1855 speech, someone shouted out, "Your allies deny that you are an abolitionist." Lovejoy responded, "If anyone denies I am an abolitionist he denies erroneously. I have no doubt what is the truth." He continued with the words of a song, "I am an abolitionist, I glory in the name."[65] But, he added, he was a different kind of abolitionist. Not until 1860 was the meaning of that statement clear to enough voters that the Republican Party could register a victory in Illinois. Lincoln's incremental acceptance that Lovejoy and his friends had been extreme abolitionists but were now pragmatic political abolitionists was critical to that victory.

The history of the usage of the term *abolitionist* to refer to immediate abolitionism and the use of invective language by the abolitionists began when William Lloyd Garrison galvanized people who were tired of waiting for gradual emancipation and were fed up with attempts at "colonization." He wrote in his newspaper, the *Liberator*, on January 1, 1831, that he promised "to strenuously contend for the immediate enfranchisement of our slave population." He confessed that he had repented before God for assenting "to the pernicious doctrine of gradual abolition" and contended that the "coarseness of his invective and the persistency of his measures were not hindering the cause of emancipation but assisting it." He galvanized a sizable group in the North for two decades.[66]

However, the immediatists' righteous judgment of the slave owners as sinners was countered by slavery supporters' exaggerated claims and vicious threats and acts of violence against the abolitionists. Such recriminations both marginalized and emboldened the immediatists. The Garrisonians blamed the churches for failing to provide full support, calling them the "bulwark of slavery." Moreover, Garrison's supporters blamed the American people for accepting the very flawed Constitution, which they believed would protect slavery in the South forever, and began calling for disunion from the southern states. And they often used self-righteous language rather than diplomacy and developed few ideas about how to assimilate freed slaves into white society.[67] Such tactics only further alienated them from the larger public, especially in the South. Lincoln and others consequently concluded that abolitionism was likely to hinder rather than help the cause of emancipation.

Most abolitionists were religious people motivated by a deep conviction that slavery was a sin against the laws of God. They articulated their principles at a December 1833 meeting in Philadelphia at which the American Anti-Slavery Society was formed. The society opposed paying compensation to planters, the principle that one human could hold property in another human, and expatriation but conceded that "Congress, under the present national compact, has no right to interfere with any of the slave States, in relation to this momentous subject." The society's members would do all that they could "to bring the whole nation to a speedy repentance. Our trust for victory is solely in GOD."[68]

Historians have defined *abolitionist* in various ways. Dwight Dumond, author of *Antislavery: The Crusade for Freedom in America*, and Betty Fladeland, writing in *Men and Brothers: Anglo-American Antislavery Cooperation*, use a broad definition that holds that abolitionists had the goal of "the ending of slavery, no matter what method is advocated."[69] Others use the word *immediatist* to refer to Garrison and others who sought immediate, complete, uncompensated emancipation and civil equality for African Americans. Some apply the adjective *antislavery* to anyone who hoped "that slavery might ultimately disappear as a result of various developments and tactics."[70] The phrase *political abolitionist* applied to those who believed political action was necessary to end slavery, while the term *Radical Abolitionist* refers to those members of the Liberty Party who refused to join the Free Soil Party in 1847 to pursue political objectives. Impelled by a strong religious motivation to bring God's kingdom here on earth, Radical Abolitionists committed to full suffrage for blacks and women and to other reform movements. Benjamin Shaw, editor of the *Dixon Telegraph* in Lee

County, next to Lovejoy's Bureau County, years later referred to Lovejoy as a "constitutional abolitionist," determined to end slavery within constitutional limits.[71]

In the mid-1850s, Lincoln recognized that slavery was immoral but had no notion of what to do about it because it was so deeply entrenched legally and socially in southern culture: speaking in Peoria on October 16, 1854, he told his audience, "If all earthly power were given me, I should not know what to do, as to the existing institution."[72] By 1858, he had developed a hopeful plan: stopping slavery's spread would eventually lead to its demise. But clearer perception, deeper vision, and wider public support would be needed before he would advocate an end to slavery.

Many constituents assumed that Lovejoy was a Garrisonian abolitionist with a vigorous plan to end slavery immediately. In truth, his immediate plan was to gain national political power, which could then be used to prohibit slavery in all the areas under the jurisdiction of the federal government. He anticipated that southern states would then do what northern states had done: end bondage because it was ineffective, inhuman, unjust, and undemocratic. However, effective southern propaganda that painted all who worked to abolish slavery as fanatics and the alienating tactics of the Garrisonians in the mid-1830s meant that Lincoln could not easily determine Lovejoy's position.

As a member of the General Assembly, Lincoln tried to walk the line between his conviction that slavery was wrong and the political situation in central Illinois. In explaining why he voted against the March 1837 resolutions restricting antislavery societies, Lincoln said, "The institution of slavery is founded on both injustice and bad policy; but that the promulgation of abolition doctrine tends rather to increase than to abate its evils." The injustice of slavery and the importance of the First Amendment apparently trumped the negative aspects of abolitionism.[73] Also, he believed that Congress had no power to interfere with slavery where it already existed but could abolish it in the District of Columbia if the people of the District agreed. Lincoln's views differed from those of almost all of his colleagues, who overwhelmingly passed the bill to limit the formation of abolition societies in Illinois.

Despite legislative intimidation, mobs, and apathy, antislavery societies flourished. By 1838, the country had more than thirteen hundred such societies with 109,000 members as well as twenty-four antislavery newspapers. Congress received 412,000 antislavery petitions in 1838 asking for measures such as the emancipation of slaves in the District of Columbia.[74] The movement was "inspired by the anticlericalism of Garrison himself, the Quakerism of John Greenleaf Whittier, and the transcendentalism of Theodore Parker."[75]

The movement received a further boost from the evangelical efforts of the Reverend Theodore Weld. According to Gilbert Hobbs Barnes, Weld created "a mighty wave of evangelical antislavery sentiment west of the Appalachians" that "brought about the formation of countless abolition societies and the arousing of a religious crusade against slavery which was more significant and important in the election of Lincoln and the outbreak of the Civil War than the work of Garrison in the East."[76]

Some historians have difficulty understanding this distinction between eastern and western abolitionists. Allen C. Guelzo, for example, believes that Lincoln's views differed significantly from the abolitionists' "romantic absolutism": "Where they preached from passion and choice, he worked from reason and prudence; . . . where they brushed aside the Constitution, Lincoln would proceed against slavery no farther than the Constitution allowed."[77] Guelzo reduces all the abolitionists to the remnant of the eastern Garrisonians, ignoring the role of Lovejoy and other western political abolitionists who were reasonable, pragmatic constitutionalists and who comprised an important part of Lincoln's Republican Party coalition.

However, Lovejoy understood the role of religion in the antislavery movement. During the winter of 1838, he confirmed his religious commitment against slavery with the leading men in the antislavery movement at the American Anti-Slavery Society's New York City office and began developing his political strategy to end it. Other leaders in this effort included Weld; James Birney, a lawyer-politician, former slaveholder, and newspaperman; Lewis Tappan, an evangelical layman, successful merchant, and generous and imaginative philanthropist who financed the movement; Henry Stanton, an antislavery organizer and government lobbyist; Leavitt; and Alvan Stewart, a noted lawyer and Liberty Party leader. These men eagerly mentored the twenty-seven-year-old Lovejoy on his mission to end slavery, providing him with the religious, political, and legal foundations that would guide and direct his ministry.

Lincoln also had a well-known group of loyalists on the Eighth Judicial Court Circuit, including Judge Davis, Dickey, Swett, Lamon, and Henry Whitney. All of these colleagues were conservative Whigs who sympathized with slavery: they had a functional respect for Lincoln and enjoyed his company but did not share his radical commitments.

Disagreeing over the Fugitive Slave Law

In their speeches on restoring the Missouri Compromise, Lincoln and Lovejoy disagreed on one of the most controversial issues of the day, the 1850 Fugitive Slave Act, which required all citizens to report any activity that involved assisting escaped slaves to freedom. In his 1854 speech, Lincoln elaborated on his support for abolitionists' insistence on restoring the Missouri Compromise and his differences with their call for the repeal of the Fugitive Slave Law: "In

Traversing Uneven Political Ground 33

both cases you are right. In both cases you oppose the dangerous extremes. In both cases you stand on middle ground and hold the ship level and steady."[78]

Lovejoy, in contrast, presented an impassioned case for the repeal of the Fugitive Slave Act. This was the most persistent difference on policy between Lincoln and Lovejoy, and it was apparent to all who compared their foundational speeches. Lincoln's reverence for law required him to obey the act as part of a national compromise—a sacred deal. It was hard to argue against the abrogation of one such national deal, the Missouri Compromise, and at the same time argue for the abrogation of the 1850 compromise. And Lincoln's quasi-sacred regard for the Constitution, which included a Fugitive Slave Clause, also made it more difficult for him to oppose the law, though he sensed its unfairness and legal excesses. For Lovejoy, however, commitment to a higher law prevented him from obeying an unjust and in his view unconstitutional law that treated humans as legal property.

Lincoln had privately admitted that fugitive slave laws were "obnoxious" and "ungodly."[79] But in his public speech, he indicated both his commitment to obeying the fugitive slave laws and some sympathy for protecting the legal rights of those falsely accused of being escapees: "I would give [southerners] any legislation for the reclaiming of their fugitives, which should not, in its stringency, be more likely to carry a free man into slavery, than our ordinary criminal laws are to hang an innocent one."[80]

At the October 1854 Republican Convention in Springfield, Lovejoy went along with the compromise platform position and did not call for the repeal of the fugitive slave laws, a position calculated to attract moderate men such as Lincoln.[81] Yet four months later, this concession had not yielded any significant increase in support from the future president or other moderate anti-Nebraska politicians. Lovejoy realized that his opposition to the Fugitive Slave Act was integral to the support and effectiveness of the antislavery organization. He said in his 1855 speech that he found the act repulsive because it required citizens to perform a "degrading service—to transform ourselves into four footed beasts and chase down the fugitive." Then he appealed to Thomas Jefferson's conviction "that God is just," saying plainly, "In the face of fines, in the face of imprisonment—and with God's grace, that stood by my brother—in the face of death itself, I tell you I will not do it."[82] Some observers have claimed that Lovejoy's active defiance of the Fugitive Slave Act by participating in the Underground Railroad was "the method of his madness."[83] Standing up for what he believed gained him respect, even from those who disagreed with him.

Lovejoy explained his position by noting that the constitution refers only to "'any person held to service or labor'—that is all the foundation the act has." But the "slave does not owe service or labor under the laws of the slave states" since he had not signed a contract and consequently did not legally owe anything to

34   CHAPTER 2

the master. "In Kentucky, for instance, he is made an article of property, by the laws, the same as a horse or an ox. The law places him as a piece of property, at the feet of the master, and he whips the labor out of him if necessary." In the case of indentured apprentices or people bound by contracts, Lovejoy supported their return. He then applied one of his stock approaches, describing a woman "fleeing from a wretched libertine who had purchased her." The fugitive slave bill "asks me to seize this young woman, to fetter and mangle her, and drag her back to the possession of that miserable Libertine."[84]

In 1838, Lincoln took the position that bad laws "should be repealed as soon as possible, [but] still while they continue in force, for the sake of example, they should be religiously observed."[85] A decade and a half later, he was not ready to work for the repeal of the fugitive slave laws, partly because he had no idea how the Constitution could be amended to do so.

Though the political, legal, and philosophical differences between Lincoln and Lovejoy over the Fugitive Slave Law lingered, the two men slowly came to appreciate and accept the advantages they gained from this difference. Lovejoy could consolidate and extend his constituency, while Lincoln could evade the "extreme abolitionist" label that Douglas tried to pin on him.

Cautious Steps toward Fusion

In January 1855, a reconstituted state central committee of the October 1854 Republican Convention met in the office of *Chicago Tribune* editor Charles Ray. In attendance were not only Lovejoy and Eastman but also John C. Vaughan of the *Tribune* and former state legislator Henry W. Blodgett, from Lake County.[86] Borrowing a tactic from the Free Democratic Party of Illinois, they unanimously rehired Codding to continue his political coalition building. Unifying various antislavery groups behind Lincoln was a formable task because of the historical barriers between the five vying political factions, but it was also necessary for Lincoln to succeed. According to historian Victor Howard, "Codding, more than any other person in Illinois, sowed the seed that Lincoln harvested in 1860."[87]

The first of these factions was the Whigs, who could usually muster a successful candidate from the Seventh Congressional District in central Illinois. Many of them were followers of Henry Clay, the U.S. senator from Kentucky and 1844 presidential candidate who had helped craft the Missouri Compromise and was committed to the nonexpansion of slavery. Their leaders were former Illinois state senator Orville Browning and former Illinois congressmen Archibald Williams from Quincy, Richard Yates from Springfield, and Lincoln.

The second faction was a new political organization, the American Party, that had recently emerged from the Know-Nothings. The American Party gained popularity by appealing to the prejudices and fears induced by the influx of Catholic immigrants. These righteous Protestants opposed the production and consumption of alcoholic beverages as well as dishonesty and corruption in government. Their leaders were highly ambitious and wanted to wield personal influence, and they included the editor of the *Springfield State Journal*, Simeon Francis; Ozias Hatch of Pike County; and Jesse Dubois of Lawrence County.[88]

The third group consisted of anti-Nebraska Democrats who were disappointed by Senator Douglas's revocation of the Missouri Compromise and disgusted by his demand that all Illinois Democrats had to agree with the Kansas-Nebraska Act. Among the members of this faction were newly appointed U.S. senator Lyman Trumbull of Alton, recently defeated congressman William Bissell of Carlinville, and State Senators John Palmer of Belleville, Burton C. Cook of Ottawa, and Isaac Arnold and Norman Judd of Chicago.

The next faction was composed of the German immigrants who lived in the Belleville area and in Chicago. They were non-Catholic, beer-loving, educated people who vigorously supported freedom. Many of them had left Germany after failing to democratize the country during the 1848 revolutions. Their leaders included Gustave Koerner of Belleville; George Schneider, editor of the German-language *Chicago Staats-Zeitung*; and Chicago banker Francis A. Hoffman.

The fifth faction emerged from the Free Democratic Party that had grown out of the remnants of the Liberty Party. Among Lovejoy's associates in this group were Eastman, Codding, and John Howard Bryant. They spearheaded the organization of the 1854 Republican conventions in northern Illinois that led to the Springfield Convention that October.

The turning point in the fusion process came at the close of a Codding lecture in Quincy in July 1855. The *Quincy Whig* reported that Williams, the defeated 1854 Whig candidate for Congress, introduced resolutions opposing the extension of slavery but pledging to refrain from interfering with it where it already existed. The meeting then called on all who concurred to unite without regard to other issues.[89] For the first time, Whigs, Free Democrats, and anti-Nebraska Democrats had achieved fusion in central Illinois. Codding predicted, "This is the inauguration of the Republican movement in Middle and Southern Illinois, and mark my word; it will be responded to and followed up throughout this region of the country."[90]

The people who had voted in favor of the fusion resolution after Codding's lecture in Quincy, together with like-minded people in other parts of the state, started calling for a fall meeting, possibly in Springfield, to consolidate the state's growing Republican interest. The *Aurora Guardian* was so encouraged by the Quincy resolutions that its editors requested that "the Republicans of Adams County . . . take the initiative" in calling for a statewide convention.[91] However, Whig editors in the central part of the state remained skeptical about Codding

36   CHAPTER 2

and Lovejoy and warned readers not to lend their sympathies or their influence to mere sectional parties.[92]

The unofficial Republican steering committee and its allies realized that no convention would be truly representative of the state unless more moderate Whigs and anti-Nebraska Democrats were included. To that end, organizers contacted Trumbull, Lincoln, and Williams.[93] On August 6, 1855, Lovejoy wrote to Williams,

> The danger to Freedom is so great & pressing that I feel willing & anxious to unite on ground where *all can* unite. For myself I should be willing to unite on a Platform in substance like yours & then we could hitch our short bob sleds to suit the inequalities of the political surface in difficult portions of the State.
>
> I think that all the Anti-Slavery men of the northern part of the State would unite on such a basis. True it would [be] deemed rather tame to some of the old Abolitionists but I think they will all see & acknowledge the necessity of not loading the Middle & Southern portions of the State with too heavy a load. I was on the [point] of writing to you to ask you what you thought of holding a State convention early this Fall at Springfield to consult together & to organize with a view of carrying the State for Freedom in 1856.[94]

Despite this letter and other conclusive evidence of Lovejoy's role in the fusion process, credit for uniting the anti-Nebraska factions is frequently given to Lincoln, who supposedly possessed a political prudence that Lovejoy and other abolitionists lacked.

Lincoln opened his August 11, 1855, response to Lovejoy's letter seeking support for a statewide anti-Nebraska convention, "Not even you are more anxious to prevent the extension of slavery than I." Then Lincoln went on to inform Lovejoy of his cautiousness in dealing with the Know-Nothings: "Until we can get the elements of this organization, there is not sufficient material to successfully combat the Nebraska democracy. I fear an open push by us now, may offend them, and tend to prevent our ever getting them." The phrase *by us now* indicates that Lincoln identified himself with the Republican movement. He also highlighted the risks that he had taken during the past year: "In many speeches last summer I advised those who did me the honor of a hearing to 'stand with anybody who stands right,'" and, he continued, "I am quite willing to follow my own advice." Finally Lincoln outlined the conditions under which he was willing to unite. "I lately saw in the *Quincy Whig*, the report of a preamble and resolutions, made by Mr. Williams, as chairman of a committee, to a public meeting and adopted by the meeting. I saw them but once, and have them not now at command, but so far as I can remember them, they occupy about the ground I should be willing to 'fuse' upon."[95] The formula for fusion had been found in Illinois. But who would do it and when and how it could be done remained unclear.

Traversing Uneven Political Ground

Lovejoy and Lincoln knew of each other's speeches. They had taken radical steps together. Both had played a significant role in getting a resolution prohibiting slavery in the territories through the lower house of the state legislature. Both had heard of Codding's success in Quincy and the support of a leading Whig, Williams, and they had independently and simultaneously reached the same conclusions about the best way forward. They were now not only reading from the same book but turning the pages together; however, Lincoln frequently read more slowly.

Both were anxious about their practical compromises and unsure about precisely how to proceed—as Lincoln wrote in his August 11 letter, "I fear to do anything, lest I do wrong."[96] On August 24, 1855, Lincoln wrote to Joshua Speed, "You enquire where I now stand. That is a disputed point. I think I am a Whig, but others say there are no Whigs, and that I am an abolitionist. . . . I now no more than oppose the *extension* of slavery."[97]

Writing more than half a century later, journalist Horace White argued that Codding and Lovejoy were "the only ones who were entirely foot-loose and had a clear view of the course before them."[98] They had known that they needed Lincoln since they heard his 1854 speech. Lincoln slowly realized that he needed their contributions as well. He soon began to perceive the strength of their political organization, their willingness to let others take the lead since they were perceived as fanatics, and their ability and courage to articulate a reasoned position with enthusiasm.

3 Standing Together Nobly, 1856

Heretofore it had been merely a "Union" party of heterogeneous
elements working together to prevent the expansion of slavery. Yet,
how nobly the elements stood together.

—N. Dwight Harris

The Republican Steering Committee, meeting in the office of the *Chicago Tribune*, decided that the fall of 1855 was not the appropriate time to call an anti-Nebraska convention to organize the various factions opposed to the Kansas-Nebraska Act. Neither Abraham Lincoln nor Lyman Trumbull was ready to relinquish his political identity, and various Whig and Democratic newspapers were not ready to support plans for fusion. However, the anti-Nebraska factions, especially the Republicans, faced the reality that the Republicans had been pilloried by much of the Illinois public. Remarks against abolitionists appeared with increasing frequency in both Whig and Democratic newspapers as the Republican political threat grew.[1] The *Joliet Signal*, for example, called the Republicans "a nigger stealing, stinking, putrid abolition party."[2] The invective continued even though Owen Lovejoy had publicly stated that the Republicans were not meddlesome abolitionists and would not interfere with slavery where it was legal in the southern states.

The opposition press accused the Republicans of instigating black violence, disturbing community safety, being unpatriotic disunionists, and being amalgamationists, but the only accusation that came close to sticking was the charge that they were criminals who were breaking the Fugitive Slave Law. Lovejoy repeatedly interpreted his activity in the Underground Railroad as an act of human sympathy for the oppressed and an act of conscience in defiance of an unjust law. He was not against the southern people, he said, but against the inhumanity of slavery.

Because the Republican Steering Committee was aware of the effectiveness of these misrepresentations, its members developed a new strategy. They would send the more experienced antislavery men such as Lovejoy to Pittsburgh to help form the National Republican Party and send those less identified with the abolitionists, including Charles Ray, to Decatur to meet with the Illinois anti-Nebraska newspaper editors. Lovejoy dubbed this "our short bob sleds" strategy, after a Maine method of bringing long logs out of the snowy and rocky terrain.[3]

Implementing the Twin Bobsled Strategy

In response to calls by the chairs of the state Republican Parties in Ohio, Massachusetts, Pennsylvania, Wisconsin, and Vermont, a national convention was held on February 22, 1855 (the 123rd anniversary of George Washington's birth) in Pittsburgh to plan for a presidential nominating convention in June. The Illinois delegation included Lovejoy, Ichabod Codding, John C. Vaughan, John Howard Bryant (Lovejoy's neighbor and backer in Princeton), and others. When organizational disputes arose, Lovejoy was quickly asked to be a part of an intense preplanning group that met the night before the convention to settle some contested procedures.[4] The group comprised one member from each state and eventually chose Francis Blair, a powerful former journalist and Jacksonian Democrat from Missouri, to preside at the meeting.

Lovejoy was asked to open the proceedings by "addressing the Throne of Grace."[5] After thanking God for a long list of blessings and invoking blessings on this special meeting, he encouraged the delegates to be inspired by the Divine Presence to reclaim the nation's principles:

> Wilt Thou remove from office the President of these United States, who has proved recreant and treacherous to the high trusts committed to his care. And wilt Thou move upon the hearts of the People to elect one to fill the Executive Chair; who will administer the Government in accordance with the great principles of Justice, Truth, and Freedom, which underlie the Constitution which binds us together as a confederacy. . . . [L]ead us to lay down such principles and to adopt such measures as are calculated to secure the results we all desire. Hear us, O Lord, in these our petitions, and graciously forgive us our sins.[6]

A little later, Codding reminded the delegates that the spirit of the martyred Elijah Lovejoy was present and introduced Owen Lovejoy as the next speaker.[7] Lovejoy thanked the convention's president for declaring that Divine Power had revealed that "there was a higher law than that created by demagogues."[8] Lovejoy later made the motion that increased the number of delegates for the national Republican Convention on June 17 from two per congressional district to three, a commitment to increased local involvement that resembled Lincoln's way of organizing Whig county nominating conventions in the 1840s.[9]

The bobsled strategy was to find the rationale for calling a convention of all the factions working against the Douglas Democrats. At the beginning of 1856,

40 CHAPTER 3

Ray had noticed that a number of newspapers were responding to an invitation to an anti-Nebraska editors' meeting at Decatur, Illinois, sent by Paul Selby, the young editor of the *Morgan Journal* in Jacksonville, who had attended the Springfield Republican Convention in 1854. Ray published Selby's invitation in the *Chicago Tribune* and promoted it vigorously.

Selby was chosen to chair the Decatur editors meeting, and Ray was chosen to chair the resolutions committee. Selby later wrote that Ray was the primary influence on the platform, "in conjunction with Mr. Lincoln in the clear enunciation of the principles of the new party on the subject of slavery."[10] Lincoln had cleverly let it be known that he would be in Decatur on that day. The Decatur meeting wrote a call for a "State Convention of the Anti-Nebraska Party of Illinois" to be held in Bloomington, Illinois, on May 29, 1856, to nominate candidates for statewide offices."[11] Attendees appointed a large statewide central committee to implement the plans for the convention. According to Selby, "There is a coincidence of no small interest in the fact" that the Decatur and Pittsburgh meetings occurred on the same day.[12]

The twin bobsled strategy was moving forward. The less radical men had stayed in Illinois. The persons with higher public visibility as former "abolitionists" went out of state; they already had useful national contacts. Lovejoy had served on the Resolution Committees and spoken at almost all the National Meetings of the Liberty, Free Soil, and Free Democratic Parties. As the May 29 Bloomington Convention drew near, Republican leaders in Chicago realized they had a problem. Some anti-Nebraska conservatives were still afraid that the early Republicans would take over. Ray reassured them in an editorial in the *Chicago Tribune* two weeks before the convention: "We wish to correct one misapprehension that has gone abroad in relation to the proposed gathering. It is this—that the Convention is to be exclusively REPUBLICAN. Such is not the case. The Republicans, so far are as we are informed, consent to be represented there purely as Anti-Nebraska men, and if there is anything in their political creed which points to more radical measures than Old Line Whigs or Anti-Nebraska Democrats can consent to, they have expressed their willingness without dissent to put such things in abeyance, and unite upon the platform upon which all Northern men who are not avowedly pro-slavery, ought to stand."[13]

The Bloomington Convention, May 29, 1856

The drama commenced the day before the convention began. As the delegates arrived, tensions were running high. Would the "radical abolitionists" keep away the conservatives? Would the extreme conservatives alienate the antislavery men? J. O. Cunningham, a respected young Champaign County newsman, noted "the athletic personality of Owen Lovejoy making love to the abolition-ist haters of the center and south."[14] Archibald Williams of Adams County was named the meeting's temporary chair.[15] Dignified Whig leader Orville Browning was asked to lead the organizing of the meeting, since Selby had been severely injured by some toughs in Jacksonville and was not able to attend.[16] Browning was a Kentuckian and personal friend of Lincoln's who had served with him in the legislature during the 1830s. However, Browning privately believed that Lincoln did not possess either the refinement or the education to serve in higher office. Browning's program committee firmly warned Lovejoy "to avoid arous-ing bitterness."[17] However, many people who heard him speak for the first time were agreeably surprised by "his eloquent appeal in favor of the cause in which they were embarked."[18]

Browning was chosen as chair of the Resolutions Committee, on which Love-joy also served. The resolutions reflected both the passionate language of Lovejoy ("The present administration has prostituted its powers") and the legal phrases of Browning ("in accordance with the opinions and practices of all the great statesmen"). The meeting unanimously nominated for state offices the balanced slate determined at the Decatur meeting. It included former Democrats, Whigs, Know-Nothings, and German Americans but no antislavery Republicans, as Ray had promised in the *Chicago Tribune*.[19]

When Lovejoy spoke during the afternoon session, many who heard him for the first time "were agreeably disappointed by his declaration of [moderate] sentiments." He merely stated that he opposed slavery's extension but went no further, offering an "eloquent appeal in favor of the cause [that] will not soon be forgotten."[20]

As the proceedings neared their close, no word had yet been heard from Lincoln. Only a handful of the three hundred official delegates were active antislavery leaders, but the gallery was packed with antislavery leaders who had traveled from all over the state, and they led the call for Lincoln to speak.[21] Joseph Medill, antislavery publisher of the *Chicago Tribune*, reportedly spread word that Lincoln would soon take the podium.[22]

He did, giving an oration that "surpassed all others—even himself. His points were unanswerable, and the force and power of his appeals, irresistible—and were received with a storm of applause."[23] According to Elwell Crissey, Lincoln "enumerated the pressing reasons of the present movement. He was here ready to fuse with anyone who would unite with him to oppose the slave power. He spoke of the bugbear of disunion, which was so vaguely threatened. It was to be remembered that the Union must be preserved in the purity of its principles as well as in the integrity of territorial parts. It must be 'Liberty and Union now and forever, one and inseparable.'"[24] Lincoln thus issued not only an impassioned reaffirmation of Daniel Webster's commitment on January 26, 1830, during the

Nullification Crisis but also a radical affirmation that the Union must be preserved in the purity of its principles. The delegates responded with a thunderous standing ovation, and the address established Lincoln as an eminent leader in the movement. More important, it convinced Ray to double his efforts to put forth Lincoln as a candidate for the U.S. Senate in 1858—for the seat held by Stephen A. Douglas.[25]

Just before the Bloomington Convention ended, former Democrat John Wentworth of Chicago moved "that the delegates in attendance from the several congressional districts be requested to suggest the names of . . . *three* persons for delegates to the national convention to be held at Philadelphia."[26] Even though the name *Republican* was omitted from the resolution, the meeting for which the delegates were to be chosen was the national Republican Party Nominating Convention. Both Lovejoy and Lincoln were elected delegates to Philadelphia, while Ray was elected one of the five members to the official state central committee.

The National Republican Nominating Convention

On June 17, 1856, the national Republican Nominating Convention opened in the historic city of Philadelphia. Those in attendance called loudly for Lovejoy to make a speech. He seized the moment, inspiring the delegates with a vision for their future: "It is the destiny of our nation to maintain and illustrate the self-evident truth laid down in the Declaration of Independence." He then attempted to leave the stage, but the attendees urged him to continue, and he responded with an exposé of the aggressions and usurpations of the South.[27]

Lovejoy subsequently played the role of a practical politician, helping to work out a sensitive compromise on the floor of the convention. The Know-Nothings had recently held a national meeting at which participants had divided on the slavery question into the northern and southern wings of the American Party. Part of the northern wing wanted to join the Republican Convention, and it was suggested that they had been invited to do so and that the convention consequently was honor-bound to accept them. Lovejoy quickly gained the floor and explained that they had not been invited as a group but had been asked "to come as individuals, and unite for Freedom." Well aware of the growing political influence of the German Americans in Illinois, Lovejoy warned the convention, "If the North Americans were received as an organized body of Know-Nothings, that demagogue, Stephen A. Douglas, would tickle the senses of the foreign born citizens of Illinois, and Illinois would be lost." The issue was relegated to a committee, which never gave a report, and the Know-Nothings were not invited to participate as a group.[28] Here again, Lovejoy's prudent political position anticipated Lincoln's.

Standing Together Nobly

The Bloomington Convention had elected thirty-three delegates to represent Illinois in Philadelphia. The delegation was considerably more conservative than the antislavery vanguard that attended the Pittsburgh planning convention. At the Philadelphia meeting, California explorer John C. Frémont, popularly called the Pathfinder, was nominated for president; he had the support of fourteen members of the Illinois delegation, while the remainder supported Supreme Court justice John A. McLean of Ohio. McLean garnered more than 50 percent of the votes of the delegates from Pennsylvania, Illinois, and Indiana, indicating the conservative nature of those states and presaging the challenge that Frémont would face in carrying them.[29]

Lincoln chose not to attend the convention for fear that he would be "plat-formed"—that is, forced to accept some more extreme antislavery platform position, such as the repeal of the Fugitive Slave Act.[30] However, Lincoln encouraged Trumbull to attend, telling both Trumbull and Elihu Washburne that he preferred the more conservative McLean as the presidential nominee.[31]

The heavy dose of antislavery talk and the nomination of Frémont, a former Democrat, disturbed some of the Illinois Whigs, especially William Archer, a good friend of Lincoln's from his state legislature days. Realizing the need to balance the ticket with a more moderate candidate, Archer quickly sought out Trumbull, John Palmer, Norman B. Judd, and other Illinois Democratic leaders to ask them to consider Lincoln for vice president. Grateful for Lincoln's support of Trumbull for U.S. senator, the Democrats heartily assented to Archer's request and set about lobbying other delegates. Lincoln received 110 votes on the first informal tally, far behind William L. Dayton's 243 votes but nonetheless making Lincoln known to hundreds of influential national Republicans.[32]

Lovejoy Nominated for Congress

Many influential antislavery leaders in the local and district Republican organizations in northern Illinois came to the conclusion that it was time to elect one of their own to wider public office. They had previously agreed that they would settle for being only foot soldiers, canvassing for others, but would not themselves run for statewide office. Now they enthusiastically went about organizing for Lovejoy to become the Republican candidate for the Third Congressional District, a move Lovejoy had been contemplating for several months. He had resigned as pastor in January 1856 to spend more time and energy on his political activities.

The biggest difficulty his backers faced in obtaining the nomination was that the southern section of his district was a stronghold of Henry Clay devotees. The leadership in that area consisted of Judge Davis's friends who traveled the Eighth Judicial Circuit together. For years they had shared the Whig agenda and

44   CHAPTER 3

the comradeship of Lincoln. Among them was Leonard Swett, an able Bloomington lawyer originally from Maine, who was the preferred Whig candidate
for Congress and was expected to gain the nomination. On Swett's side was
General Asahel Gridley, a wealthy Bloomington banker. A former member of
the state legislature, he had helped bring the railroads to Bloomington, and he
was now a member of the state central committee formed at the Bloomington
Convention.[33] Other prominent citizens who favored Swett included Isaac Funk,
the region's largest landowner and farmer, and Judge T. Lyle Dickey, an avid
supporter of Clay for president and a friend of U.S. senator John Crittenden
from Kentucky.

Lovejoy, too, had prominent supporters. John Howard Bryant and his brother,
Cyrus, who had helped organize the Bureau County Republican Party on July 4,
1854, pushed the movement for Lovejoy for Congress. Burton C. Cook, a former
Democratic state senator from nearby Ottawa, was the son of one of Lovejoy's
colleagues, the Reverend Chauncey Cook. And lawyer Charles L. Kelsey held
behind-the-scenes positions in the regional Republican Party.

Much was at stake for both sides as well as for the fledgling Republican Party.
The party held its nominating convention on July 2, 1856, in Ottawa. Twenty-
five-year-old Parker Earle was the youngest delegate, indicative of the younger
men moving into the area who were attracted to Lovejoy's politics, and half a
century later, he recalled,

> I was one of the two delegates from Grundy County, Judge Redding being the
> other. The Judge was the leading lawyer of the County and a pronounced conser-
> vative politician, while I was a somewhat radical young fellow. . . .
> Every possible influence was used with me. But I was born in Rutland, Ver-
> mont and reared in an atmosphere of hostility to slavery; and I personally knew
> Mr. Lovejoy, and shared his political beliefs, and admired his great courage and
> wonderful ability as a public speaker; and I could not be persuaded to vote for
> Mr. Swett. The vote was taken very calmly[,] every man feeling that it portended
> great results. Mr. Lovejoy was nominated by a majority of one.[34]

A rally for Frémont and the Republican ticket was held on July 4, 1856, in a
lovely wooded area called Bryant's Grove at the south edge of Princeton. Lincoln
had been invited to introduce himself to the people of the area and to give one
of the day's many speeches, but he hesitated because of his disappointment that
Swett had not been nominated. (Lincoln wrote to Davis that he "went blind"
on hearing the news.)[35] Nevertheless, Lincoln went to Princeton. Lincoln knew
John Howard Bryant, a former Democratic member of the state legislature, as
well as his brother, William Cullen Bryant, the well-known poet and editor of
the *New York Evening Post*, and stayed with John Howard Bryant after the rally.

According to the *Tiskilwa Independent*, the rally attracted between eight
thousand and ten thousand people, and Lincoln's speech, which stressed the

idea the "Declaration made to the world by our Fore Fathers, 'That all men are born free and equal,'" generated "loud and enthusiastic cheers." Lovejoy then took the opportunity to highlight his moderate position, telling the crowd that "he was aware the idea had gone out to the world that he was a rank abolitionist, but he said he was not in favor of meddling in the institution where it is but he is a sworn enemy to letting any more slave territory come in. . . . He is opposed to interfering with slavery where it exists by law but will not consent to another foot of slave territory where freedom now exists." According to the newspaper report, Lovejoy had been nominated "in spite of old fogy wire-pullers, whose diluted politics have brought the country to the very brink of destruction." Lovejoy, in contrast, was among those "who fully comprehend the crisis, and whose hearts are fully devoted to the cause." But he was also no extremist but was rather "a man of prudence and discretion," "free from the ultraism so abundantly charged upon him." His work in the state legislature, at the Bloomington Convention, and at the national convention in Philadelphia "by common consent placed him among the ablest leaders in this great movement." Predicted the *Independent*, "The PEOPLE will send Mr. Lovejoy to Congress, backed by a 5,000 majority."[36]

As at Bloomington, Lincoln and Lovejoy were addressing each other's constituencies. After the rally, Lincoln wrote to his friends in the Third Congressional District, advising them that it would be helpful if they could dissuade Dickey from running against Lovejoy as a Republican: "Seeing the people there—their great enthusiasm for Lovejoy—considering the activity they will carry into the contest with him—and their great disappointment if he should now be torn from them, I really think it best to let the matter stand."[37] Lincoln's decision disappointed some of his conservative friends, but he had correctly assessed the situation. Lovejoy won by 6,069 votes.[38]

Different Campaign Tactics

During the first official national Republican contest in Illinois in 1856, both Lincoln and Lovejoy seemed driven to campaign vigorously. Lincoln claimed that he gave more than fifty speeches on Frémont's behalf, primarily in the central and southern districts of the state.[39] For reasons that are unknown, Lincoln became depressed after hearing that 110 people had voted for him for vice president at the Philadelphia Convention. He initially mocked himself, and his speeches from this period became "flat," lacking their previous inspirational tone. On July 17, the *Dixon Telegraph* lauded him, noting, "As a close observer and cogent reasoner, he has few equals," but the newspaper did not mention his positions on the issues in an overwhelmingly Republican district.[40] Moreover, though state party leaders ran announcements of Frémont rallies in the papers, they hesitated to label him a Republican, suggesting their fears that the party's

46   CHAPTER 3

name still had negative effects. The Democratic *Illinois Register* played on this ambivalence by referring to the party as the "What-y-call-ems."[41]

Democratic newspapers also criticized Lincoln personally, with one claiming that he was "desirous of climbing up the ladder of fame . . . until the Whig party was no more, then he joined the Republicans, and is now working side by side with John Wentworth, Lovejoy & Co. During the last session of the Legislature he was a candidate for U.S. Senator to fill the place of Shields, but his Abolition friends deceived him and elected Trumbull. The defeat set hard upon him, for he confidently expected to have been Senator."[42] This distortion blamed the antislavery forces rather than Democrats for Lincoln's defeat.

Antislavery Republicans and the official Illinois Anti-Nebraska Central Committee, which was organizing county groups, were having difficulty hitching together their bobsleds, as evidenced by Lincoln's lingering reluctance to appear in public with Lovejoy. The two men are known to have stood on the same platform only six times—on September 17 in Urbana, September 24 in Decatur, September 25 in Springfield, September 30 in Lacon, October 7 in Ottawa, and October 8 in Joliet.[43] In addition, the central committee deliberately avoided having Lovejoy campaign in the central and southern parts of the state.

Lovejoy accurately described his campaign as "arduous."[44] He repeated his July 4 speech wherever he could, disclaiming fanaticism, proclaiming practicality, and exposing and confronting the persistent demagoguery of his opponents with simple references to the Bible. No confrontation was more famous, more dramatic, or more successful than his speech before a hostile audience at the "Bolters' Convention," whose participants planned to nominate a candidate to run against Lovejoy at a time when the party was striving to hold together a fragile political alliance. About twenty people met on the afternoon of July 16 at the Bloomington courthouse, with Funk chairing the gathering. Those present unanimously nominated Dickey.[45]

A rally that evening in the courthouse square drew as many as a thousand people for a public ratification of Dickey's nomination. Jesse Fell had been at work behind the scenes promoting the meeting.[46] Fell had publicly supported Swett for Congress but had been in the East during the Ottawa Convention that nominated Lovejoy.[47] When he returned, however, he declared his support for the duly nominated Republican candidate. The support of Arthur and John Howard Bryant, fellow horticulturalists, would have gone a long way with Fell, as it did with young Earle. Fell would have understood that disharmony among the Republicans would be harmful for Lincoln and more dangerous for the new party than for Lovejoy.

The adroit and sarcastic General Asahel Gridley stirred up the meeting, denouncing Lovejoy as an abolitionist and "nigger thief" and saying that he wished Lovejoy and Preston Brooks had cut each other's throats.[48] At the close of Gridley's address, the meeting was declared adjourned, but someone called for Lovejoy to speak, alerting the crowd to his presence. Most of those present knew him only through his "prominent abolitionist" reputation, and many considered him "to wear both hoofs and horns."[49] Despite the unsympathetic audience, Lovejoy gave a speech that not only displayed his courage and oratorical talents but also demonstrated that the use of biblical language could have a compelling effect on listeners. His address was "based on the opening sentences of the Declaration of Independence and the Golden Rule" as well as a common appreciation of chapter 25 of Matthew: "I am accused of aiding fugitive slaves. I do not know that I ever gave aid to a slave. My Bible tells me to feed the hungry and clothe the naked, and I have done so to the best of my ability without reference to whether the applicants were bond or free, white or black, or some other shade of color. I cannot say that any of them were slaves, because, as a matter of fact, I do not know. When a poor wanderer comes to my door, hungry and asking for bread, or in tattered garments asking for clothing, I do not stop to institute an investigation as to whether he is a slave or not before relieving his wants. It is enough for me to know that he or she is a fellow creature in need of food, clothing, or shelter."[50] Two nights later, attendees at a Bloomington meeting led by Fell heartily endorsed Lovejoy, indicating a significant shift in public sentiment in the southern part of his district.[51] Within two weeks, Lovejoy had the support of Funk and Dr. Harrison Noble, who had previously lent their names to the Bolters' cause.

Lovejoy's supporters in the area were subsequently disappointed that he spent so little time there, and he wrote to Fell to explain that the circumstances of his campaign prevented him from returning to Bloomington: "God knows that I have worked as hard & as constant as I am able to do & that there is no county where I would sooner work than in old McLean. . . . The tone of the letter I recvd was a little discouraging. I must throw myself on the kindness of my friends in your county." He asked Fell to do what he could to get out the vote, suggesting that supporters "hold meetings in the School Districts." Lovejoy continued, "Every town ought to be canvassed & the name of every voter put on a list so that it may be known who has voted & at noon send for those who have not voted. We have votes enough to carry the state if they are all out." And, Lovejoy concluded, "Will you please write me & let me know how things stand in McLean."[52]

Dickey wrote to Lovejoy, challenging him to answer specific questions on his antislavery position and hoping that his responses would damage his campaign. Unintimidated, Lovejoy replied with a lengthy and forthright letter.[53] Lovejoy's popularity presented Dickey with a problem, a state of affairs acknowledged by Dickey's supporters, including Judge Davis, who wrote, "It would not profit us to inquire in this letter what has brought this about, but I am led to the

48   CHAPTER 3

conclusion that it is a melancholy fact."[54] On September 13, Dickey publicly removed himself from the contest. He nonetheless remained hostile to Lovejoy, bothered that public opinion in his area had shifted to the antislavery cause, and in 1858, he became a Democrat.[55]

Not all of Lincoln's conservative friends opposed Lovejoy. A number of others changed their minds, as Funk and Fell did. One such political associate, J. E. McClun of Platt County, wrote to Lincoln that Lovejoy had done himself much credit in the 1855 state legislature. "He is with us on the Republican platform and is an able vindicator of it. Even if he has been somewhat ultra in the past he is glad of the opportunity that this Republican movement has given him to take a more conservative shot in politics."[56]

Lovejoy was denigrated as an extremist throughout the campaign, with opponents misrepresenting his positions much more extensively than they would during the 1858 and 1860 contests. After the election, the *Bloomington Weekly National Flag* expressed its displeasure with the results by announcing, "The notorious Abolitionist and 'nigger stealer' is elected to Congress from the district."[57] The tactic apparently fell out of favor because it cost his Democratic opponent votes rather than gaining them. Two years later, when strategists expressed their fears that his positions would frighten the Kentuckians in the southern part of the district, he responded, "Now I submit that was tried on in '56 till it was worn out."[58]

Until August 27, 1856, Lincoln did not directly address the subject of abolitionism. However, when he was invited to speak at a pro-Frémont rally in Kalamazoo, Michigan, attended by twenty thousand enthusiastic opponents of slavery, he experimented with new language defining the abolitionists: "They tell us that we are in company with men who have long been known as abolitionists. What care we how many may feel disposed to labor for our cause? Why do not you . . . come in, and use your influence to make our party respectable? . . . So sure as God lives, the victory shall be yours."[59] His words here echoed those Lovejoy had spoken at the opening of the Springfield Convention: "Let us trust in God and God's truth. He is for us; who can be against us. His truth is what we are contending for, and victory will crown our efforts."[60]

After the 1856 election, Lovejoy explained to a valued acquaintance, "A part of my district extends to the middle of the State. One of the principal charges against me was the 'running off niggers' as they call it. I owned up as we say to the charge so far as feeding and keeping them was concerned which is what they mean by the phrase, & justified it & the people sustained me."[61]

Davis had predicted in July that "the outrages in Kansas & the general conduct of the administration, with the attack on Mr. Sumner have made abolitionists of those, who never dreamed they were drifting into it. . . . The readiness with which many persons support Lovejoy is surprising. . . . I think the grand reason after all is—that his views and opinions are becoming the views and opinions of a majority of people."[62] Don E. Fehrenbacher agreed, claiming that the "disorder and violence in Kansas verging at times on civil war . . . kept the anti-Nebraska coalition alive."[63] In addition, Lovejoy benefited from the fact that he was an energetic campaigner and organizer who had the fortitude to stand up to public derision and personal threats. His courage and integrity were readily recognized by those who met him. His ability to inform, entertain, and persuade audiences was effective. The earnestness of his commitment to the cause and his ready name recognition as Elijah Lovejoy's brother were also assets. He had a genius for tapping into the religious sentiments and basic humanitarian instincts of his listeners. And the large numbers of new people from New England and New York moving into northern Illinois were more open than the natives and were ready to be organized.

Lincoln had calculated with considerable accuracy that in a three-way race, the American Party candidate, Millard Fillmore, was a problem. Lincoln did his best to persuade the Fillmore enthusiasts to vote for Frémont, though underestimated the total number of votes that would be cast for Fillmore (predicting 11 percent rather than the 15 percent he actually received). If Lincoln's gallant effort had reduced Fillmore's support to 10 percent of the total vote, Frémont would have been victorious in Illinois.[64] However, Republicans took all of Illinois's statewide offices.

In sum, according to N. Dwight Harris, author of *The History of Negro Servitude in Illinois*, "This triumph in 1856 gave the new party in Illinois immense prestige within the State, and inspired its members to more extensive efforts. Heretofore it had been merely a 'Union' party of heterogeneous elements working together to prevent the expansion of slavery. Yet, how nobly the elements had stood together. The abolitionists led by Lovejoy, the Whigs headed by Lincoln and Yates, and the Anti-Nebraska Democrats inspired by Palmer, Judd and Wentworth had labored in the greatest harmony and union throughout the campaign. Every leader realized fully the victory was due to the efforts of each faction and to the unity of all." Lincoln and Lovejoy had clearly done more than their share and as much as anyone else to form what would become the Illinois Republican Party, as is evidenced by the role they played at a victory celebration in Chicago. In Harris's words, "On Wednesday evening December 10, 1856, a great banquet was held at the Tremont House in Chicago, in celebration of the memorable victory. Lincoln, Lovejoy, Turner of Freeport (President of Illinois Assembly in 1855), James Miller, J. J. Beardsley, and B. C. Cook delivered rousing speeches, and great enthusiasm prevailed."[65]

A Republican newspaper reported the next day, "It was an event which will mark in history's page the point of which despotism ceased and where the principles of constitutional freedom commenced—where clamor of demagogues failed, and the simple story of the honest freeman achieved a victory." The article went on to mention the thirteen toasts that were made by able speakers. Lincoln's toast was "To the Union—the North will maintain it—the South will not depart there from." Lovejoy's words were "To the Congressmen Elect—Loyalty to Republican principles will be fidelity of their constituency." Cook ended the toasts with, "There's a good time coming boys!"[66]

But Lincoln and Lovejoy were aware that much remained undone in the process of melding the factions more permanently, especially overcoming the differences between their two constituencies. Each man set to work reflecting on the campaign and observing the unfolding events to generate new themes and tactics that would energize the Republican movement.

4 Disputing the Supreme Court Decision, 1857

"[Negroes were regarded as] so far inferior that they had no rights
which a white man was bound to accept."
—Chief Justice Roger Taney

Both Abraham Lincoln and Owen Lovejoy disparaged the Supreme Court's political abuse of judicial power displayed in the Dred Scott decision written by Chief Justice Roger Taney. They abhorred the Court's interpretation that the Constitution provided federal authority to reduce human beings to property without rights. Both waited for an opportune moment to fasten the abuses of the justices and of southern slaveholders securely onto the public mind. The 1856 caning of Senator Charles Sumner on the Senate floor had represented a stark symbol of southern power's encroachment on northern rights and interests, but the Dred Scott decision alerted even more northerners to the erosion of their political rights.[1]

By the time Dred Scott's case reached the U.S. Supreme Court, he had been seeking his freedom and that of his wife, Harriet, for more than a decade. The March 1857 decision that the Scotts remained enslaved despite their residence in the free state of Illinois—and more severely, that slaves were not citizens and indeed "had no rights which a white man was bound to accept"—outraged many northerners and deepened the Lincoln-Lovejoy relationship. The Dred Scott episode provided them with opportunities to express in new ways that people cannot be legally reduced to things, to focus on emancipation for all those enslaved, and to develop pragmatic techniques for exposing their opponents' distortions and falsehoods. It was not by accident that these issues emerged from Missouri, the first new slave state bordering on a free state since the ratification of the Constitution in 1788.

Illinois Precedent with Slave Transit Law

Both Lincoln and Lovejoy had direct experience dealing with the legal status of slaves seeking freedom. The Illinois Supreme Court had issued a series of

52   CHAPTER 4

somewhat confusing rulings on slaves brought into the state. In a case involving
Lovejoy, the court briefly established the principle in Illinois that a slave brought
into the state by his or her master was not considered a fugitive and was granted
free status if he or she escaped. Lovejoy had been indicted for "harbouring and
secreting" an African American woman, Agnes. Testimony at the October 1843
trial revealed that Agnes's owner was bringing her in transit from Kentucky to
Missouri (both slave states) via Illinois when she escaped. Lovejoy then cited
English law and lore, quoting William Cowper,

> Slaves cannot breathe in England, if their lungs
> Receive our air, that moment they are free—
> They touch our country and their shackles fall.[2]

Lovejoy continued, "If this is the glory of England, is it not equally true of Illinois, her soil consecrated to freedom by the Ordinance of 1787 and her own
constitution?"[3] Bureau County Circuit Court judge John D. Caton instructed
the jury, "By the Constitution of this State, slavery cannot exist here. If, therefore, a master voluntarily brings his slave within the State, he becomes from
that moment free, and if he escapes from his master while in this State, it is not
an escape from slavery, but is going where a free man has a right to go; and
the harboring of such a person is no offense against our law; but the tie which
binds a slave to his master can be severed only by the voluntary act of the latter."
Because Agnes's owner had brought her into the free state of Illinois, the jury
acquitted Lovejoy of the charges of harboring Agnes, and the Illinois Supreme
Court confirmed Caton's reasoning in its 1845 *Jarrot v. Jarrot* decision, a case
argued by Lyman Trumbull that confirmed the principle that a slave voluntarily
brought into a free state by a master was legally free.[4]

In a subsequent decision, the Illinois Supreme Court upheld that principle but
found Quincy abolitionist Dr. Richard Eels guilty of harboring a slave because it
was not proved that the owner had voluntarily brought the slave into the state.[5]
However, in another case, in which Jacksonville abolitionist Julius A. Willard
was charged with aiding a fugitive slave who was traveling with his master from
one slave state to another, the court reversed the principle of a slave becoming
legally free once freely brought into a free state, ruling that transit privilege
meant that "a slaveholder has a perfect right to pass through Illinois with his
slaves and comity between the States will protect him in regarding the slaves as
such, while within our limits." This was the final case in which a northern court
denied the right of a slave to escape while in a free state and upheld slaveholders'
right to pass through a free state without risking loss of their property.[6]

During this period, Lincoln was working actively with the Illinois Supreme
Court and would undoubtedly have heard of these cases, although he did not
comment publicly on them. He had participated in two court cases involving

Disputing the Supreme Court Decision

transiting slaves. In 1841, Lincoln defended Major David Bailey, a friend with whom Lincoln had served in the Black Hawk War. Bailey was being sued by the estate of Dr. William Cromwell for refusing to pay to Cromwell's estate four hundred dollars for an "indentured servant," Nance Legins-Costly. In 1836, when he was moving to Texas, Cromwell had arranged to have Bailey purchase the services of the unwed and pregnant Nance. In exchange, Bailey, an abolitionist, signed a promissory note agreeing to pay Cromwell four hundred dollars when he received legal proof of Nance's indentured status. Lincoln won the case on the basis that involuntary servitude was illegal in Illinois and that Cromwell's estate could not produce the record of the woman's voluntary indentured status. Nance was free.[7]

In the second case, which took place in 1847, Lincoln represented a slave-holder, Robert Matson of Coles County, who sought to repossess his slave woman, Jane Bryant, and her four children. Lincoln's client claimed that his situation fell under the transit law, since he had not brought Bryant to Illinois as a permanent resident. However, evidence indicated that she had resided in Illinois for two years, and she was declared free, meaning that Lincoln lost the case.[8] Both of these cases upheld the idea that an enslaved African American brought into Illinois from another state had been freed by virtue of Illinois being a free state, or if transit law was invoked, by virtue of being a permanent resident in a free state.

These experiences with the laws regarding fugitive slaves had prepared Lincoln and Lovejoy to respond to the Dred Scott decision. Both men saw the case as a blatant disregard for the established legal precedent that freedom had accrued to any slave who resided in a free state after voluntarily having been brought there by a master, and both men saw the decision as an excellent opportunity to highlight the Slave Power's encroachment on northern sovereignty. Lincoln forcefully challenged the Supreme Court's legal and political maneuverings and developed ways to appeal to both legal conservatives and radical Republicans, while Lovejoy completely rejected the decision as an irresponsible abuse of political power.

No Federal Right to Make a Person Property

Lincoln and Lovejoy had contended for years that humans could not legally be reduced to property under the Constitution. They reluctantly had to admit that the Constitution allowed existing southern state laws to permit this practice, but human beings were no longer considered property in northern states. They had dealt with this radical distinction personally, professionally, and politically, and they would articulate and promote it to facilitate their rise to national political power.

54   CHAPTER 4

During the second session of Lincoln's term in the House of Representatives, he had cast two votes that illustrated his radical commitment that federal law did not reduce persons to the status of property. The first was precipitated by Daniel Gott's 1848 bill to prohibit the slave trade in the District of Columbia, which passed by a ninety-eight to eighty-seven vote.[9] Lincoln seized the opportunity and took the floor to discuss the District of Columbia Emancipation Act, which "had absorbed his interest for years." He had worked on it with Ohio congressman Joshua Giddings.[10] Lincoln's bill would have called for compensated, gradual emancipation for the slaves in the District if the city's voters consented by referendum. Lincoln claimed that fourteen leading local citizens supported his bill, but when called on to produce their names, he remained silent and on the following day failed to introduce his bill. Southern opposition to Gott's bill and the controversy it generated then led to the measure's reconsideration and eventual defeat.[11] Northern Whigs' reluctance to support ending the slave trade in the District signaled that Lincoln's proposal would not succeed. Nevertheless, by making his proposal, Lincoln had indicated publicly that he backed the radical idea of freeing slaves where he considered it legally possible to do so.

The second issue was even more significant. It concerned the fundamental recognition of slaves as property. Antonio Pacheco had filed a claim for a thousand-dollar payment for his slave, Lewis, who had been sent west with the U.S. Army. The case was referred to the Committee on Military Affairs, whose chair supported the claim. However, he was aware that in the past, such claims had been denied on the constitutional grounds that human beings could not be considered property. But southerners on the committee were eager to reverse that precedent.[12]

Congressman Giddings was just as determined to preserve the precedent, to resist the southerners, and to refuse the claim. He foresaw that if slaves could be considered property under the Constitution, the slaveocracy would have won a major victory. Having earned respect as the chair of the Claims Committee, he persuaded a minority of the Committee on Military Affairs to present a negative report denying Pacheco his claim, and the committee members invited Giddings to write the report. During the legislative process, Giddings realized that another vote would take place and that it would probably affirm the claim.[13]

On January 6, 1849, Giddings, in poor health, spoke against the majority committee report favoring Pacheco's claim. Giddings "insisted that the Declaration of Independence and the principle of natural rights barred the federal government from acknowledging such a property right."[14] The discouraged Giddings believed that he was speaking only for the record and posterity and had no expectation of changing the minds of the members of Congress. But he slowly became aware that his words were receiving studied attention.[15] He told his audience that robbery and piracy were crimes of small importance compared with slavery. The slave states might keep their "foul contagion," but they could not make "slave dealers" or "traders in humanity" of residents of other states.[16] Sensing that the moment had come, he called for the final vote on the majority report to award Pacheco his claim, hoping that the motion would fail. It did, by a vote of ninety to eighty-nine. Lincoln cast one of the votes to defeat the bill. Giddings wrote in his journal, "I rejoiced greatly, and really now think those among the happiest moments of my life."[17]

Just under two weeks later, the decision was reconsidered and overturned by a 101–95 vote.[18] However for that brief time, the core of the southern establishment had been threatened. With this radical risk-taking vote, Lincoln had demonstrated to himself and others the vulnerability of the southern slave strategy; the "Liberty party principle of 'freedom national' had suddenly entered the mainstream of congressional debate."[19] The South's attempt to federalize its local laws that declared African Americans to be property met stiff resistance from the North, which increasingly considered the desires of the southern Slave Power injurious to northern interests. And Lincoln had joined in taking that radical stand.

Lincoln and Lovejoy on Religion and Politics

One of the major tactics available to Lincoln and Lovejoy to expand their growing political base was to use descriptions of injustices and immoral actions to appeal to sensitive listeners. The two men did so by utilizing the language, symbols, and insights of the prevailing moral and religious ethos of the period—Protestant evangelicalism. This crucial appeal to religious sentiments to expose the immorality of reducing a person, created by God, into a piece of property lay at the heart of their effort to inspire a vision of hope that these abuses could be stopped.

Lincoln was aware of the evangelical Protestant sources of antislavery energy even though he disagreed with the abolitionist commitment to the higher law. On the one hand, according to Richard Carwardine, Lincoln "argued his antislavery case in terms which he knew would stir up the antislavery moderates of the mainstream churches."[20] Lincoln used a mixture of Jeffersonian and scriptural precepts set in the context of Whiggish self-improvement. On the other hand, Allen C. Guelzo sees the religious righteousness of the abolitionists as a problem for Lincoln: "The absolutism that drove William Lloyd Garrison . . . to attack the Constitution as an 'infamous bargain' . . . was precisely what alienated Lincoln from the abolitionists." In Guelzo's view, Lincoln disagreed with Henry David Thoreau's belief that "a righteous reform" could not be accomplished "by the use of 'expediency.'"[21] Lincoln's prudence led him to "regard constitutional means as being fully as sacred as abolitionists' ends." Guelzo insists that prudence rather than a radical religious commitment drove Lincoln to seek emancipation through legislative solution.[22] But the fact that Lincoln was driven by a moral commitment to end slavery was itself radical. Lincoln came to understand that religious language was a helpful tactic, and he applied it wisely. More important, Guelzo does not appreciate that at that point Lincoln was no different from Lovejoy and the other radical political abolitionists with whom the future president cooperated to achieve their mutual goal.

Both Lincoln and Lovejoy knew that religious sentiments clothed in behavioral terms could be an effective method for influencing people to do good. Each man had delivered a formative speech back in 1842 that indicated his personal perception of the role of religion and politics. Lincoln, more keenly aware of the manipulative emotional abuses of religion, used more poetic language; Lovejoy was more at home with the traditional language of God. But both were concerned with human responses and interpretations of life-shaping events. Comparing these differences and similarities provides some background for their next major joint political step.

In 1842, Lincoln delivered a Washington's birthday speech to the Washington Temperance Society, which sought to give hope to destitute alcoholics as the first president had brought the hope of survival to a new nation, a method of encouraging sobriety in a nonjudgmental atmosphere that had recently become popular. Washington had been Lincoln's boyhood hero, and he told the society's members, "To add brightness to the sun, or glory to the name of Washington, is alike impossible. Let none attempt it." He praised the society's successes, likening the new movement to a "powerful chieftain, going forth 'conquering and to conquer'" and to an archangel invading the devil's den. He described drunkards as overcoming the "*great adversary*," the demonic forces of deception. Although he never mentioned God, he alluded to Christian customs—rites, altars, worship, sacrifice, and especially the "last trump" (the trumpet sound of judgment). In his view, "Success is so much greater *now* than *heretofore*, . . . doubtless owing to rational causes"—the work of the "all conquering mind." He also ruminated on the tactics and motives of earlier, failed reformers: "It is so easy and so common to *ascribe* motives to men of these classes, other than those they profess to act upon. The preacher, it is said, advocates temperance because he is a fanatic and desires a union of Church and State; the lawyer from his pride and vanity of hearing himself speak; and the hired agent, for his salary."[23]

At the time Lincoln delivered this speech, he was struggling with his own weakness—his inability to keep his promise to marry Mary Todd. He wrote to his good friend, Joshua Speed, on July 4, 1842, "I must regain my confidence in my own ability to keep my resolves when they are made. In that ability, you know, I once prided myself as the only, or at least the chief gem of my character. That gem I lost—how, and when, you too well know. I have not yet regained

Disputing the Supreme Court Decision 57

it; and until I do, I can not trust myself in any matter of much importance."[24] According to historian Stewart Winger, Lincoln's temperance address "was the first great installment of Lincoln's romantic and Christian political thought."[25] The Washington Temperance Society redeemed alcoholics by encouraging former drinkers to reason with those afflicted and give them hope rather than by denouncing them as condemned sinners with no chance of renewal. Said Lincoln, "Love through all their actions runs, and all their words are mild. . . . And when such is the temper of the advocate, and such of the audience, no good cause can be unsuccessful."[26] Lincoln thus "addressed the evangelicals *on their own terms*," displaying a "full command of a form he would bring to perfection at Gettysburg. . . . He used the language of disinterested benevolence that was fundamental to the antebellum reform movements."[27] This speech offered as moving a rendition of a spiritual transformation as any Methodist evangelical preacher could have produced; the only difference was that the agent for the transformation was not an inspired Christian but a former alcoholic: "But when one, who has long been known as a victim of intemperance, bursts the fetters that have bound him, and appears before his neighbors 'clothed, and in his right mind,' a redeemed specimen of long lost humanity, and stands up with tears of joy trembling in eyes, to tell of the miseries once endured, now to be endured no more . . . however simple his language, there is a logic and eloquence in it, that few, with human feelings, can resist."[28]

Though Lincoln appreciated the witness of a transformational experience honestly given in simple language, he also understood the pitfalls of authoritarian judgmentalism: "To command his action, or to mark [the person denounced] as one to be shunned and despised, and he will retreat within himself, close all the avenues to his head and his heart and . . . you shall no more be able to pierce him, than to penetrate the hard shell of a tortoise with rye straw. Such is man, and so must he be understood by those who would lead him, even to his own best interest."[29]

Lincoln believed that human beings naturally rebel against coercion and domination by creating defenses that become impenetrable to themselves as well as others. But he believed that "therein is a drop of honey that catches his heart, which, when once gained, you will find but little trouble in convincing his judgment of the justice of your cause, if indeed that cause really be a just one."[30]

On July 21, 1842, Lovejoy preached a sermon on "Religion and Politics" that was published in the *Western Citizen* on January 20, 1843.[31] Lovejoy shared Lincoln's preference for mild, loving words to those in need. His father, the Reverend Daniel Lovejoy, had struggled with depression before hanging himself in the family barn a decade earlier.[32] Lovejoy began his sermon by quoting from II Timothy 2:25: "Well we must have compassion on the weak, pulling them out

58 CHAPTER 4

of the fire and the mists, as the case may be: 'Meekly instructing those who oppose themselves,' is the divine instruction."[33] However, he differed with Lincoln on the separation of church and state. In Lovejoy's view, "Religion and politics have been separated long enough. It is just a separation as the *Adversary of Good* loves to see."[34] Lovejoy advocated not a union of church and state but rather a judgment on the state by the church, similar to Lincoln's "last trump."

Lovejoy's sermon was based on King David's last words, "He that ruleth over men must be just, ruling in the fear of God": "I am prepared to say that the commands, precepts and instructions directed to the king, magistrates, rulers and other kinds of offices, are in their general principles applicable to every voter in this country; that whatever the Bible, reason, justice and humanity require of lawmakers, judges, and executives, and other such offices, they require of every elector."[35] Lovejoy took the revolutionary view that in a republic, each voter was a sovereign and combined it with the Old Testament tenet that a sovereign must be just. He also reached out beyond the authority of the Bible to those authorities developed by the Enlightenment and classical training: reason, justice, and humanity.

Lovejoy claimed that "every voter is responsible for the laws which are enacted and the manner of their execution," citing the example of the wrongful indictment of mutiny brought against the Mendi Africans on the ship *Amistad*: "Who does not remember, and remember with indignant shame, that it was the People of the United States vs. Cinque and his companions? Our Attorney General pled against them, and was paid in our money. Now there certainly is individual responsibility in this thing, whether we feel it or not."[36]

Lovejoy also claimed that it was practicable and possible to combine religion and politics, saying, "Some men seem to have settled down with the conviction that it is utterly impossible for a man to be honest while making and executing laws, and in discharging other political duties—that honesty and politics must be forever divorced. . . . The notion is losing ground that religion must be confined to the sanctuary and the Sabbath." For Lovejoy, "Public morals require that we should carry our religion to the polls." He illustrated the negative consequences of having "unjust and profligate" political leaders. He accused President John Tyler of profanity and labeled him "a slaveholder, and consequently a robber and oppressor of the poor." He also noted "the criminal and murderous practice of dueling. How is this kept in countenance by those men whom Christians apparently delight to honor?"[37]

Continuing on the subject of slavery, Lovejoy declared, "Abolitionists are charged with being enemies of their country. But it is not so. [William] Cowper said, 'England, with all its faults, I love thee still.' So can I say of my own land and I love it nonetheless, because I would remove an element, which, *if allowed to remain, will work out its ruin, as surely as there is a God of justice on the throne.* . . . Some fear lest religion should, in the attempt, be overwhelmed and polluted.

Disputing the Supreme Court Decision

But I fear it not. It may have many severe struggles, but the Gospel will triumph. . . . God has expressly enjoined this."[38]

Lovejoy concluded his sermon by applying it to the issue before the voters the next day: "And now, brethren, what will you do? What ought you to do? What does God require you to do? Tomorrow this thing is to be tested. We are to be just, voting in the fear of God; or unjust, voting in the fear of the devil. I do not decide what you shall do, nor for whom you shall vote. To your own God and judge you stand or fall; but in the name of Jehovah, the rock of Israel, I require you to vote in the fear of God."[39] Much of the speech was antithetical to the positions of the anticlerical and politically neutral William Lloyd Garrison, yet Lovejoy never abandoned a keystone of Garrison's thinking—"the sin of slavery."[40] In fact, Lovejoy reenergized the Illinois antislavery political movement in the early 1850s by helping to organize Christian antislavery societies with the Reverend Jonathan Blanchard and Frederick Douglass.[41]

Lincoln's address and Lovejoy's sermon indicate that both men had reflected seriously on the Calvinistic tradition and had moved beyond a predetermined future for individuals, though they still maintained a commitment to the divine sovereign power that required justice. Lincoln provided a profound, radical response to the Supreme Court's interpretations of the Constitution that was formulated on the basis of his poetic, romantic, and pragmatic use of religious language. Lovejoy also provided such a response but formulated it on the basis of his traditional, dramatic, and pragmatic use of religious language.

Lincoln and Lovejoy Respond to the Dred Scott Decision

Lincoln looked for a way to interpret the issues of the Supreme Court decision to the people. He was in a quandary. In 1838 he had insisted, "Let reverence of law . . . become the political religion of America."[42] But in the words of historian David Donald, "Lincoln's faith in the impartial, rational judiciary was shaken; never again did he give deference to the rulings of the Supreme Court."[43] Said Lincoln, "We think the Dred Scott decision is erroneous . . . and shall do what we can to have [the Court] to over-rule this."[44] Lincoln could not denounce the decision outright. Doing so would have made him appear to be a Garrisonian abolitionist and cost him the support of his conservative constituency. Yet if he did not find new common ground with the antislavery wing of the Illinois Republican Party, he would be out of the Senate race before it started. He knew well the importance of taking time to observe and reflect. As he wrote two years later, "To be fruitful in invention, it is indispensable to have a *habit* of observation and reflection."[45] So he meditated on this quandary.

He also delayed his public response for practical reasons. During those hard economic times, he had to earn money before he could turn to active campaigning. Also, he needed to know what position Senator Stephen A. Douglas

60   CHAPTER 4

was taking. On June 12, Douglas obliged by making a speech in Springfield in which he called for respect for and obedience to the U.S. Constitution, expressed his horror at the idea that equality would lead to amalgamation of the races, and explained his view that the Declaration of Independence applied solely to whites.[46]

Exactly two weeks later, Lincoln responded, addressing the concerns of his conservative friends, his antislavery friends, and the general public. He reminded conservatives that Douglas had wrongly accused his opponents of criticizing the final verdict. Lincoln explained that although the process had been erroneous, the verdict that Scott was still an enslaved person under Missouri law was correct, and the Court should have considered that point alone. Lovejoy, in contrast, considered both the process and the verdict wrong.

Lincoln was well aware that Douglas's statement that there was a "natural disgust in the minds of nearly all white people" at the idea of racial amalgamation was a tactic to attract some conservative voters. Lincoln claimed that Douglas thought he could "fasten the odium of that idea upon his adversaries" and thus "struggle through the political storm." Lincoln accused Douglas of basing his political hopes on "being able to appropriate the benefits of this disgust to himself. . . . He clings to this hope as a drowning man to the last plank." Then Lincoln mocked Douglas's "counterfeit logic that because I do not want a black woman for a slave I must necessarily want her for a *wife*." And he drove the point home by turning the disgust back on to the slaveholders: "These statistics show that slavery is the greatest source of amalgamation," as children were conceived by the "forced concubinage of their masters."[47]

To appeal to those with antislavery sympathies, Lincoln cited Justice Benjamin R. Curtis's dissent from the Dred Scott decision. In response to Taney's claim that African Americans now received more respect in society than had been the case during the revolutionary era, Lincoln pointed out that although African Americans in New Hampshire, Massachusetts, New Jersey, New York, and North Carolina had voted to ratify the Constitution at proportionally the same rates as whites, those five states no longer allowed blacks to vote.[48]

Lincoln described a slave as locked into "a prison house . . . bolted in with a lock of a hundred keys, which can never be unlocked without the concurrence of every key; the keys in the hands of a hundred different men, and they scattered to a hundred different and distant places." And, he added, slaveholders were still musing about "how to make the impossibility of his escape more complete than it is."[49]

As far as Lincoln could see, it was impossible to contemplate a way to free the slaves in the South. But he was determined that the South dare not contemplate building new prisons anywhere else, and he further recognized that mammon, ambition, philosophy, and the theology of the day were combining to pin the

Disputing the Supreme Court Decision

slaves in their place. Lovejoy, however, had a plan for exposing the false religious claims implied in the Taney decision.

Lincoln also returned to a common theme stressed by Lovejoy and the radicals. The Declaration of Independence had previously been "held sacred by all; but now, to aid in making the bondage of the negro universal and eternal, it is assailed and sneered at, and construed and hawked at, and torn, till if its framers could rise from their graves, they could not at all recognize it." He especially assailed Douglas for saying that the signers of the Declaration of Independence "referred to the white race alone, and not to the African when they declared all men to have been created equal—that they were saying that British subjects on this continent were equal to British subjects born and residing in Great Britain." At that point, Lincoln held up a copy of Taney's decision and urged his listeners to "read that carefully over some leisure hour, and ponder well upon it—see what a mere wreck—mangled ruin—it makes of our once glorious Declaration. . . . And now I appeal to all—Democrats as well as others—are you willing that the Declaration shall be thus frittered away?"[50]

Lincoln directly confronted Taney's abuses to the Declaration while Lovejoy alluded to Taney's abuses of religion. However, Lincoln and Lovejoy agreed with the Republican Party's view that Taney had been incorrect in asserting that according to the Constitution, slaves were property under federal law. Lincoln declared forthrightly, "The Republicans inculcate, with whatever of ability they can, that the negro is a man; that his bondage is cruelly wrong, and that the field of his oppression ought not to be enlarged."[51] Lincoln was moving toward a more forceful appeal to the party's antislavery base.

Lovejoy waited until he had a platform in Congress to respond to the Dred Scott decision. On February 17, 1858, he vehemently challenged its contentions that "human beings are property" and that "the system of American Slavery was right, having the sanction of a natural and revealed Religion." Said Lovejoy, "As the whole of this discussion, in its real merits, hinges on this principle or dogma, I confront it at the very threshold and deny it. I affirm that [slavery] has not the sanction of natural or revealed religion, or of the Constitution.[52]

Lovejoy argued, "Indeed, till within a very few years, Slavery was acknowledged by all classes, in the slave no less than in the free States, to be an evil, social, moral, and political—a wrong to the slave, a detriment to the master, and a blight on the soil; its very existence deplored, and its ultimate termination looked forward to with earnest and often impatient hope." Lovejoy then used picturesque language to claim that this new and pernicious doctrine that slavery was a right was being carried into the free states on "a constitutional *palanquin*," or fancy litter. The new doctrine was "manufactured and borne aloft on the one side by a Democratic Executive [Buchanan] and on the other by a

62 CHAPTER 4

Democratic Jesuit Judge [Taney]!" Lovejoy also employed another vivid image to reveal the destructive power of the Dred Scott decision: "The President and Chief Justice, by new, unheard of, and most unwarrantable interpretations of the Constitution, are endeavoring to enthrone and nationalize Slavery, and make it the dominant power in the land."[53]

Lincoln had similarly claimed that Douglas and Taney sought to make slavery "universal and eternal" and had focused his strongest feelings against the misrepresentations of the Declaration and Constitution. Lovejoy even more forcefully and categorically contended that "in no article, in no section, in no line, word, or syllable, or letter, is the idea of property in man expressed or implied" and that alleging otherwise was "absolutely untrue and slanderous toward the framers of the Constitution." Like Lincoln, Lovejoy admonished Douglas for reducing Thomas Jefferson's declaration "that all men are created equal" to all British men. And, Lovejoy thundered, the Taney decision was based "upon the false, atrocious, and *impious argument that human beings are property! Again I meet this doctrine, and spurn it. The Supreme Being never intended that human beings should be property*. . . . [W]hen you call upon me to keep step to the sound of clanking chains and of human manacles, to the wild shriek of human agony and suffering, I cannot do it. It grates upon me like the very dissonance of hell. I cannot keep step to such music."[54]

Lovejoy followed up this impassioned argument by reiterating his Republican confidence in the doctrine of the consent of the governed. "If a majority of a people of a Territory or of a State will vote that they themselves and their children shall alike be slaves, I am content. But that a majority have the rightful power to take away the natural rights of any one single human being, I deny."[55] This idea had formed the core of Lincoln's argument from the beginning.[56]

Lovejoy and Lincoln Prepare for the 1858 Elections

Lincoln's response to the Dred Scott decision had encompassed elements of the conservative, moderate, and radical positions. By the end of 1857, he was preparing to overcome the huge barriers necessary to become the next U.S. senator from Illinois. It would be an uphill climb to expose the Little Giant's weaknesses and win over enough people to defeat the state's well-organized and controlling Democratic Party. Could he accomplish the tricky task of winning with a diverse coalition of formerly antagonistic political factions? Could he find new themes and tactics to hold them together and move forward?

Before Lovejoy could leave for Washington, he needed to prepare his family and church for his departure. His parishioners encouraged him to continue to speak truth to power. At a farewell gathering, the members of Princeton's Hampshire Colony Congregational Church expressed their gratitude for "his efforts in the pulpit and in the philanthropic and reformatory movements of the day" and noted that he had gained the respect of the entire community for exerting "a controlling and far reaching influence in forming the sentiment and molding the character of our population."[57]

Living in Washington would require Lovejoy to make a number of adjustments. He would need someone he trusted to assist him with his correspondence. He would need friends and acquaintances to help him navigate an environment where men whose names he would recognize behaved much like common folk. He would be a novice navigating in alien waters with rapid currents of unfamiliar institutional patterns and labyrinthine procedures. Could he adapt the pragmatic skills he had used to achieve political power so that he could retain it? Could he find the themes and images he needed and develop a cadre of people who shared his radical vision?

5 Trusting Those Who Care for the Results, 1858

"Our cause, then, must be intrusted to, and conducted by its own
undoubted friends, those whose hands are free, whose hearts are in
the work—who care for the result."
—Abraham Lincoln

Abraham Lincoln ended a politically sensitive March 8, 1958, letter to Owen Lovejoy, "Let this be strictly confidential. . . . I have some valued friends who would not like me any the better for writing it."[1] This cautionary tone demonstrates that Lincoln trusted Lovejoy enough to risk giving him candid information. Lincoln was taking risks to win the favor of the more radical opponents of slavery.

Lincoln also gave Lovejoy a friendly warning about some machinations against his reelection in DeWitt County, the most conservative county in Lovejoy's congressional district. The details represent a significant step in the relationship between the two men: "I have just returned from court in one of the counties of your District where I had an inside view that few will have who correspond with you; and I feel it rather a duty to say a word to you about it. Your danger has been the democracy would wheedle some republican to run against you without a nomination, relying mainly on democratic votes. I have seen the strong men who could make the most trouble in that way, and find that they view the thing in the proper light, and will not consent to be so used. But they have been urgently tempted by the enemy; and I think it is still the point for you to guard most vigilantly."[2]

Lovejoy responded by sending a form letter warning his supporters about the Democratic scheming.[3] The letter so upset one conservative antiabolitionist that he wrote to Judge David Davis, "We are thrashed out completely. You never saw abolitionists flock out so in your life. Lovejoy has sent confidential letters, to every Abolitionist in the county and probably in the district. I saw one, day before yesterday, an appeal to the Sympathizers and Abolitionists; every one of them turned out to the rescue. I am not only mad, but tired of this Nigger Worshipping. If Lovejoy is to be the nominee, I am ready to vote for a Douglas

Democrat."[4] On June 7, Davis wrote to General William Wallace, "If it was not for saving Lincoln for the United States Senate a pretty great outbreak would follow. I don't believe Lovejoy can be beaten if nominated and there is no use of bolting."[5]

The troublemaking continued even after Lovejoy was nominated for a second term. T. Lyle Dickey of Ottawa had been stymied in both 1856 and 1858 in his efforts to run against Lovejoy as a Republican. He was now convinced that his friend Lincoln had gone over to the "Abolition Party" and needed to be separated from it for his own good. Dickey and the members of his camp falsely claimed that Lovejoy was secretly supporting "pure abolition candidates" for the state legislature who would vote against Lincoln for the U.S. Senate.[6]

Lincoln's young legal protégé from Champaign, Henry Clay Whitney, shared Dickey's ardent antiabolitionism, writing to Lincoln, "True, Lovejoy may be invincible in that district but the loss of two or three members of the Legislature through the greediness of those *stinking abolitionists* may cost you the election. . . . [I]f Lovejoy & c. get a balance of power of Abolitionists in the Legislature they will demand Lovejoy for the Senate &c. . . . [T]here is more danger in it to my notion than in everything that Douglas can accomplish by scouring the Country." Lincoln risked losing the votes of his avid antiabolitionist friends. Whitney warned, "It is not so clear that such republicans as Coffing [Churchill, Whig lawyer from Peru, Illinois,] & a host of others who hate abolitionism will support avowed Abolitionists."[7]

Immediately after getting Whitney's letter, Lincoln wrote to Lovejoy and their mutual friend, State Senator Burton C. Cook. "I have a letter from a very true friend, and intelligent man, insisting that there is a plan on foot in LaSalle and Bureau to run Douglas republicans . . . for the legislature in those counties." According to Lincoln, in exchange for Democratic support for some extreme abolitionists for the state legislature, Republicans in the district would support Democratic nominees for the legislature.[8]

Lovejoy replied immediately after receiving Lincoln's letter, assuring him that the rumors had had minimal effect and that they could be interpreted as efforts among a few legislative candidates jockeying for their own advantage. According to Lovejoy, "This county will send a clean Republican to the Legislature whatever his antecedents. I am assured that Lasalle is all right, I think the rumors that are afloat are but efforts to secure the nomination & that when the nominations are made the people will sustain them whatever a few may say or do. I mean to try & keep my district all right & the counties connected with it. I was at Clinton & our friends assured me that D[ouglas] lost ground while there."[9] The trusting collaboration between Lincoln and Lovejoy was growing deeper. They were turning another political page.

The possibility that Lincoln would win the Senate seat was increasing. Republicans had won many races both in Illinois and nationwide in 1856. The anti-Nebraska Democrats who had blocked his first bid for the Senate now supported him. His June address on the Dred Scott decision satisfied many voters. Then, however, some powerful eastern Republicans became enamored with Douglas's efforts to delay Kansas's admission as a slave state.

Douglas had reconsidered the implications of his 1854 concept of popular sovereignty for Kansas statehood. He realized that if the popular vote of a territory was not representative of the people, it made a mockery of his concept. Douglas began a series of complicated maneuvers in March 1858 to prevent the Democratic Buchanan administration from admitting Kansas as a slave state. In August, the people of Kansas in essence voted to become a free state.

The matter was finally settled, much to the distress of Buchanan and the Democrats, and with much appreciation from Lovejoy and Republicans for Douglas's assistance. However, Douglas's active role in preventing Kansas from becoming a slave state doomed his presidential chances. In the words of Robert W. Johannsen, the crisis over Kansas's statehood "left a legacy of party disruption and sectional hatred from which the nation would not recover."[10] This deep dissension among the national Democrats buoyed the Illinois Republicans and Lincoln, but not for long.

Several prominent leaders recognized a measure of statesmanship and integrity in what Douglas had done. Horace Greeley, the ambitious editor of the Republican *New York Tribune*, wrote that Douglas's "course has not only been merely right, it has been conspicuously, courageously, eminently so."[11] Republicans in the East suggested that the Illinois party support Douglas's reelection. Lincoln's friend Elihu Washburne had worked with Douglas in Congress to help delay the Kansas vote; he picked up Greeley's battle cry of support for Douglas. But Illinois senator Lyman Trumbull confided to Lincoln "that some of our friends here act like fools in running after & flattering Douglas." But, Trumbull reassured Lincoln, "I have no sort of idea of making Douglas our leader either here or in Ills. He has done nothing as yet to commend him to any honest Republican—He still endorses the Dred Scott decision & no man who does so ought to be thought of as deserving Republican support."[12]

Lincoln responded to Trumbull, "What does the New-York Tribune mean by it's constant eulogizing, and admiring, and magnifying [of] Douglas?"[13] Trumbull advised Lincoln to send his law partner, William Herndon, to consult with Douglas and Greeley. Herndon returned from the East gravely concerned and wrote a stern letter to Washburne telling him "Illinois is not for sale. We here are not willing to be sacrificed for a fiction—national maneuvers."[14]

Lovejoy was among the Republicans who appreciated Douglas's efforts to keep Kansas free. Lovejoy believed that when Kansans voted again, they would prohibit slavery in their new constitution, thus making Douglas an unexpected supporter of the nonextension of slavery. The *Springfield Journal*, now a Re-

Trusting Those Who Care for the Results 67

publican paper, charged the Democratic *Springfield Register* with hypocrisy for pillorying the "Black Republicans" since Douglas had taken the same policy position.[15]

Exposing Douglas's contradictions helped Lincoln with the antislavery wing but not with the conservative Republicans and Democrats whom Greeley was hoping to entice into the antislavery movement by nominating a Democrat. To secure the endorsement of the Illinois Republicans and win the Senate seat, Lincoln needed a new tactic, with new language, to appeal to conservatives, radical antislavery Republicans, and the general public.

Most Illinois opponents of the Kansas-Nebraska Act still distrusted Douglas. All of the antecedent parties of the Republican coalition had reason to be displeased with him. In fact, defeating Douglas became a basic factor uniting the factions in the Republican Party. The party's county leaders eagerly included nominations for the U.S. Senate on their convention agendas, directly appealing to active citizens to get involved in the nominating process for Lincoln. The tactic of encouraging countywide conventions had been used by both Lincoln and Lovejoy since the mid-1840s, but it had seldom been used for nominating a U.S. Senate candidate because senators were elected by the state legislatures rather than by direct vote of the people. On June 12, 1858, when the Bureau County Republican Convention nominated Lovejoy for his second term in Congress, it also nominated Lincoln for the Senate.[16] Cook, Lake, LaSalle, Henry, Livingston, and Stark Counties made similar nominations at about the same time.[17] Capable leaders emerged from both the former Whig and Democratic Parties in northern Illinois to strengthen the Republican Party, while activists from the Free Democratic Party, who had built up county political networks in 1854 and 1856, added their loyalties and energized this endeavor.

Claimed the *Ottawa Free Trader* on July 24, 1858, "That convention which nominated Owen Lovejoy for Congress in this district was composed nine-tenths of old line abolitionists—the 'Libertymen' of five or six years ago—no one will dispute, for we have their names and political history before us and can furnish the proof. These men, not only in that convention, but *at all the conventions and meetings* of the so called 'republican party,' do most of the moving and talking, and pull all the wires."[18] Illinois historian Arthur Charles Cole reported that at the state Republican Nominating Convention in Springfield on June 16, more than a thousand people gave Lincoln a standing ovation and a unanimous vote and that "ninety-five county meetings had given such an endorsement to Lincoln."[19]

Lincoln accepted the nomination with his now-famous House Divided speech in the Hall of Representatives in the State Capitol. He was now ready to announce publicly a hopeful, rational, radical plan to free the slaves from their prison—to contain the injustice of slavery so that the South, like the North,

68   CHAPTER 5

would eventually free them. The Slave Power's celebration of the Dred Scott decision, the dissension in the Democratic Party over Kansas, and the lingering disgust over the betrayal of the Missouri Compromise by the Kansas-Nebraska Act had created widespread outrage in Illinois. Lincoln had new hope.

Lincoln may well have remembered the thoughts of his political hero, Henry Clay, that the people's aspirations for liberty cannot be ignored indefinitely without drastic results. Eulogizing Clay in 1852, Lincoln had alluded to the Kentucky senator's courage in standing up to the southern slaveholders over the Missouri Compromise. Lincoln quoted a speech Clay had given in 1827: "If they would repress all tendencies towards liberty and ultimate emancipation . . . they must penetrate the human soul, and eradicate the light of reason, and the love of liberty. Then, and not till then, when universal darkness and despair prevail, can you perpetuate slavery."[20]

Lincoln might also have been inspired by Lovejoy's February 1858 speech to the U.S. House of Representatives, "Human Beings Not Property," which was widely distributed at the time and remains Lovejoy's best-known address. It not only used the term "ultimate termination" but, more important, looked forward "with earnest and often impatient hope."[21] Lincoln was ready to ignore the political advice of his old friends and risk charting a new path.

The House Divided speech began, "If we could first know *where* we are, and *whither* we are tending, we could then better judge *what* to do, and *how* to do it."[22] A year earlier, he had seen slavery as an entrenched, morally wrong institution that nevertheless had to be tolerated. Now he saw it as a moral wrong that should eventually be terminated. He redefined the condition of slavery for the public mind. It would no longer be seen as a hopeless struggle between two poles—those agitating for its immediate abolition versus those insisting on slavery as a positive good in perpetuity. Neither of these positions had ever claimed the hearts of the masses North or South.

Lincoln noted that the agitation over slavery had worsened since the passage of the Kansas-Nebraska Act and that the Union could not last indefinitely at this rate of decline: "In my opinion, [the agitation] will not cease, until a crisis is reached and passed." He continued by arguing in words that are now familiar, "A house divided against itself cannot stand. I believe this government cannot endure, permanently half *slave* and half *free*. I do not expect the Union to be *dissolved*—I do not expect the house to *fall*—but I *do* expect it will cease to be divided. It will become *all* one thing or *all* the other."[23] With this sentence, Lincoln was emphasizing the encroachment of slavery into the North, hinting that slavery could be reintroduced even in Illinois.

His listeners would have been well aware that the phrase *a house divided* came from Jesus—specifically, Matthew 12:25. Jesus was admonishing the Pharisees for using duplicitous language to confuse his disciples. Lincoln would use the speech to admonish the Democrats, claiming that the national political house was built on the duplicitous language used in the decisions made by the Slave Power through the voices of President Franklin Pierce, Chief Justice Roger Taney, President James Buchanan, and Senator Stephen Douglas.

Then Lincoln applied a phrase, *ultimate extinction*, which would provide hope that slavery could eventually be eliminated. In so doing, Lincoln shifted the stereotypic understanding of abolition from its old connotations of agitating for immediate emancipation to a new understanding of a rational plan to end slavery by stopping its spread: "The *opponents* of slavery, will arrest the further spread of it, and place it where the public mind shall rest in the *belief* that it is in the course of ultimate extinction." He concluded by placing his confidence in the people of Illinois's political and religious antislavery movement: "Our cause, then, must be intrusted to, and conducted by its own undoubted friends—those whose hands are free, whose hearts are in the work—who *do care* for the result."[24]

Lincoln had helped define the emerging political ground.[25] Clothing his ideas in religious language, he gave people the hope that if they admitted that slavery was wrong, prevented its spread, and defeated its defenders, especially its chief spokesman in the North, Senator Douglas, it would be on the road to extinction. Lincoln hoped and expected that over time, the southern states would repeal the laws that supported slavery.[26]

The speech left Democrats aghast. The party's defenders of the slaveholders' interests claimed that Lincoln had made "an implied pledge on behalf of the Republican party to make war on the South and destroy the Union."[27] Douglas insisted that Lincoln was now a Garrisonian abolitionist, unabashedly painting Lincoln as a supporter of full African American equality.[28] Frederick Douglass later said that no man of his time had done more than Douglas "to intensify hatred of the negro."[29] Conservative Whigs scolded Lincoln, warning that his "speech would injure his chances in central Illinois, enabling Democrats to portray him as a dangerous radical."[30] Lincoln later redirected his political language and focused on defending himself against Douglas's charges that he backed Negro equality, but the moderate antislavery principles of nonextension and noninterference had been defined in memorable terms.[31] According to Douglass, "The speech helped the friends of freedom recognize Lincoln as a statesman who could unite the political forces [opposed to] the slave power."[32] For his part, Lincoln later stated that if he could choose to be remembered for only one thing, "I should choose that speech and leave it to the world unerased."[33]

Lovejoy rejoiced on reading Lincoln's speech. "It sounds like God's truth from the mouth of the prophet. . . . It will shatter the doubtings of thousands of weak and timorous souls who are under the ban of pro-slavery sympathizing and small despots all about us. They can now defy these in the strength of Lincoln's leadership. To the faithful it is a new hope."[34] Lincoln was on board with the

70   CHAPTER 5

plan to put an eventual end to slavery, as Lovejoy had advocated since 1843—a religiously motivated ethical imperative to prohibit slavery incrementally and politically in areas where the Constitution allowed that prohibition. Lincoln was taking a calculated risk based on his experience of the reliability of the Illinois antislavery constituency, of which Lovejoy was the leading voice.

Lovejoy's Renomination Speech

On June 30, 1858, Lovejoy accepted his unanimous renomination to Congress with a revealing and strategic speech. He introduced his plan to proceed. He reminded his supporters that he was not a Garrisonian abolitionist advocating the immediate end of slavery. "For myself, I hate slavery with a deathless and earnest hatred, and would like to see it exterminated, as *some time by some means* it must be. But because I thus feel towards slavery, it does not follow that I shall seek its extermination in unjustifiable modes." He assured his critics, "I am told that fears are expressed about the southern part of the District and the southern part of the State,—fears that Lovejoy will frighten away Kentuckians. . . . I have had many a cordial pressure of the hand and kindly gleam of the eye from those same Kentuckians. After hearing me advocate my principles, and God knows I never concealed them, they have often said to me: 'I am just as much of an abolitionist as you are.' I do not care to make any allusion to the campaign of 1856 which might have the appearance of boasting, but I must be permitted to say that anyone who talks about Lovejoy loading down the ticket must himself be ignorant of the history of that period, or presume on the ignorance of others." Lovejoy was proud to be a Republican, telling his listeners, "The sooner we forget what we have been, and only remember that we are Republicans now, the better. The original and variant elements of our party had to be melted in the crucible of our common cause." He claimed that when he was often accused of becoming less radical and rabid, he would reply, "It is no matter who has changed, so that we are all right and all together *now*."[35]

Two weeks before the renomination speech, Lincoln wrote to encourage his friend, Ward Lamon, not to resist Lovejoy's renomination: doing so would "result in nothing but disaster all around." Lovejoy "has been known as an abolitionist, but is now occupying none but common ground." Concluded Lincoln, "As to the inclination of some Republicans to favor Douglas, that is one of the chances I have to run, and which I intend to run with patience."[36]

Lovejoy repaid the favor in his speech, offering a wholehearted endorsement of Lincoln:

It is asked if I am for Lincoln. My reply is that the Republican Party was not organized for the benefit of any man—it was not made for Lincoln or Lovejoy, or any one else, but it was organized for the purpose of giving political efficiency to those principles of freedom with which, in theory, our government is distinct, but which have of late in its administration been crucified. I am no hero worshipper. . . . And now I am prepared to say that I am for Lincoln, not because he is an old line Whig—to me this is no objection and it is no commendation—but I am for him because he is a true hearted man, and that, come what will, unterrified by power, unseduced by ambition, he will remain true to the great principles upon which the Republican party is organized.[37]

Lovejoy then reiterated that loyalty to the cause was what mattered:

I am for him for the same reasons that you and those you represent are for me.— Why have the people of this District risen in their majesty, and poured out to the primary meetings in multitudes through streams and mud, and honored me with this unanimous nomination by acclamation? Was this because they wanted to honor me as an individual? Not that, but because they thought I had been true to those principles which they cherish and love as above all price and above all individuality. For this reason I am for Lincoln.

He ended, "Let us be true to our principles and God will crown our efforts with success."[38] Two weeks later, Lovejoy sent Lincoln a copy of an extra edition of the *Bureau County Republican* that contained the full text of Lovejoy's speech.[39]

The Negro Equality Issue

On August 4, Lovejoy wrote to Lincoln, bringing him up to date and sharing opinions on Negro equality:

I do not know of any Douglas Republicans in this county unless it means Douglas men who are becoming Republicans. . . .
I showed up Dred Scottism & P[opular] S[overeignty] as irreconcilably opposed as well as I could. I had a cordial reception. I believe that the bugaboo of Negro Equality has pretty much lost its power. . . . Is it true that [John] Crittenden [Whig senator from Kentucky and friend of Lincoln's] is exerting his influence for Douglas? . . .
I think you said the whole in a word when you said that the mistake of Judge D[ouglas] was that he made slavery a little thing when it was a great thing.[40]

Lovejoy knew that the phrase *Negro equality* was used to scare people who felt threatened by the ideas of interracial marriages, black job competition, black voting, and integrated schools. Lovejoy and Lincoln tried to mitigate the effectiveness of the Negro equality charge and dampen its sting by recognizing it to some extent. That effort provoked some of Lovejoy's abolitionist friends. Lincoln distanced himself from support for Negro equality in large part because he recognized whites' deep hatred for African Americans. Indeed, many whites—in keeping with the Dred Scott decision—considered African Americans an inferior species not worthy of any rights. Lincoln also understood that the political concept of race was a powerfully effective weapon used by slaveholders to maintain political power.

Sometimes Lovejoy would ambiguously speak about African American inequality or "concede the Negro is inferior," but he always affirmed that blacks were human beings created by God and argued that slavery caused that inequality by subjecting blacks to a poor diet and denying them education, in keeping with the Reverend Hosea Easton's observation that "the slave system is an unnatural cause, and has produced its unnatural effects, as displayed in the deformity of two and a half millions of beings, who have been under its soul-and-body-destroying influence."[41] When Lovejoy was in Congress, he enraged slave masters by highlighting their complicity in amalgamation. His commitment to equality was exhibited in all his relationships and constituted a core principle that guided his life. Lovejoy had less firsthand experience than Lincoln did with white brutality against blacks and at times preferred to see whites' fear of Negro equality as annoying and baseless—almost a quirk that needed to be expressed and counteracted with religion, humor, or explanation.

At times, practical considerations interfered with Lovejoy's commitment to African American equality. For example, Lovejoy previously had publicly supported African American suffrage but considered it a political impossibility during the 1850s. Consequently, he joined with Joshua Giddings in opposing Frederick Douglass's motion to include Negro suffrage in the 1852 Free Democratic Party platform. However in 1853 and 1855, Lovejoy sought to expand African Americans' rights by working hard (though unsuccessfully) for the repeal of Illinois's Black Codes.[42] In the 1858 election, members of the small Radical Abolitionist Party, which demanded immediate full political rights for African Americans, refused to endorse Lovejoy's reelection.[43] Moderate positions and understandings assisted both Lincoln and Lovejoy in defining and appealing to the Republican base.

Lincoln and Lovejoy had taken another step together as they coped with their integrity of means and ends in dealing with the "bugaboo of Negro equality."[44] Lincoln did not dare openly endorse Lovejoy for fear of alienating the sensitive balance of power in the politically mixed central Illinois counties. However, both men realized that Lovejoy did not need Lincoln's support. They also knew that Lincoln would probably receive the votes of the members of the northern Illinois antislavery base because of his stand in the House Divided speech. What would help Lincoln most was for the general public to see that he was not an extreme antislavery man. His debates against Douglas provided the opportunity to clarify that distinction.

The Lincoln-Douglas Debates

The relatively unknown Lincoln negotiated with the well-known Douglas to have a debate in each of Illinois's seven congressional districts. Douglas believed that he could easily persuade conservatives that Lincoln was too antislavery while convincing the antislavery men that Lincoln did not share their commitment. This task turned out to be more difficult than Douglas realized. He assumed that if Lincoln were forced to separate himself from the antislavery wing, its members would become disenchanted with him. Outside of Lovejoy's district, much of the public did not think of Lovejoy as a former abolitionist, since many still believed that he was an extreme Garrisonian. Whatever Lovejoy could do to dismiss that misrepresentation of himself would help both him and Lincoln.

For his part, Lincoln still needed to find ways to put political distance between himself and "Lovejoy & Co." In the debates, Douglas defined Lincoln time after time as a "Black Republican" abolitionist, likening him to Lovejoy thirty-seven times.[45] Fortunately for Lincoln, during the first debate on August 21 at Ottawa, in Lovejoy's district, Douglas overreached, enabling Lincoln to create the necessary distance from Lovejoy without alienating most of Lovejoy's friends. Douglas overconfidently and zealously claimed that Lincoln had "learned Parson Lovejoy's catechism by heart."[46] But Lincoln never used the standard antislavery phrases and rallying points that comprised Lovejoy's "catechism." Lincoln never said, "Slavery is a sin against the laws of God." He never publicly uttered a supportive word for Lovejoy's reelection. All he had done in public was to come up with some compromise language recommending a long and indirect process to place slavery on track for its demise.

Douglas claimed incorrectly that Lincoln had been present at the 1854 Springfield Republican Convention and that it had passed radical proposals, including one favoring the repeal of the 1850 Fugitive Slave Act. Much to his distress, the crowd, estimated to be as large as twelve thousand people, cheered.[47] In his rebuttal Lincoln quipped, "My fellow citizens, when a man hears himself misrepresented, it provokes him—at least I find it so with myself; but when the misrepresentation becomes very gross and palpable, it is more apt to amuse him."[48] Charles Lanphier, the editor of the Democratic *Illinois State Register*, had either intentionally or accidentally given Douglas a copy of the Aurora platform, not a copy of the Republican platform agreed to at the Springfield Convention.[49]

Lincoln adroitly disposed of Douglas's charges against him. "There was a call for a Convention to form a Republican party at Springfield, and I think that my friend Mr. Lovejoy, who is here upon this stand, had a hand in it. I think this true and I think if he will remember accurately, he will be able to recollect

74   CHAPTER 5

that he tried to get me into it, and I would not go in."[50] Lovejoy nodded in the affirmative. By identifying Lovejoy as his friend, Lincoln avoided alienating the antislavery majority. Lincoln continued his rebuttal with a refutation of Douglas's charge that he had agreed "to sell out the old Whig party." Lincoln clarified that the opposite was true: "I know that after Mr. Lovejoy got into the Legislature that winter [1855], he complained of me that I had told all the old Whigs in his district that the old Whig party was good enough for them, and some of them voted against him because I told them so."[51] Here again Lincoln demonstrated his friendly relationship with Lovejoy while indicating their differences. In Paul Angle's words, Lincoln "dissociated himself from Abolitionists without quite repelling them."[52]

Those in the audience who had doubted that Lincoln could hold his own with the Little Giant went away quite disappointed in Douglas's coarseness and inability to make his points consistently. Observed one DeKalb resident, "Douglas roared out 'I will bring him to his milk,' which brought Lincoln to his feet, with a stern expression on his face. But before he had time to interrupt, as apparently he intended, Lovejoy, sitting behind, grabbed his coat, pulled him back and whispered something that induced him to resume his seat. Douglas's speech gave me the impression that he was as ready to appeal to prejudice as to reason."[53]

Lincoln and Lovejoy dined that night at the home of Ottawa mayor Joseph O. Glover. After dinner, Lovejoy was escorted by a "large deputation of Republicans, headed by a band of music," to the courthouse, where he spoke to a crowd of fifteen hundred, removing his tie and collar and delivering an oration one observer described as "full of eloquence and magnetic power."[54]

Unlike Lincoln, Lovejoy was not amused at being misrepresented by Douglas. Six days after the Ottawa debate, Benjamin Shaw, the editor of the *Dixon Telegraph*, met Lovejoy on the train on the way to the Freeport debate. He found Lovejoy "not in a pleasant humor" about being labeled in the "radical class" by Douglas in his Ottawa speech.[55] In the second debate, Douglas asked Lincoln seven questions. The first was based on faulty information: Did Lincoln still "stand in favor of the unconditional repeal of the fugitive slave law?" Lincoln emphatically replied, "I do not now, nor ever did, stand in favor of the unconditional repeal of the fugitive slave law." He subsequently elaborated, "I think, under the Constitution of the United States, the people of the Southern States are entitled to a Congressional Fugitive Slave Law." But, he said, "I think it should have been framed so as to be free from some of the objections that pertain to it, without lessening its efficiency."[56] Douglas had again made a mistake that provided Lincoln with an excellent opportunity to distance himself from both Lovejoy and radical abolitionism.

That evening, after Douglas had retired to his hotel room, friends of Lovejoy, encouraged by Shaw, set out a box under Douglas's window and invited a very willing Lovejoy to stand on it and make a few remarks. Shaw called them "scathing philippics" against Douglas and those who voted for the Fugitive Slave Law. Taking the Pythagorean idea of transmigration, Lovejoy transformed the soul of Douglas into a savage bloodhound on the track of a slave escaping from bondage.[57] With this speech, Lovejoy both inspired the large antislavery Republican base in the Freeport area and demonstrated the major difference between himself and Lincoln. Lovejoy's speech benefited Lincoln by exposing the inhumanity of the Fugitive Slave Law and ridiculing Douglas.

Over the course of the debates, Lincoln equivocated about the extent of his support for ending slavery. But when at the last debate at Alton, he sounded a clarion call equal to Lovejoy's. Madison County was an auspicious place for Lincoln to test his new plan for the gradual ending of slavery. Located on the Mississippi River, across from St. Louis, the county was home to a mixture of slavery-sympathizing Democrats and Whigs with long-standing ties to southern trade and commerce built on slavery. Outside of the town of Alton, on the hill in Upper Alton, resided northern entrepreneurs from New York and New England. Elijah Lovejoy had ministered there and been murdered there in a clash between these two subcultures. Many Alton residents felt a lingering sense of guilt about Elijah Lovejoy's death and consequently were receptive to Lincoln's message.[58]

In the Alton debate, Lincoln reminded his southern-oriented listeners that Kentucky Whig Henry Clay had included the nonextension of slavery in the Missouri Compromise. Lincoln also reminded them that the word *slavery* did not appear in the Constitution and that the document's references to fugitives concerned "persons held to service or labor" who had signed contracts—the same distinction that Lovejoy had made in his 1855 Springfield speech. Lincoln teased that Douglas was opposing the Buchanan administration over Kansas and chided him for having supported the Missouri Compromise before arranging for its repeal.[59] After defending his House Divided speech, Lincoln said, "What I understand to be the *real issue* in this controversy between Justice Douglas and myself . . . is the sentiment on the part of one class that looks upon the institution of *slavery as a wrong*, and another class that *does not look* upon it as a wrong." The Republican Party, he continued, saw slavery "as being a moral, social and political wrong" but nevertheless had "due regard for its actual existence among us."[60] Lincoln defined who was a Republican and who was not—who was too conservative on slavery and who was too radical. He claimed that Republicans insisted that slavery should as far as possible "*be treated* as a wrong, and one of the methods of treating it as a wrong is *to make provision that it shall grow no larger. They desire a policy that looks to a peaceful end of slavery at some time.*" But two extremes of people were not in the Republican Party: "If there be a man amongst us who does not think that the institution of slavery is *wrong in any one of the aspects* of which I have spoken, he is misplaced and ought not to be with us. And if there be a man amongst us who is *so impatient of it as a wrong* as to disregard its actual presence among us and [to disregard] the difficulty of *getting rid of it suddenly in a satisfactory way*, and to disregard the constitutional obligations thrown about it, that man is misplaced if he is on our platform."[61] According to Timothy S. Good, with these statements, Lincoln "ignored the known sympathies of the audience, ignored his political instinct, ignored the advice of Davis, and acted like Lovejoy, standing there not as a politician solely seeking votes, but as a statesman standing for what he had always believed, and always would."[62]

The 1858 Election

Lovejoy was reelected by a 7,325-vote margin, an increase of 1,318 over 1856. Lincoln, however, lost the vote to become a U.S. senator, receiving support from just forty-six of the one hundred legislators.[63] The legislators who supported Lincoln received 51.9 percent of the total vote in the state, while those who supported Douglas accounted for only 45.3 percent, but the less populated conservative districts in the south and central parts of the state dominated the Illinois House.[64]

According to Allen C. Guelzo, "If only *three* more Whig Belt districts [in central Illinois] had gone to Republicans," the party would have controlled the legislature and Lincoln would have been sent to Washington. Both William Herndon and Joseph Medill believed that a letter sent by Crittenden, a prominent Whig and friend of Lincoln's, damaged the Republicans more than any other factor. Dickey had requested the letter and sent it out to voters in central Illinois a week before the election, and in Herndon's view, it was the reason that "thousands of Whigs dropped us on the eve of the election." Dickey had lost to Lovejoy in 1856 and was irritated at Lincoln for encouraging their mutual colleagues not to support Dickey. Moreover, Dickey was concerned that Lincoln's House Divided speech supported abolitionism and feared that the Republican movement would dissolve the Union, so he switched parties and became a Democrat. Lincoln's rebuff of Dickey in supporting Lovejoy behind the scenes in 1856 and 1858 was a major factor in Lincoln's defeat for the Senate in 1858, and the loss of Dickey's friendship pained Lincoln deeply.[65]

The defeat left Lincoln depressed and believing that his political career was over. He wrote to a confidant, Dr. Anson G. Henry, "I am glad I made the late race, it gave me a hearing on the great and durable question of the age, which I could have had in no other way and though I now sink out of view, and shall be forgotten, I believe I have made some marks which will tell for the cause of civil liberty long after I am gone."[66]

The clouds lifted a few weeks later, and some of Lincoln's conservative friends, including Davis, still felt that by keeping his principles and coming too close to Lovejoy, he had made the wrong choice. However, Lincoln disagreed, telling a small group at the Urbana court, "I used to think the Abolitionists and their detractors a little noisy, but I got along so that the agitation never hurt me.... I used to be more afraid that we Old-line Whigs would drive the Abolitionists out of the Party, but I found out later that it was useless uneasiness and that there wasn't enough of us, all told, to scare anybody!"[67] He had come to know who really cared about the results, and they had come to trust him. Said one supporter, "He lost the Senatorship; but no man ever won more conspicuous distinction and widespread reputation in his party."[68] The so-called radicals, who were really antislavery men and women, may have helped shut the door on Lincoln's Senate hopes, but they had helped open the door to the presidency.

6 Remaining Steadfast to the Right, 1859

"You Republicans of Illinois have deliberately taken your ground.
... All you have to do is to keep the faith, to remain steadfast to the
right, to stand by your banner."
—Abraham Lincoln

With Owen Lovejoy winning by a wider margin in 1858 and Abraham Lincoln winning the support of legislators representing the majority of voters though losing in the state legislature, both men were positioned to enhance the opportunities for a Republican victory in Illinois in 1860. They were recognized leaders in the state as well as known in national circles. Lincoln's debates with Stephen A. Douglas received extensive coverage in local newspapers, and the telegraph, a recent invention, quickly spread the news of their intriguing interplay to major cities across the nation. Douglas's attacks on Lovejoy in the debates and Lovejoy's distribution of his own congressional speeches, combined with his martyred brother's well-known name, helped Lovejoy, too, gain national recognition.

Shortly after Lincoln's defeat, some newspapers recognized him as a man of principle and ability and suggested his name as a presidential candidate.[1] Lincoln at first said that he was not qualified to be president, but his wife, Mary Todd Lincoln, changed his mind.[2] The possibility of his candidacy soon appealed to him, and he went to work collecting and publishing various accounts of the debates.[3]

Among the factors that encouraged Lincoln to consider the presidency more seriously were the widening divisions within the Democratic Party. The Supreme Court's Dred Scott decision and President James Buchanan's actions alienated some northern Democrats. Knowledge of the fire-eaters' support for an independent southern nation and the reopening of the African slave trade frightened both northern and southern Democrats. The Democrats were obviously vulnerable.

In light of these divisions, Douglas sought to build a new political alliance that would include northern Democrats, conservative Whigs, and Republicans who were dissatisfied both with the southern disunionist fire-eaters and the extreme abolitionists. It was a shrewd move, appealing to those who wanted to hold the Union together and prevent sectional conflict while ignoring the horrific consequences of slavery.

The prevailing mood of the white people of the North and part of the South had for decades been symbolically expressed in Methodist Church policy in Illinois. Becoming an ordained minister required candidates to declare that they neither backed slavery nor advocated abolitionism.[4] With this requirement, the Methodist establishment was accepting the present condition of slavery in society as long as neither side made things worse. However, the General Association of Illinois Congregational Churches, of which Lovejoy's Hampshire Colony Congregational Church in Princeton was a member, accepted only ministers who considered slavery an evil that made the conditions of society worse.[5] Lincoln's middle position that extending slavery worsened the situation shared some ground with both religious traditions. Douglas was now trying to create a new middle political position by claiming that both the fire-eaters and the immediate abolitionists were causing the situation to deteriorate and that slavery should be left in its current position.

Lincoln also needed to demonstrate his identification with the growing moral indignation regarding slavery and the growing political hope that something could be done to limit its impact on the nation. Doing so required Lincoln to refine his strategy and continue to separate himself from the negatives of the abolition label. Lovejoy continued to aid him by taking the fanaticism of abolitionism out of the antislavery movement—that is, by continuing to distance himself from the Garrisonians who insisted on immediate abolition.

Douglas published a major article in the September 1859 issue of *Harper's Magazine* in which he defined his new application for popular sovereignty.[6] He claimed that the will of the people in the territories would neither allow the southern fire-eaters to impose slavery nor allow the abolitionists to prohibit it through congressional action. Douglas worked to label both Lincoln and New York senator William Seward as old-line abolitionists. He quoted from the House Divided speech and Seward's Irrepressible Conflict speech to argue that the current state of affairs would lead to sectional warfare. Douglas cast both Lincoln and Seward as extreme politicians whose methods were analogous to those of the southern fire-eaters.

From Lincoln's point of view, this ploy was frightening, offering a way to extend the immoral system of slavery. Lincoln decided to intensify his political efforts in 1859 by continuing to expose Douglas's distortions of both popular sovereignty and the Declaration of Independence. On March 1, he spoke to Chicago's Republican leaders, many of whom were Lovejoy's friends. Lincoln began his speech by expressing his appreciation for audience members' support for his principles during the previous campaign and assured them that he stood with them in the effort to stop the spread of slavery.[7]

When Douglas decided to go to Ohio to implement his new strategy, Lincoln followed him, presenting major speeches in Columbus, Dayton, Hamilton, and Cincinnati. In Dayton on September 17, Lincoln centered his speech on Douglas's claim that the Founding Fathers had considered slavery desirable. Lincoln presented a condensed "history of the government [showing] that the framers of the government found slavery already existing when the Constitution was formed, and got along with it as well as they could in consummating the Union of the States, anticipating the advent of the period when slavery in the United States should no longer exist."[8]

Lincoln wrote in his notes that the Republican Party sought to address the "danger that slavery will be further extended, and ultimately made national in the United States; and to prevent this incidental, and final consummation."[9] To that end, southern politicians might seek to pass a congressional slave code for the territories, revive the African slave trade, and engineer a second Dred Scott decision. Though these possibilities "are not just now the chief dangers to our purpose, these will press us in due time, but they are not quite ready yet—they know that, as yet, we are too strong for them."[10]

Lincoln perceived the danger that the North was being lured away from its essential moral commitment—that slavery was wrong—and that Douglas was behind that effort: "We want and must have a national policy, as to slavery, which deals with it as being wrong."[11] In Chicago in March, Lincoln had claimed that slavery should be treated "with the fixed idea that it should come to an end." And he challenged the Republicans to avoid straying "from the strict part of our duty by such a device as shifting our ground and throwing ourselves into the rear of a leader who denies our first principle"—that slavery is wrong. He concluded, "You Republicans of Illinois have deliberately taken your ground. . . . All you have to do is to keep the faith, to remain steadfast to the right, to stand by your banner. . . . Remember how long you have been in setting out on the true course; how long you have been in getting your neighbors to understand and believe as you now do. Stand by your principles; stand by your guns; and victory complete and permanent is sure at the last."[12] Lincoln was delivering Lovejoy's sentiments to Lovejoy's men. Lincoln was working with them in their common cause, not distancing himself from them but letting them know that he was with them and encouraging them. He did not stand in their way, and they did not stand in his.

When Lovejoy arrived in Washington in late November 1858 for the second session of the Thirty-Sixth Congress, he went about shoring up the antislavery Republican base. Many House Republicans were conciliatory moderates or conservatives, avoiding confrontation with southern Democrats. One of the meeting places for the radicals since the mid-1850s had been at the home of the editor of the *National Era*, Gamaliel Bailey, whose knowledge and insights were highly respected among the antislavery faithful. Lovejoy and other Republican congressmen now visited Bailey almost every day. According to Mary Abigail Dodge, a writer for the *National Era*, Lovejoy at times was indignant and loudly eloquent about the wickedness of slavery, yet he was also willing to be interrupted or criticized: "He was always tolerant of the hand that pulled the valve-string of his balloon, and he ever came earthward again with a half-ashamed smile, with a deprecatory look, or a mock ferocious threat."[13]

Election Impact on Kansas and the Fire-Eaters

With the Republican Party's success in the 1858 elections, the winds of change in the North were evident. The results reflected the northern dissatisfaction with the Dred Scott decision and Buchanan's attempt to make Kansas a slave state. Southern Democratic congressmen were reeling from the failures of the northern branches of their party at the polls and of slaveholders' major effort to bring Kansas in as a slave state. Led by Alabaman William L. Yancey, the fire-eaters set about gaining support from moderate southern unionists. According to Yancey, the South needed to "insist that slavery is right, that the protection of territorial slavery is right, and that Northern Democrats must pass a reasonable test that slavery's blessing would be protected."[14] Such talk was designed to intimidate and disturb.

In response, Lovejoy planned to be fearless but not rash, firm but not obstinate.[15] He had listened to a good deal of abuse from the other side, had been called a fanatic for twenty years, and name calling held no terrors for him.[16] He was well aware of the effectiveness of truthful statements distorted into incendiary quips designed to discredit the abolitionist voices in New England. The southern press effectively equated nineteenth-century antislavery activists with the self-righteous seventeenth-century New England puritans who accused their opponents of being witches and burned them.[17] Southern demagogues made such outrageous claims as, "The North, who having begun with burning witches, will end by burning us."[18]

An astute student of human nature, Lovejoy understood the tendency to blame others for one's own faults. In response to slaveholders' accusations that he supported intermarriage between blacks and whites, Lovejoy contended that the idea must have been "running in the head of these gentlemen, this amalgamation idea, I mean." Laughter usually followed.[19] Lincoln was also aware of the tendency to blame others for ones' own wrongdoings, and he closed his Cooper Union Address by saying, "Neither let us be slandered from our duty by false accusations against us, nor frightened from it by menaces of destruction to the Government nor of dungeons to ourselves."[20]

Lovejoy worked to shift the stigma away from the abolitionists and toward the real fanatics—slaveholders and their defenders. On February 21, 1859, he delivered "The Fanaticism of the Democratic Party," an address that called for the system of slavery supported by the Democratic Party to be wiped out.[21] It was published in at least a dozen major newspapers, bringing him national attention.[22] The *Bureau County Republican* claimed that the speech "evidences as ever the unfathomable depth of purpose, and the intuitive drift of design, that have of late years cheered the hearts of the humane."[23] The *New York Tribune* called it "an uncommonly effective and telling speech to a very large audience." Lovejoy's "directness of thought sustained by affluence of imagery, and extraordinary command of language, enable him to send his satire, his sarcasms, his arguments and his invectives, through and through the subjects at which he aims." Concluded the *Tribune*, "He had come into Congress with a high reputation for popular oratory, which he has fully sustained thus far in his Congressional career."[24]

In the speech, Lovejoy observed that three decades earlier, "slavery was deemed a moral, social and political evil"; now, however, "this strange fanaticism deems Slavery not an evil, but a blessing." Democrats were fearful zealots who silenced dissenting opinions, and "the reason our principles do not circulate in the slave States is that this despotism has, like another Napoleon, crushed out the freedom of speech and of the press. Allow us free access to the minds of the non-slaveholders of the South, and in one year we would have more Republican votes in proportion, in the slave States, than there are Democratic votes in the Free States." Lovejoy continued, "The strangest and most impious phase of this fanaticism is that it claims the sanction of the Bible for American slavery. . . . If the Bible sanctions slavery at all, it is of white men." He chastised the slave system for breaking up families, contradicting the biblical injunctions to "Honor thy father and thy mother" and "What God hath joined together, let no man put asunder."[25]

Furthermore, Lovejoy noted, Democrats claimed to have a great horror of African Americans, but their acts belied their words: a southerner "draws the milk which makes his flesh and blood and bones from the breast of a nigger . . . ; he is undressed and put to bed by a nigger . . . ; he is washed, dressed, and taken to the table, by a nigger, to eat food prepared by a nigger. . . . [W]hen he reaches manhood, he invades the nigger quarters, to place himself in the endearing relation of paternity to half niggers. Finally, if he should be ambitious, it may occur that he will come to Congress to represent a constituency, three-fifths of whom are niggers."[26]

His aid to fugitive slaves had earned Lovejoy accusations that he was a thief. He turned the opprobrium back on the Democrats, claiming that they turned northerners into bloodhounds. And, he thundered, "I never will do it. Owen Lovejoy lives in Princeton, Illinois, three-quarters of a mile east of the village, and he aids every fugitive that comes to his door. Thou invisible demon of

Remaining Steadfast to the Right 83

Slavery, dost thou think to cross my humble threshold, and forbid me to give bread to the hungry and shelter to the houseless! I BID YOU DEFIANCE IN THE NAME OF MY GOD."[27]

Joseph Lovejoy's Betrayal

As Lincoln had been betrayed by his friends T. Lyle Dickey and John Crittenden, Lovejoy, too, was betrayed by one of his intimates. On March 20, 1859, the Democratic *Washington Union* printed an article as an open letter to Owen Lovejoy from his brother, Joseph. A cadre of slavery supporters connected to the liquor industry had invited Joseph to visit with them in the South and evaluate the slave system for himself. Joseph accepted their hospitality and concluded that his former beliefs about slavery had been in error.[28]

Joseph attacked Owen's February speech point by point, defending slavery on constitutional and biblical grounds. Joseph had decided that slaveholders were "benefactors to the country and to the human race" and that American slavery was "a redemption, a deliverance from African heathenism." Joseph claimed that the speech had only "irritate[d] the south and alienate[d] one section of the Union still more from the other."[29]

Owen did not respond publicly to Joseph's attack, and no private response has been found. Many families were quarreling over slavery at that time, so such strain was not uncommon, but few people had been as deeply involved in the antislavery movement as Joseph and reversed their course. On November 30, while traveling from Illinois to Washington, Owen attempted to mend his relationship with his brother by visiting his home in Cambridgeport, Massachusetts. Although Joseph had left the house, his wife, Sarah, and several of their children welcomed Owen for dinner, and they visited several old friends together. Soon thereafter, Joseph received a job in Washington from the Democrats; he moved there, while his family remained in Cambridgeport. He continued voting for that party in the following years. During the Civil War, when Owen became very ill, Joseph stopped by to see him and several times helped Owen meet constituent needs.[30] Lincoln similarly did not retaliate after Dickey's and Crittenden's betrayals: he grieved the loss of Dickey's friendship but still considered Crittenden a friend.[31]

However, Joseph Lovejoy's actions raise a core question: How intolerant of slavery was the North? The *Washington Union* interpreted his change of heart as a sign of the general decline of antislavery influence in the North, opining, "The production [of the letter] is the more remarkable as the expression of the sentiments, not alone of the individual author of it, but of an immense class of honest men at the North who are sick to disgust of the abominable fallacies of anti-slavery fanaticism. It is the production of a 'representative' mind, and

84 CHAPTER 6

the conclusions which it enforces are those, we doubt not, of an *immense majority* of honest, candid men in the Northern States."[32] Southern newspapers promoted Joseph's account as demonstrating the "Decay of Abolitionism in New England."[33] But Joseph's prediction that substantial numbers of moderate northerners were about to become defenders of slavery was unfounded.

Representatives of both the North and the South intentionally blurred the major distinction between the nonextension of slavery and its immediate abolition. Southern writings elided the pacifist, moral, religious, and egalitarian aspects of immediatism, thereby enabling readers more easily to envision the North invading their privacy, denying their rights, burning slave owners, and encouraging slave insurrections.

The myth of the benevolent master espoused by southern propagandists and Joseph Lovejoy was strongly disputed by those fleeing slavery. Accounts of "despotic police methods" used to contain slave unrest, including torture, sent "shock waves through American society from bottom to top," accelerating the momentum of the antislavery movement and raising tensions within the Slave Power.[34] In that light, both Lincoln and Lovejoy recognized the value of the radical symbolism of bringing a highly intelligent, broadly respected African American figure such as Frederick Douglass before the public to provide further impetus to the abolition movement.[35]

The Wounded Lion, John Brown

White abolitionist John Brown shocked the nation by raiding the federal arsenal at Harpers Ferry on October 16–17, 1859, seeking weapons to help free slaves. The raid ended with fourteen persons dead, nine of them Brown's men, including two of his sons. Brown was captured, severely beaten, and then hastily tried on charges of murder, conspiring with slaves, and treason. After a weeklong trial, he was convicted and hanged on December 2, 1859. Fire-eaters used the incident to frighten nonslaveholding southern whites, but the incident was less effective as a Democratic weapon against the Republicans in the North. Instead, it provoked a new round of northern debate on the rightness or wrongness of slavery and played into Lincoln and Lovejoy's strategy of emphasizing its immorality.

An indication of Illinois's shifting attitudes toward slavery can be seen in the town of Toulon, twenty miles west of Princeton. An Illinois Underground Railroad operator and friend of Lovejoy's, the Reverend Samuel G. Wright, found out that Brown's self-sacrifice and death were causing the townspeople to reflect deeply and search their consciences. When he announced that he was presenting a sermon on slavery and Brown's execution, local Democrats predicted that the sermon would be another political attack against them. But it was not so. According to Wright, "The house was crowded beyond what it ever was before on the Sabbath—people came from miles, and it was said every Democrat was there. I tried to improve the occasion to make a deep impression of the wickedness of the system of slavery." Wright had "never seen a more attentive audience" as he told his listeners that slavery hurt whites as much as blacks.[36]

In keeping with his prudent approach to abolition and his emphasis on reforming the system through legal means, Lincoln told an audience in Elwood, Kansas, on December 1, "We have a means provided for the expression of our belief in regard to slavery—It is through the ballot box—the peaceful method provided by the Constitution. . . . John Brown has shown great courage, rare unselfishness. . . . But no man, North or South, can approve of his violence or crime." Similarly, speaking in Leavenworth, Kansas, the day after Brown's hanging, Lincoln said, "Old John Brown has just been executed for treason against a state. We cannot object, even though he agreed with us in thinking slavery wrong. That cannot excuse violence, bloodshed, and treason."[37] On December 6, Lincoln claimed that he "had yet to find the first Republican who endorsed the proposed insurrection," but "if there was one, he would advise him to step out of the ranks and correct his politics. But slavery was responsible for their uprisings. They were fostered by the institution."[38] Lincoln benefited politically from Brown's use of violence: as Michael Burlingame notes, Lincoln "seemed acceptably moderate compared to Seward and acceptably radical and energetic compared to [former Missouri attorney general Edward] Bates."[39]

Lovejoy was much closer to this drama than was Lincoln. Lovejoy personally knew several of the men who had helped or been consulted by Brown and admired his audacity. Lovejoy knew he would have to incorporate the incident into the Republican Party's 1860 presidential campaign strategy, whomever the party selected as its candidate.[40] Brown's actions caused many problems. The raid and the trial elicited reflection on the causes of violent revolt.[41]

Brown's action increased the difficulty of convincing southern congressmen that the Republicans did not intend to invade the South or remove slavery where it already existed. Not until April 5, 1860, did Lovejoy publicly address the Harpers Ferry raid, saying, "This affair of John Brown brings us to the reality of things. This raid confronts us with slavery, and makes us ask, is slaveholding right? And, if so, what rights has it?"[42] Lovejoy also sought to use the speech to clear the name of Ohio congressman Joshua Giddings, who had been falsely accused of being in on Brown's plot, and to highlight the beating that Brown had received while he was captured:

> When the curtain rose and startled the nation with this tragedy, John Brown lay there like a wounded lion with his head upon his paws, a saber cut on his brow, bayonet gashes in his side, the blood oozing out, and life itself apparently ebbing fast; around were certain little specimens of the canine species, snuffing and

86 CHAPTER 6

smelling, and finally one of them yelped out: "Mr. Lion, was the old war-horse that pastured on the Western Reserve [Giddings] with you on this expedition?" The lion slowly raised his head, cast a disdainful side glance upon the inquirer, growled out a contemptuous negative, and reposed his head as before.[43]

Lovejoy then turned to his audience: "In regard to John Brown, you want me to curse him. I will not curse John Brown—You want me to pour out execration upon the head of old Osawatomie. Though all the slaveholding Balaks[44] in the country fill their houses with silver and proffer it, I will not curse John Brown. I do honestly condemn what he did; from my standpoint, and with my convictions I disapprove of his action, that is true."[45] But Lovejoy also said that he believed that Brown's "purpose was a good one; that so far as his own motives before God were concerned, they were honest and truthful; and no one can deny that he stands head and shoulders above any other character that appeared on the stage in that tragedy, from beginning to end; from the time he entered the armory there to the time when he was strangled by Governor 'Fussation.'"[46] In Lovejoy's view, Brown was guilty of neither murder nor treason, though he had "unquestionably violate[d] the statute against aiding slaves to escape; but no blood was shed, except by the panic stricken multitude, till Stevens was fired upon while waving a flag of truce. The only murder was that of Thompson who was snatched from the heroic protection of a woman, and riddled with balls at the railroad bridge. Despotism has seldom sacrificed three nobler victims than Brown, Stevens and Hazlitt." Finally, Lovejoy suggested that "the lessons which the slave States ought to have learned from John Brown and from all these events, are not these expressions of rage and vengeance. Instead of being stimulated to revenge, Virginia ought to have learned the lesson of penitence."[47]

Lincoln's approach had been more cautious, as he sought to pacify northern conservatives by stating that the lesson to take from the raid was that white men would not succeed in inciting blacks to violence: "The raid on Harpers Ferry was not a slave insurrection. It was an attempt by white men to get a revolt among slaves, in which the slaves refused to participate."[48] Lovejoy, in contrast, predicted that Brown's hanging had made him a martyr and would consequently expand the raid's meaning beyond the expectations of all involved. Lovejoy referred to a sonnet by William Wordsworth that described the spread of religious freedom in England after biblical scholar and reformer John Wycliffe's bones were exhumed, burned, and spread by state authorities.

> The Avon to the Severn runs
> The Severn to the Sea;
> And Wickliffe's dust shall spread abroad
> Wide as the water be.[49]

Likewise, Brown's death would not make southern whites safer; rather, the truth of the immorality of slavery would spread far outside the South. According to Lovejoy, "It will mix with the waters of the ocean; the whole civilized world will snuff it in the air; and it will return with awful retribution on the heads of those violators of natural law and universal justice. I cannot say when, or what form; but depend upon it, if such acts take place, then slavery must look out for the consequences."[50]

As a pragmatist, Lincoln distanced both the Republican Party and himself from the unsuccessful use of violence by a misguided and unrepresentative northern white man; as a radical, he blamed the raid on the outrage of the institution of slavery. Lovejoy's first response was to comfort the pain of his associates—especially Douglass and Giddings—who shared Brown's outrage regarding slavery and admired his courageous but foolish actions. His second response was like Lincoln's but used much more forceful, religious, and historic language as he informed the Slave Power that the incident had provided the movement with another martyr.

First Session of the Thirty-Sixth Congress

On December 5, 1859, three days after Brown was hanged, the first session of the Thirty-Sixth Congress opened. As Lovejoy climbed up the granite steps of the Capitol, he understood that the political battle had turned: with 109 seats, the Republican Party had a plurality in the House. The deepening fractures among the Democrats and the growing unity among the Republicans produced unprecedented feelings of vulnerability among the southern congressmen. Yet their fears only increased their arrogance, belligerence, and often ludicrous behavior. Because the Republicans did not have a clear majority, a fierce battle for Speaker of the House began immediately.

The first salvo was fired by unpopular Missouri Democrat John Clark, who moved that any congressman who had approved of the *Compendium of the Impending Crisis*, by Hinton R. Helper, was not fit to be Speaker.[51] The maneuver would have prevented almost all antislavery republicans from assuming the speakership: according to the *New York Herald*, sixty-six Republican members of the Thirty-Fifth Congress had recommended the controversial book, and forty—including Lovejoy and Indiana congressman Schuyler Colfax—had been reelected.[52] Though the resolution was never adopted, it served its purpose. Front-runner John Sherman of Ohio, who had endorsed Helper's book, was effectively ruled out.

The struggle over the speakership continued for nearly two months, until February 1, 1860, when William Pennington, the moderate former Republican governor of New Jersey, was elected. Pennington did not personally favor the

88   CHAPTER 6

repeal of the Fugitive Slave Law, but he appointed Free Soilers as committee chairs. Lovejoy became chair of the Committee on Public Lands. Lovejoy used his new position to engineer House passage of the Homestead Act of 1860. He had been a supporter of homesteading since 1848, and he believed that the new measure would help build an independent-thinking middle class, which he saw as more "than any other class, the hope of the country."[53] The law was a huge accomplishment, popular in the North, and it earned him acclaim as the "Farmer's Congressman."[54] However, President Buchanan vetoed the act, providing Lovejoy with an electrifying issue that he could use on behalf of the Republican cause during the 1860 campaign.

Preparing for the 1860 Election

Both Lincoln and Lovejoy sensed the beginning of a new political day filled with great promise for the Republicans. Their next step: elect Republican majorities in the House and Senate and put a Republican in the White House. Both they and the Democrats were beginning to look for presidential candidates.

Lincoln was in Springfield with his finger on the pulse of Illinois politics. Lincoln recognized that Seward's supporters in northern Illinois and Bates's more conservative backers in the central part of the state preferred to select delegates district by district rather than at a single statewide convention, an approach that would guarantee each camp some delegates. However, Lincoln preferred a unified state delegation and carefully selected a team to help him achieve that goal. Two conservative former Know-Nothings who had been elected in 1856, secretary of state Ozias Hatch and auditor Jesse Dubois, would influence central Illinois leaders. Norman B. Judd and his archrival, John Wentworth, had pull in the Chicago area. Together, these four men convinced the Republican Central Committee to hold a statewide convention in Decatur on May 9–10, 1860, to elect delegates for the Republican Presidential Nominating Convention in Chicago.[55]

In the fall of 1859, Lovejoy asked Hatch for an annual railroad pass and reminded the secretary of state that he had sought to campaign in southern Illinois in 1854 and 1856 but had been prevented from doing so. Lovejoy believed that he could help any 1860 Republican candidate in the state by campaigning in the Democratic stronghold because "you can never catch the Devil napping. . . . You have got to meet him face to face and hit him between the horns." He chastised Hatch and other leaders for their lack of confidence in him and pointed out that the overwhelming number of voters in the northern part of the state had swept candidates from the southern part—including Hatch—into state offices.

> Some of your chaps got into the Kingdom without much of crucifixion it is true, but it was through the various sufferings of the northern half of the State. One thing

Remaining Steadfast to the Right

I hold certain that we cannot beat the Democrats by strategy, cheating, or lying but we *can* beat them by the open manly and earnest discussion of our principles. I hold to no sentiment in regard to the character of slavery, and to no measure for its removal that has not been the recorded sanction of Washington, Jefferson, and the other sages and fathers of the republic, and I believe consequently what I think a large majority of people believe and when we come to understand each other we are together. This is the whole of it.[56]

Lovejoy adopted the same tactic while vigorously campaigning for Lincoln in 1860.

On November 23, 1859, Lovejoy went to New York City to confer with Republican leaders, among them Colfax and editor Horace Greeley. The group invited the recovering Senator Charles Sumner to make a public address either at the New York Academy of Music or at Henry Ward Beecher's Plymouth Church in Brooklyn. The group discussed a response to the raid on Harpers Ferry, the selection of a Speaker of the House, and proposed House and Senate legislation.[56] Lovejoy had become an important and respected leader in the party's core radical group.

7 Disenchanting the Nation of Slavery, 1860

> "Here and now I break the spell, and disenchant the Republic . . . of this stupid wrong."
> —Owen Lovejoy

In his politically diverse Illinois, Abraham Lincoln had learned to harness various political forces and pull them together. Could he transfer this knowledge to a wider political arena? His verbal slings during his debates with the popular Stephen A. Douglas fit a good David and Goliath story line. His friends had spread the story of the emergence of a strong, rail-splitting young man from a meager background. But Lincoln knew he needed more national exposure if he was to win the presidency as a compromise candidate from a necessary state.

In Illinois, Owen Lovejoy had been instrumental in convincing the populace that slavery ran contrary to the Gospel and the Declaration of Independence. After three years in Congress, with name recognition stemming from his martyred brother, his oratorical abilities, and his mastery of the issues, he had become a leader among his peers. Like Lincoln, however, Lovejoy sought wider national recognition.

Lincoln at Cooper Union in New York City

Lincoln's opportunity came from an unexpected source. He was invited to speak as part of the Plymouth Church Lecture Series in Brooklyn, New York, on February 27, 1860.[1] The church's pastor was Congregational minister Henry Ward Beecher, one of the most popular preachers in America. Beecher's congregation raised money to buy freedom for young female slaves, and he was the brother of Harriet Beecher Stowe, whose wildly popular 1852 novel, *Uncle Tom's Cabin*, had exposed the inhumanity of slavery. He was also known for sending aid, including Bibles and rifles, to Kansas settlers in the mid-1850s.[2] Moreover, his brother, Edward Beecher, had been with Owen and Elijah Lovejoy in Alton, Illinois, just hours before Elijah's murder.

Plymouth Church's congregation included many businessmen, among them Henry Bowen, a member of the church's board of directors, who was married to the daughter of antislavery entrepreneur Lewis Tappan. Bowen was also the publisher of the antislavery *New York Independent*, which Rev. Beecher had helped popularize. A "tired and woebegone Lincoln" visited Bowen in his office on the Saturday before the lecture. Bowen reminded Lincoln that the Republicans needed a presidential candidate who "could draw the Border States that had gone to the Democrats in 1856." William H. Seward had been labeled a radical abolitionist and faced strong opposition, so Bowen and others were looking for an alternative. Bowen informed Lincoln that the venue had been changed from the church in Brooklyn to the Cooper Union in New York City in hopes of attracting a larger attendance.[3] Consequently, an invitation from an institution built by eastern religious, political, and antislavery forces provided the foundation for Lincoln's national acclaim.

The speech was considered "vehement in tone and moderate in policy."[4] Lincoln appealed to the rich heritage of patriotism among people of the Northeast. He carefully undercut Douglas's assertion that the "Constitution forbids federal governance to control slavery in the federal territories," using detailed legal and historical arguments of the Founding Fathers of the nation. In sum, he said, "As those fathers marked it, so let it be again marked, as an evil not to be extended, but to be tolerated and protected only because of and so far as its actual presence among us makes that toleration and protection a necessity." Lincoln continued in a conciliatory manner, "Let all the guaranties those fathers gave it, be, not grudgingly, but fully and fairly maintained. For this, Republicans contend, and with this, so far as I know or believe, they will be content."[5]

Next, Lincoln had some harsh words for the defenders of slavery: "I consider that in general qualities of reason and justice you are not inferior to other people. Still, when you speak of us Republicans, you do so only to denounce us as reptiles or, at the best as no better than outlaws. . . . You say we are sectional. We deny it. . . . [T]he fact that we get no votes in your section, is a fact of your making, and not of ours." Lincoln went on to argue that in the Constitution "the right of property in a slave is not 'distinctly and expressly affirmed.'"[6]

He then turned to the Republicans: "Even though much provoked, let us do nothing through passion and ill temper." "In all our platforms and speeches we have constantly protested our purpose to let them alone; but this has had no tendency to convince them."[7] Then in Lovejoy style, Lincoln asked, "What will convince them? This, and this only: cease to call slavery wrong, and join them in calling it right." "Can we yield to them? Can we cast our votes with their view, and against our own? In view of our moral, social, and political responsibilities, can we do this?" "Can we, while our votes will prevent it, allow it to spread into the National Territories, and to overrun us here in these Free

States?" He concluded by appealing to the religious, political, and antislavery principles of his hosts: "Neither let us be slandered from our duty by false accusations against us, nor frightened from it by menaces of destruction to the Government nor of dungeons to ourselves. LET US HAVE FAITH THAT RIGHT MAKES MIGHT, AND IN THAT FAITH LET US, TO THAT END, DARE TO DO OUR DUTY AS WE UNDERSTAND IT."[8] Lincoln related the universal term *faith* to moral principles that could be applied to everyone of goodwill, while he alluded to the prophetic Old Testament principle from Micah 6:8 that one should do justice and walk humbly. As the meeting came to a close, organizers announced that "'one of three gentlemen will be our standard bearer'—William Henry Seward, Salmon Chase or 'the gallant son of Kentucky who was reared in Illinois and whom you have heard tonight.'"[9]

Members of the audience included such Republican stalwarts as William Cullen Bryant of the *New York Evening Post*, Horace Greeley of the *New York Tribune*, and former New York governor John Alsop King.[10] Greeley published the speech in its entirety, calling it "the most systematic and complete defense yet made of the Republican position with regard to slavery."[11] Lincoln was not yet a declared candidate, but he accepted nine opportunities in twelve days to speak in New England.[12]

Lovejoy's Barbarism of Slavery Speech

For four months after the beginning of the congressional session in December 1859, Democrats had launched a steady fusillade of pro-slavery arguments in dozens of speeches. With several exceptions, the Republicans had intentionally restrained themselves from responding. Lovejoy initially stayed in the background, but after the House passed his homestead bill, he asked Speaker William Pennington to put his name on the agenda for an hour's speech. On April 5, 1860, Lovejoy delivered what became known as the Barbarism of Slavery speech.[13]

Lovejoy began with a frontal attack:

> The Republican Party, of which I am a member, stands pledged since 1856 to the extermination, so far as the Federal government has the power, of the twin relics of barbarism, slavery and polygamy. They have this power in the Territories of the United States.
>
> Now sir, as we anticipate a deathblow has been given to one of these twins [polygamy], I propose to pay my respects to the other.[14]

He defined slavery as "the sum of all villainy," with "the violence of robbery, the blood and cruelty of piracy. . . . [I]t has the offensive and brutal lust of polygamy. Put every crime perpetuated among men into a moral crucible, and dissolve and combine them all, and the resultant amalgam is slaveholding."[15]

After recapitulating the main justifications for slavery and its expansion, Lovejoy began to rebut them, point by point. First, he took on the argument that African Americans were inferior, retorting that even if that statement were true, "it does not follow, therefore, that it is right to enslave a man simply because he is inferior." By that logic, "If a man is a cripple, trip him up; if he is old and weak, and bowed with the weight of years, strike him, for he cannot strike back; if idiotic, take advantage of him, and if a child, deceive him."[16]

While he was speaking, Lovejoy wandered in front of the Democrats' desks in the House chamber. An incensed Roger Pryor of Virginia sprang forward, shaking his fist and exclaiming, "It is bad enough to be compelled to sit here and hear him utter his treasonable and insulting language; but he shall not, sir, come upon this side of the House, shaking his fist in our faces." A brawl immediately broke out, with thirty or forty congressmen on both sides of the aisle shoving and shouting.[17] A couple of men cocked their pistols, and a toupee was knocked loose.[18] Lovejoy stood his ground, announcing, "I will not be intimidated," and he later wrote, "I had made up my mind to sell out my blood at the highest possible price."[19]

After twenty tense minutes, Speaker Pennington pounded his gavel and order was restored. Lovejoy took up again where he had left off, refuting the argument that slavery was consonant with Christianity and spreading civilization. He then spoke against the idea that the Constitution protected slavery: "In no article, in no section, in no line, in no word, in no syllable, can there be any recognition or sanction of human slavery found in the Constitution of the United States. It is for liberty." He continued, "The world is watching to see if we will live up to our declaration of equality. Our image in the world depends on ending slavery." When a southern congressman accused Lovejoy of stealing slaves, he responded vehemently, "Who steals? I tell you that I have no more hesitation in helping a fugitive slave than I have in snatching a lamb from the jaws of a wolf, or disengaging an infant from the talons of an eagle. Not a bit. Long enough has this nation crouched and cowered in the presence of this stupid wrong." Then, he thundered, "Here and now *I break the spell, and disenchant the republic* from the incantation of this accursed sorceress—slavery. . . . The question is: Whether the 28,000,000 people who favor the free labor system shall be accommodated or the 2,000,000 people wrapped up in the slave system. Is this a democracy or not?"[20]

Then Lovejoy suggested that the South could be permitted up to fifty years to end slavery, using words that clearly echoed Lincoln's support for the "ultimate extinction" of slavery: "I tell you of the slave States that you must emancipate your slaves. It belongs to you and not to us. You must transform them from slaves into serfs, and give them homes, and protect and guard the sanctity of the family. We shall not push you. If you say that you want a quarter of a century you can have it; if you want half a century you can have it. But I insist that this system must ultimately be extinguished."[21]

Virginia's Elbert S. Martin responded to Lovejoy's words with a threat: "If you come among us we will do with you as we did with John Brown—hang you up as high as Haman," the villain from the Bible's Book of Esther. Lovejoy's retort highlighted the Slave Power's erosion of northern rights: "I have no doubt of it."[22]

Fifty-five newspapers across all regions of the country reported on Lovejoy's speech.[23] Some of slavery's supporters threatened Lovejoy's life, while others called for his expulsion from the House. In Senator Henry Wilson's estimation, Lovejoy's opponents were maddened by the accuracy of his charges. Then they "revealed by their language and manner their principles and purposes of action, stigmatizing him with rude and vulgar words" for criticizing their "monstrous iniquity."[24]

The speech had precisely the effect that Lovejoy had hoped, giving him the national platform he needed. The next day, he wrote to his wife, Eunice, "You will see before this reaches [you] by the papers that I made my speech yesterday. I was so fatigued last night that I could not write. I do not know what the account in the papers will be but probably correct. . . . The Republicans were on hand to behave nobly. I think we should whip them badly if they began it. . . . I preached the gospel pure and simple. It is the common topic of conversation this morning. They threaten to bring in a resolution to expel me but I think they will not be fools enough for that. It seems like old times to be in a storm."[25]

Thus, in the late winter and spring of 1860, both Lovejoy and Lincoln were important national political figures, and both had reached that stage by way of vehement yet conciliatory speeches. Lincoln offered more of an appeal to his listeners' logical state of mind, while Lovejoy was more provocative, engaging their emotions and sense of justice—a kind of "good cop, bad cop" approach that was indicative of their broader collaboration.

The Presidential Nomination

Encouraged by his trip East, Lincoln returned to Springfield highly motivated to win the Republican presidential nomination. His wife, Mary Todd Lincoln, was quite convinced that he could do it; he was also encouraged by a small group of men who were both eager to improve their own positions and aware of Lincoln's skills and opportunities. According to David Donald, these campaign managers "were not an organized or unified group. Throughout Lincoln's career, his advisers felt connected only to him, not to each other or to some larger cause." They were frequently jealous and feuded with each other. The two Democrats in the group, Norman B. Judd and John Wentworth, hated each other. Leonard Swett

Disenchanting the Nation of Slavery

did not get along with Richard Yates, but they joined together to take on Judd. Wentworth also attacked the Know-Nothings, Jesse Dubois, and Ozias Hatch. According to Donald, "This decentralized command structure" encouraged each man to believe that "he alone understood Lincoln and gave him helpful advice." Most advisers felt that Lincoln needed encouragement and protection because he was such "a guileless man," an assessment that Donald thinks Lincoln would have found very amusing because of his self-reliance.[26]

The Republican Platform was a future-oriented document containing major innovations for the nation's emerging technological, industrial, and geographical expansion. After a section "abhorring Disunion" and proudly recognizing "that no Republican member of congress has uttered threats of Disunion" as well as a section vowing support for the right of each state "to order and control its own domestic institutions" came some strong antislavery measures repeated from the 1856 platform.

> The Present Democratic Administration has far exceeded our worst apprehensions, in its measureless subserviency to the exactions of a sectional interest; especially evinced in its desperate exertions to force the infamous Lecompton Constitution upon the protesting people of Kansas; . . . in construing the personal relation between master and servant to involve an unqualified property in persons; . . . and in its general and unvarying abuse of the power intrusted to it by a confiding people. . . . The new dogma that the Constitution, of its own force, carries Slavery into any or all of the Territories of the United States is a dangerous political heresy.[27]

The platform provided that no person should be deprived of his or her constitutional right of life, liberty, or property by those trying to establish slavery in the territories. But overt support for the Declaration of Independence was not included in the Platform Committee's report. Joshua Giddings took the floor and moved to include a reference to the Declaration, which was voted down. George William Curtis of New York then asked the delegates "whether they are prepared to go on record before the country as voting down the Declaration of Independence?" The motion to reconsider passed unanimously. It was ultimately incorporated into the final version of the platform, making it comply more fully with Lincoln's public positions.[28]

Lincoln shrewdly understood the dynamics of the balloting process in a five-way race that also included Edward Bates, a conservative Free Soil Whig from Missouri, and Simon Cameron, a favorite son from Pennsylvania. Lincoln astutely worked the system with the help of his capable political associates, including Judd, a member of the Republican National Committee; Gustave Koerner, a leader in the German American community; Orville Browning; and Judge David Davis.[29] Lovejoy had observed the value of Lincoln's approach in 1854 and 1856 and carefully refrained from making any public statements that

96   CHAPTER 7

might unnecessarily alienate others. He had close relations with Senator Seward in Washington and had worked with Chase in the Liberty Party and had gone with him into the Free Soil Party. And Lovejoy had worked with Lincoln to build up the Illinois Republican Party. In the spring of 1860, he kept his presidential preferences to himself. Lovejoy's primary goal was putting a Republican in the White House, and he did not want to do anything that might hurt the chances of any of the antislavery candidates. However, once Lincoln was nominated, Lovejoy was jubilant, writing a June 10 letter offering his "sincere" congratulations and stating, "I have seen enough of political life to know that it is not altogether a bed of roses. You have the advantage of being without entanglements & will go into the White House as free I trust as you are now." He also mentioned that he had sent a book to Mary Lincoln.[30] These actions strengthened the connections between the two men.

Electing Lincoln

In May 1860, Lovejoy requested that Jesse Fell, editor of the *Bloomington Pantagraph*, print an early full endorsement of Lovejoy's renomination to Congress. He also asked Fell to inquire whether Judge Davis intended to endorse Lovejoy.[31] Davis had never liked Lovejoy, blaming Henry Clay's failed 1844 presidential bid on the Liberty Party.[32] Lovejoy's 1856 defeat of Swett for the 1856 congressional nomination increased Davis's resentment. If Davis refused to back Lovejoy this time, Lovejoy was willing, "with all cordiality," to let matters take their course.[33]

Lincoln became the buffer between the two men. On June 8, 1860, he wrote an anonymous letter to the *Chicago Press and Tribune*, offering assurances that "Judge Davis expects Lovejoy to be nominated and intends to vote for him."[34] Since Davis had previously worked against Lovejoy's nomination, this statement helped ensure the support of Lovejoy's constituency for Lincoln's presidential candidacy. With the backing of Davis and Fell, Lovejoy's renomination was assured, freeing him to campaign for Lincoln throughout Illinois and in neighboring states.

Lovejoy had stayed in Washington until the end of the session on June 25 and so was not part of the Republicans' Chicago Nominating Convention. Having won the nomination, Lincoln sought to get his former rivals, including Bates and Seward, to work on his behalf. Lincoln asked Lovejoy to bring Seward into the campaign and to give some speeches in New York; after doing so, Lovejoy reported in late June, "Everything looks promising."[35]

On July 24, Lovejoy wrote to ask Seward for a "very great favor": speak in Lovejoy's congressional district, where the disappointment was "sore and deep" that Seward had not been nominated. Lovejoy's political benefactor, John Howard Bryant, was also asked to help persuade Seward to speak in the Princeton area, probably because of the influence of Bryant's brother, William Cullen Bryant.[36]

Disenchanting the Nation of Slavery 97

Seward ultimately graciously and vigorously supported Lincoln, putting the Republican cause above his own candidacy. Though he did not come to Princeton, he spoke in Chicago on October 2, giving a rousing endorsement speech for Lincoln that included a fine tribute to Lovejoy. Seward shared his hopes for the election of more men who were "as brave, as truthful, as fearless and as firm as Owen Lovejoy," a comment that received loud applause. Lovejoy also spoke to the gathering, and he, too, received an enthusiastic response.[37]

The Campaign

According to the custom of the times, Lincoln did not make campaign speeches promoting his own candidacy. But he did work behind the scenes. He at first concentrated on soothing his disappointed rivals and their chief supporters, reminding them, via intermediaries, that he would not favor any one group but would provide "justice and fairness to all," a motto that raised many hopes but made no firm commitments.[38] He also worked to prepare materials that would enable journalists and others to present him, a relatively unknown candidate, to the public.

Since the northeastern states were quite solidly behind him, with his commitments to patriotism, freedom, and stopping the spread of slavery, Lincoln sought to highlight other planks in the Republican platform to appeal to residents of Pennsylvania and some midwestern states. His surrogate speakers across the country drew not only on the platform but also on Lincoln's themes during the 1858 debates and his 1859–60 speeches.

In Illinois, the surrogates for Lincoln included Browning, a former Whig state senator; Yates, a former congressman and current gubernatorial candidate; former Democrats John M. Palmer, who had chaired the Bloomington Convention, and Lyman Trumbull, who was running for reelection to the U.S. Senate; German Americans Koerner and George Schneider; former antislavery orator Ichabod Codding, who wrote an 1860 campaign booklet; and, of course, Lovejoy. All of these men not only shared Lincoln's principles but were able orators, yet according to Trumbull, "No man in the State, if any in the nation, ever exerted a greater influence on the masses by his speeches than Owen Lovejoy."[39]

The Wide Awakes

Especially in Illinois, the work of these field commanders was supplemented by the Wide Awakes, a symbolic army of political young foot soldiers. They had organized in Hartford, Connecticut, in 1859 to protect and promote the Republican gubernatorial candidate during a tension-filled campaign. They came to the Chicago Republican Convention and demonstrated their techniques, and by the end of the summer, at least one hundred thousand young men were rallying

98 CHAPTER 7

on behalf of the Republicans.[40] The Wide Awakes were a young men's social club whose members wore enameled shimmering capes and soldiers' boots and caps and carried torches. They marched through the streets in military fashion.[41]

Regional Wide Awake groups operated wherever the fight was hottest on the borders between strong Democratic and strong Republican constituencies, such as central Illinois, southern New Jersey, and southern Maine. Chicago had forty-eight such groups.[42] When they marched silently late at night carrying their flaming torches, stomping their boots in unison, or in huge numbers in parades, they presented an intimidating presence. Symbolically, they were standing up to the southern demagogic forces that were encroaching on their rights and interests.

Lovejoy understood intimidation. He declared at the Wigwam campaign rally that the time when the South could intimidate the nation as a whole for the sake of the slaveholders was coming to an end: "Companies of Wide Awakes will . . . organize themselves in defense of the constitution and the Union." Southerners had already begun to argue in favor of secession, citing the Wide Awakes as one of the reasons why that action was necessary.[43]

The Princeton Wide Awakes were noted for "their superior drill and general Zouavity of demeanor." A September 29 Princeton rally for Lincoln drew thousands of Wide Awakes, who marched with bands, flags, and banners "in grand and imposing style."[44] They enlivened Lincoln's campaign in Illinois, and Lovejoy appreciated the enthusiasm, commitment, and symbolism they brought to the campaign.

Holding Together the Factions

Lincoln was confident that the Republicans would win in 1860 if the "discordant and rival elements that composed the party could work together."[45] In Illinois, the various antecedent factions of the party needed to cooperate on five major political fronts to win: first, hold the Frémont antislavery base of 1856 in the northern districts; second, persuade conservative Whigs and Democrats who were dissatisfied with Douglas to support Lincoln; third, capture the German American vote without alienating the Know-Nothing vote; fourth, capture the Know-Nothing vote without alienating the German American vote; and fifth, persuade new voters to back the Republican candidate.

To secure the antislavery base in northern Illinois, Lovejoy campaigned with stinging humor, charming illustrations, bright metaphors, commonsense logic, and moving oratorical flourishes. Some of these speeches were two to three hours long, delivered to the largest audiences ever assembled in Illinois politics until that time, with women, children, and even Democrats flocking to hear him. The Democratic press was less than complimentary, with one paper

Disenchanting the Nation of Slavery

labeling Lovejoy the "negro equality preacher" and another claiming that he "turned himself into a circus clown, mimic, a buffoon, an ape, to make a few score of witlings laugh, as many more young women blushed."[46] Opined the *Salem Advocate*, Lovejoy "has talent and so have monkeys; he has a heart and so has a hyena; The Devil himself was once an angel; Lovejoy without having been an angel, already is possessed with all the malignity of an arch fiend."[47]

Lovejoy believed that Lincoln could win the presidency by conveying a clear message against the extension of slavery into the territories on the grounds that northern rights were threatened and that the abusive and corrupt Slave Power dominated the Democratic Party. These issues were spelled out in the Republican platform and articulated by Lincoln's spokesmen.[48]

At Chicago's Wigwam on October 15, Lovejoy defended his use of indignant language against slavery:

> I have no right to indulge in the spirit of retaliation or revenge. I do not denounce slavery because a brother's blood mingles with the Mississippi as it flows down to the land of slavery. I do not denounce slavery because I saw him there, in the bloom of manhood, shot down like a very beast, while the mob cheered over his prostrate lifeless body. It is not for that; it is because slavery is wrong. It is because slavery is a curse. If there is not enough in slavery to move any human heart to the use of indignant language; then I have no business to use such language. . . . Nobody wants to invade [the South]. Nobody wants to take away one iota from the constitutional rights of the South—never. But when you talk of slavery and its extension that is another question. Here, my friends, I come to the living practical issue of the day; shall slavery be allowed to extend to the Territories of the United States?[49]

Just over a month earlier, in Freeport, Lovejoy had both mocked Douglas and compared him to the devil, borrowing from poet John Milton to describe the Democrat as "a serpent to whisper sin in the ear of Eve." Then he urged former Whigs to remember their "uncompromising hostility to slavery extension" and to avoid being seduced by Douglas's whisperings.[50] When Benjamin Shaw, editor of the *Dixon Telegraph*, claimed that the radical abolitionists in his district were not supporting Lincoln, Lovejoy urged them to vote for the Republican candidate because despite his imperfections, he was the best available choice.[51]

Lovejoy's stump speeches did not directly address the Fugitive Slave Law because the Republican platform did not call for the measure's repeal. However, radicals and Democrats among his listeners frequently shouted out, "What about the Fugitive Slave Law?" or asked whether he had helped runaways. On October 15, he responded, "I told them in Congress, when they wanted to know whether I [aided escapees]—I marched right up to the confessional and told them I aided every fugitive slave who came and asked it. I said to them, if the

100 CHAPTER 7

demon of slavery expects to cross my threshold and bid me not feed the hungry and shelter the houseless, I bid it defiance in the name of Almighty God."[52]

Lovejoy's role in the campaign provided ammunition for Democratic attacks on Lincoln. Douglas and his supporters claimed that Lovejoy was a "Black Republican" abolitionist who favored immediate emancipation and full Negro equality and then tried to extend that characterization to the candidate. When Lovejoy was slated to campaign in a particular town, the Democratic press would run long articles describing him as the "high priest of Abolitionism" and twisting his words to convey the idea that he wanted an immediate end to slavery by any means.[53]

Democratic papers often quoted the contention in the *Chicago Democrat*, published by Long John Wentworth, a renegade Democrat who became the Republican mayor of Chicago in 1860, that if Lincoln were elected president "no man would enjoy [his] confidence to a greater degree than Mr. Lovejoy."[54] This statement simultaneously won Lincoln antislavery votes in northern Illinois and cost him Democratic votes in the southern part of the state. According to Judge Davis, Wentworth's "extreme abolition generally does us harm, Great Harm."[55]

But Lovejoy and Lincoln's other campaign surrogates also worked to attract conservative voters, in part by connecting the Republican platform to Henry Clay's position as articulated in the debates over the 1820 Missouri Compromise—that is, allowing slavery to continue where it already existed but prohibiting it in the new territories. These campaigners also claimed this viewpoint resembled that of Founding Fathers George Washington and James Madison. This approach met with at best mixed success.

Lovejoy also sought to entice conservatives by painting the Democrats as having violated northern rights, an idea that he had embraced as far back as 1838 and that Lincoln had highlighted in the House Divided speech. In Freeport on September 12, Lovejoy told his audience that slavery had negative effects on freedom of the press, freedom of religion, freedom of schools, and freedom of speech.[56] The Freeport speech is a masterpiece of political oratory and well encapsulates Lovejoy's effectiveness as a campaigner. He not only embraced his reputation but explained to his listeners why they did, too:

> Yes, I *am* an Abolitionist, you are an Abolitionist, and every *man* is an Abolitionist if he brings the question home to himself....
>
> ... There is a feeling deep down in *every* man's heart that *repudiates* the atrocious doctrine of ownership in man....
>
> ... Mr. Douglas is inferior to me in size, in weight; must he therefore be my slave? Does inferiority disqualify a man for his right to life? Certainly not! To freedom? No! I say every man; the black man also, has as good a right to life and liberty as you and I.
>
> The Negro is here—*God* made him; I didn't. God made him black, but he made him a MAN! Though before a pro-slavery court he is property, yet before the court

of Heaven he is a man. And there he will witness against you, because you *robbed* him of his manhood. . . . You call me radical! What does radical mean?—*To go to the bottom of things!* Such a radical was Christ. He was a Negro equality man, for his divine precepts apply to ALL men.[57]

The effectiveness of Lovejoy's effort to woo conservatives is difficult to assess. If nothing else, seeing him in person demonstrated that he did not have hoofs and horns, and hearing him in person counteracted misrepresentations of his views in the press. On July 20, Palmer introduced Lovejoy prior to a speech at Macoupin with the words, "I have no doubt, from the reports which have been circulated in reference to the gentleman, that many of you are prepared to see him wearing all the outward insignia of this Prince of Darkness. . . . I now have the pleasure of introducing him to you."[58]

Lovejoy was particularly well positioned to help the Republicans walk the tightrope necessary to attract both the antiforeigner and anti-Catholic Know-Nothings and the German American voters. Many Germans were Catholic, and most drank beer or wine with meals. Lovejoy, a Protestant minister with leanings against papal authority and a proponent of the temperance movement, had credentials that appealed to Know-Nothings; however, he was also not a nativist and had excellent relationships with German Americans, to whom he had reached out for support for the Homestead Act.

Finally, Lovejoy helped Lincoln's campaign attract new voters as well as appeal to a constituency that could not vote and had previously been largely ignored but that nevertheless wielded tremendous influence: women. Between 1856 and 1860, the number of Illinois voters who cast ballots in the presidential election grew from roughly 239,000 to 339,000, with the rolls swelled not only by migrants from other states, mostly in the North, but also young men and foreign-born men who were newly eligible to vote.[59]

One tactic that Republicans used to capture these new voters was encouraging political participation by women. Some Wide Awake chapters featured young women draped in robes on floats representing the states. In at least one speech, Lovejoy aimed part of his explanation of the advantages of the Republican form of the Homestead Bill to the young women in the audience: he described a young man who wanted to go west to "build a log house, turn over a few acres and have things comfortable generally, and then go and marry Jane. Will you still vote the Democracy that tells you, you can't have the land unless you are the head of the family? How do *you* like it girls? I advise you to ask the boys, when, next Sunday night they come to see you, whether they are going to vote with a party that will morally compel William to marry Mary, and then expose her to all the hardships."[60] On another occasion, Lovejoy said, "But if the men do not vote down and clear out of sight this sham Democracy that is doing all it can to unmoor the government and convert it into an old despotism, I ask the

102   CHAPTER 7

women to sweep them with their brooms into the Atlantic or in Lake Michigan, if it is deep enough to bury them and their sins."[61]

Education was another issue that Lovejoy used to attract young voters. Unlike the northern states, the southern states refused to fund public education. "In these free states we have free schools," he told an audience; in the South, however, "a man, who swears that he is a pauper, can send his children to a pauper school, and that is about all the free school they have."[62]

German American antislavery leader Carl Schurz urged Lincoln to have Lovejoy travel to southern Indiana to "make a few calm, dispassionate, discreet speeches, placing himself upon your ground." Such speeches "would do more to conciliate the people of this section of Republicanism, than anything else."[63] Like southern Indiana, southern Illinois was regarded as hostile territory for opponents of slavery, and party leaders had barred Lovejoy from campaigning there in 1856 and 1858. In 1860, however, Fell, now serving as secretary of the State Republican Committee, persuaded committee members to allow Lovejoy to go south.[64] Lincoln likely supported Fell's recommendation.[65]

On July 20, Lovejoy spoke to a crowd of twenty-five thousand in Macoupin County, south of Springfield. Lovejoy described the gathering as "overwhelming in numbers and irrepressible in enthusiasm. I had, as they say, a perfect success."[66] Baptists predominated in the region, and Lovejoy's position as a Congregational minister enabled him to speak their language. He selected twelve people from the audience and asked them to be his jury. Then he described a scenario in which a "young handsome woman" escaped into the swamps when the plantation overseer "sought to persecute her when she would not assent to his advances." He closed by implying that his actions amounted to no more than feeding the hungry, clothing the naked, freeing the oppressed, and sheltering the fugitive, just as the Bible instructed. Then he asked the "jury" to determine whether doing so was wrong. Its members answered that it was not and that he was no more an abolitionist than they were.[67]

Lovejoy worked tirelessly to convince voters to cast their ballots for Lincoln. Speaking in Chicago on October 15, he told the audience, "I am worn out and cannot go on. I have been working for weeks. All last week, I was at work, speaking and traveling in the [railroad] cars from place to place, and I will be at work next week."[68] He later reflected that he had "labored for [Lincoln's] election as I never labored for that of any other man": he "was almost daily engaged in the canvass" from July 20 until Election Day.[69]

Lincoln's Victory

On November 6, 1860, Abraham Lincoln was elected the sixteenth president of the United States, defeating not only Stephen A. Douglas but also John C. Breckinridge of the Southern Democratic Party and John Bell of the Constitutional Union Party. Though Lincoln won by a comfortable margin nationwide and in the Electoral College, he took Illinois by a mere twelve thousand votes. Because the majority was so slim, every faction in the coalition could claim responsibility for his victory. Lovejoy's work was instrumental in securing the state for Lincoln.

Lincoln received 66 percent of the ballots marked by Illinois's new voters, an edge of about twenty-three thousand votes. In all but one county where Lovejoy spoke, Republican yields increased over the party's 1856 tally by an average of 71 percent.[70] According to historian of the Republican Party William Gienapp, the Republicans won in 1860 as a consequence of three important shifts: "First, the growing support of non-Catholic immigrants. . . . Second, the disproportionate strength among younger native-born voters. Finally, the overwhelming backing Lincoln won among the former Know-Nothings."[71] Lovejoy's congressional district gave Lincoln thirty thousand votes, the most of any of the state's districts; Lincoln held a majority of forty-one thousand votes in the northern part of the state.[72]

Though Lovejoy and Lincoln privately agreed on the basic principles of the fight against slavery, they differed on tactics, and each man maintained the public persona he had carefully crafted. In so doing, they not only shored up their political bases and kept them in the Republican camp but also upheld their mutual goal of eliminating slavery. However, both men continued to believe that the southern states, not the North, should free the slaves residing below the Mason-Dixon Line. Lovejoy closed his Wigwam speech by presenting precisely that challenge to the South: If the slave states would travel down the road to emancipation, they could rid the country of a very great evil, resulting in "a free American Republic reposing proudly among the nations of the earth."[73]

Abraham Lincoln, Princeton, Illinois, July 4, 1856. Photograph by William Masters. Courtesy of the Owen Lovejoy Papers, Bureau County Historical Society, Princeton, Ill.

Owen Lovejoy, ca. 1860. Courtesy of the Chicago History Museum, Chicago (ICHi-30804).

I have pondered this subject earnestly & constantly & with what ability God has given me, since the breaking out of the rebellion and I here declare to you my deep & solemn conviction that the Emancipation of the Slave is essential to the safety & perpetuity of the Republic. I do this as I have already intimated with no offensive or dogmatic pretension of infallibility. I have seen too many older & much wiser & abler statesmen utterly at fault in their predictions concerning this rebellion to be over-confident of my own prophicies.

"The Emancipation of the Slave Is Essential": Excerpt from the manuscript of Owen Lovejoy's Cooper Union Address, June 12, 1862. Courtesy of the McLean County Museum of History, Bloomington, Ill.

Lincoln's words of remembrance for Owen Lovejoy: Excerpt from Abraham Lincoln to John Howard Bryant, May 30, 1864. Courtesy of the Bureau County Historical Society, Princeton, Ill.

Abraham Lincoln, Washington, D.C., ca. 1863. Photograph by Alexander Gardner. Courtesy of the Chicago History Museum, Chicago (ICHi-11424).

Owen Lovejoy, ca. 1858. Courtesy of the Lovejoy Society.

PART 2

Maintaining Political Power, 1861

8 Holding Firmly to Their Promises, 1861

"Let there be no compromise on the question of extending slavery.
. . . Hold firm as with a chain of steel."
—Abraham Lincoln

Shortly after midnight on November 7, 1860, amid boisterous cheers and clanging church bells, an exuberant Abraham Lincoln hurried to his Springfield home, where he announced to his wife, Mary Todd Lincoln, "We are elected."[1] The next day, he wrote down the names of eight of his most helpful advisers, six of whom would become members of his cabinet.[2]

At the same time, South Carolina senator James Henry Hammond was struggling with his response to Alfred Aldrich, a leading state legislator and disunionist. On one hand, Hammond was advocating a delaying tactic to move the Secession Convention from December to January. On the other, he was complaining that the Union "drains us of our money" and "deprives us . . . of our good name." Then he made his decision. To "be freed from the antislavery agitation . . . would be a greater blessing to the South even than all the blessings of the Union."[3] Hammond, under pressure from his state legislature, joined South Carolina's other senator, James Chesnut, in resigning from Congress.

On hearing the news of these resignations, a confident Lincoln assured his friends that he was not disturbed by the "blustering of the disunionists and traitors."[4] Owen Lovejoy had said much the same thing in his final campaign speech in Chicago. Lincoln believed that the southerners respected the law and expected that they would give him a fair chance to prove that he would protect their rights. In addition, presidential candidates opposed to disunion had outpolled the secessionist candidate in the South.[5] Nevertheless, on December 20, 1860, South Carolina's Secession Convention declared the state an "Independent Commonwealth."[6]

One of Lincoln's most respected southern congressional friends, Alexander Stephens, meekly opposed secession in a speech to the Georgia legislature. He pointed out that Lincoln had been constitutionally elected and would control only one branch of government. He advised the legislature to wait until Lincoln violated the Constitution before seceding. However, Stephens also described Georgians as ready to defend their rights, interests, and honor if Lincoln signed an "aggressive act" of Congress "to exclude us from the territories with our slave property."[7]

This was a direct challenge to the root of Republicanism. Lincoln had written to Stephens on December 22 and defined the difference between them: "You think slavery is right and ought to be extended; we think slavery is wrong and ought to be restricted."[8] Stephens responded that he was not afraid that the administration would attack slavery but rather dishonored that Republicans wanted only to put the southern states "under the bar of public opinion and national condemnation," a position that was "enough to arouse . . . revolt."

Honor and Dishonor in North and South

Honor was a compelling influence in both southern and northern cultures. It was a way of publicly justifying one's personal and social identity. Religious principles, government laws, and social mores defined what was honorable. Bertram Wyatt-Brown has concluded that rather than fear of slave insurrections and northern power, "a primary and perhaps primitive dedication to the code of honor was the South's undoing." He quotes Hammond: "Reputation is everything." According to Wyatt-Brown, the antebellum southerner "could hardly escape doubts that his section was perceived by the world as inferior, morally and materially."[9]

There is little doubt that the South felt dishonored. For thirty years before the war, "American abolitionists had denounced the South's planter class as cruel, debauched, self-serving, unchristian and doomed to eternal damnation."[10] Some revisionist historians in the 1950s claimed that these extreme verbal denunciations were to blame for the extreme actions taken by the South to silence political dissent, threaten violence, and let loose vigilante groups. In this view, extremists on both sides bore equal responsibility for causing a preventable war. As early as 1842, Lincoln had realized that dishonorable behavior was frequently reciprocal. He wrote that "not to meet denunciation with denunciation . . . was a reversal of human nature, which is God's decree and never can be reversed."[11] By 1865, he had become adept at respectfully bringing judgment in religious language, and he expected that his Second Inaugural Address would "wear as well as—perhaps better than—anything I have produced; but I believe it is not immediately popular. Men are not flattered by being told there has been a difference between the Almighty and them." And he accepted his share of the blame for dishonoring the South: "Whatever of humiliation there is in it, falls most directly on myself."[12]

Holding Firmly to Their Promises   109

Lovejoy also was not governed by the need to be popular. In a tribute to Lovejoy penned on May 30, 1864, Lincoln wrote that his friend had "bravely endured the obscurity which the unpopularity of his principles imposed, and never accepted official honors, until those honors were ready to admit his principles with him."[13]

Crisis and Compromise

The winter of 1860–61 saw escalating possibilities of a divided nation and of armed conflict. The most immediate danger was the threat of organized physical violence. On the same day that South Carolina seceded, lame-duck president James Buchanan appointed a fellow Democrat, Edwin Stanton, a loyal Unionist, as attorney general. Stanton discovered that army officers were redeploying personnel and munitions to positions advantageous to the South and became worried that if Maryland and Virginia seceded, Washington would be defenseless. In late December, after Buchanan ignored Stanton's concerns, which included information about a plot against Lincoln, the attorney general took them to New York senator William H. Seward.[14]

Lovejoy, too, heard about the rumored plot and allowed a group headed by Joseph Medill of the *Chicago Press and Tribune* to use his franking privilege to inform Lincoln, a move that suggests that Stanton, Lincoln, and Lovejoy shared information and cooperated to develop responses to events from the beginning of the administration. According to Medill, a secret organization, the Disunion Vigilance Committees, intended to assassinate Lincoln on his way to his inauguration in Washington and replace him with the Southern Democratic Party presidential candidate, John Breckinridge.

The escalating tension produced a growing gulf between conservative Republicans and the leaders of the antislavery wing of the Republican Party, creating the possibility that the party would fragment before Lincoln took office, thereby effectively nullifying the election results. Opponents of slavery feared that conservative Republicans would unite with members of other parties to save the union by allowing slavery to expand, that the Buchanan administration would transfer enough military resources to the control of the South to endanger the Capitol, or that Lincoln would assume his office but find Republican political power in Congress sapped of its strength.

In mid-December, with the southern states, led by South Carolina, contemplating secession, nearly all sides began pressuring Lincoln to find a way to preserve the Union. Congressman John Crittenden proposed that new states formed below a line extending from Missouri's southern border to the Pacific Ocean be admitted as slave states, while all new states above that line would prohibit slavery.[15] The situation was complicated by the fact that Lincoln was

110   CHAPTER 8

not expected to make public statements until after he was in office in March and by the fact that he was relatively unknown and untested.

As events proceeded, some northern congressmen continued to believe that if Congress compromised with the South, the seceded states would return. Lovejoy disagreed. Lincoln characteristically tried to appeal to both those favoring compromise and those opposing it, using the same two basic principles on which he and Lovejoy had been campaigning for years: nonextension of slavery and noninterference with it in the South. On the one hand, the president-elect sent conciliatory messages through his surrogates. According to Lyman Trumbull, the Republicans were about to demonstrate that "they will leave the Southern States and their property alone."[16] Illinois congressman William Kellogg assured a House subcommittee that Lincoln favored enforcement of the Fugitive Slave Act and the repeal of personal liberty laws passed by northern legislatures.[17] Lincoln privately encouraged Seward to support a constitutional amendment preventing Congress from abolishing or interfering with slavery where it already existed.[18] Lincoln also sent confidential messages informing a few friends that he would not compromise on the nonextension of slavery, a position that "kept his party in line."[19]

Though the president-elect took no public position on Crittenden's compromise, he privately shared his views with several Illinois members of Congress, including Trumbull, Elihu Washburne, and Kellogg: "Let there be no compromise on the question of extending slavery. . . . Have none of it. Stand firm. . . . Hold firm as with a chain of steel." To Seward he wrote, "I am for no compromise which assists or permits the extension of the institution on soil owned by the nation." He continued, "I have all the while said, that on . . . the question of extending slavery under the national auspices—I am inflexible." Lincoln declared the idea of compromise "obnoxious" since it would "put us again on a high-road to a slave empire."[20]

Lovejoy, too, played an important role in the effort to avoid compromise. On January 23, 1861, he spoke on the floor of the House of Representatives on the subject, addressing his remarks to anxious conservative Republicans who might be wavering: "You are asked to desert the party and the principles which you were proud to uphold before the people, and when you entered this House at the opening of the session; and the question is, shall we abandon the cardinal article of our faith—prohibition of slavery in the Territories of the United States? Perhaps this drift towards a compromise foreshadows a purpose to organize a new party, 'sloughing off,' as the phrase is, the extremes, both North and South. In this new arrangement all the radicals like myself are to be left out. I wish you a merry time of it, my masters. A very interesting play, Hamlet with Hamlet left out!"[21]

Lovejoy was also aware of an attempt to form a Union Party, an approach resembling the plan that Stephen A. Douglas had suggested in his 1859 *Harper's*

Holding Firmly to Their Promises

article. Proponents of the new Union movement hoped that peace could be preserved by bringing together Republicans and Democrats in a compromise that would allow slavery to continue indefinitely. Lovejoy, however, maintained that trying to push antislavery Republicans out of the picture as "extremists" would not work because the 1860 election had indicated that they represented the Republican Party's core values:

> We made the issue squarely, distinctly, without hypocrisy or disguise, before the people, and they decided that a President should be elected who was opposed to the extension of human slavery. They elected him in a constitutional mode; and all that we ask is, that he shall be inaugurated. And let me tell you, gentlemen, who are friends of compromise, who want these differences settled, let me tell you that one twelve months of the administration of Abraham Lincoln will do more to disabuse the public mind than all the compromises and peace measures that can be patched up in Congress. Let him have a trial, a fair trial. We will abate not one jot of our principle, or add anything to our creed.[22]

Lovejoy and Pennsylvania congressman Thaddeus Stevens, assisted by Washburne and Roscoe Conkling, arranged a series of delays in an effort to thwart any major compromise. They succeeded. The compromisers won only minor victories that came too late to make a difference, and the Senate defeated Crittenden's plan by a single vote on March 2, two days before Lincoln's inauguration.[23]

Some analysts have argued that a pragmatic Lincoln overrode the radicals to save the Union; others have contended that a conservative Lincoln would have thwarted the radical agenda had they not forced him to take a harder stand. Neither view is accurate. The radicals in Congress in 1861 dramatically demonstrated their ability to use the levers of political power—parliamentary maneuvers, speeches by noted congressmen, and behind-the-scenes collaborations with other leaders, most notably the prospective chief executive.

Perceiving the Task before Them

In February 1861, with the inauguration only weeks away, Lincoln in Springfield and Lovejoy in Washington were maneuvering to keep the Republicans in Congress united. Both realized that the old ways in the Capitol were going to change; they must hold the government steady while seeking to keep the compromisers and slavery sympathizers in check and working to reestablish the nation's founding principles. At this critical time of transition, the two men played significant roles in appropriating their new political power. As he prepared to leave his hometown for an unknown future, Lincoln gave a farewell speech before boarding the train for Washington. He expressed his

112   CHAPTER 8

trust in Divine guidance by asking God to accompany him in his presidential duties: "I now leave, not knowing when or whether I may return, with a task before me greater than that which rested of [George] Washington. Without the assistance of that Divine being who ever attended him, I cannot succeed. . . . Trusting in Him who can go with me, and remain with you, and be everywhere for good."[24] Lovejoy had often revealed similar beliefs. Three years earlier, as he was taking on the responsibilities of national leadership, he had said, "Gentlemen, if I have uttered one heart-prayer to my God, it was for His aid, wisely to discharge the duties of my position, and faithfully to meet the trust committed to my care. That I have performed these duties imperfectly, and with inexperience, no one can be so well aware as myself. That I have performed them honestly, I am conscious before my God."[25] Lovejoy had sent the speech to Lincoln.[26] These two men spoke less of doctrine and more of faith, and both were willing to be judged by God's sovereignty. This perspective was the foundation of their deepening trust in their radical vision, in the American people, and in each other.

Lincoln Takes Office

Lincoln spent nearly two weeks traveling to Washington, making dozens of stops along the way on a tour of the country. He arrived on February 23 after sneaking into Washington incognito. On March 4, he was sworn in as the sixteenth president of the United States. Two weeks earlier, Jefferson Davis had assumed the presidency of the Confederate States of America after six more southern states had joined South Carolina in seceding from the Union.

In an atmosphere of great tension, Lincoln delivered his inaugural address, which he composed in consultation with some trusted friends, among them Orville Browning, Seward, and Lovejoy. The New York senator felt that the speech's initial tone would be too provocative for the "defeated, irritated, angered, frenzied" southerners and suggested a more conciliatory approach. In response, Lincoln composed his stirring and ultimately well-known closing: "We are not enemies, but friends. . . . The mystic chords of memory . . . will yet swell the chorus of the Union, when again touched, as surely they will be, by the better angels of our nature."[27]

From the beginning of the administration, Lovejoy occupied a unique place with Lincoln as a member of the Illinois Republican delegation in Washington. The congressman was a frequent visitor at the White House, both to conduct business and to socialize. According to Robert Browne, a young admirer of both Lincoln and Lovejoy, early in the new administration, Lincoln invited Stevens, who had become the powerful chair of the House Ways and Means Committee, to come to the White House for a private evening chat: "Come this evening at eight o'clock. Mr. Lovejoy will be in at nine. He is one of our home folks, and if we talk a little long, he can come again. These Illinois friends have a habit of coming in at the side door; but are never bothered, or out of sorts, when I am busy and can not entertain them." Stevens responded, "Seeing the way you keep house, I think I shall want to join in and get on the footing of your Illinois friends. If it will suit your pleasure, as I know it will his, I shall be pleased to have you admit Mr. Lovejoy as a party to our talk as soon as he arrives, he is on my side, or perhaps rather, I am on his."[28]

Defending the Union

The war began at Fort Sumter on April 12. Three days later, the president called for seventy-five thousand troops to defend the United States, and by early June, four more states left the Union to join the Confederacy. Governor Richard Yates summoned six thousand volunteers from Illinois. Lovejoy was in Princeton at the time, and he joined in the enlistment effort. By the end of May, at least six companies had been formed in Bureau County, including a full regiment that Lovejoy had helped raise. It was accepted on July 31.[29] As these men and boys went off to war, Lovejoy offered only brief remarks: "It seems to me that the booming of cannons against the forts of the United States, the seizure of federal property, and the dishonoring of our flag for the first time since we became a nation, ought to arouse our patriotism without much speech-making." In response to his own question, "What was the cause of this rebellion?," Lovejoy told those assembled, "There was no cause, and the United States did not commit any aggression." But, he continued, the South "wanted to control the federal government, and when the power passed from them they got up this rebellion. The leaders misrepresented the views of the north on the subject of slavery; and I have no doubt their representatives caused many of the people to believe that when Mr. Lincoln was inaugurated he would invade their States with arms and free the slaves. But from whatever cause this rebellion comes, it is upon us and we must meet it." He concluded with a sober and somber appeal to the honor, sense of duty, and bravery of his fellow residents of Bureau County: "I am not going to urge the young men to enlist under a fit of enthusiasm or whiskey. If you enlist I shall expect to hear that you have done your share; and if you die or get killed, we will embalm your memories in our hearts."[30]

Special First Session of the Thirty-Seventh Congress

Lincoln called a special session of the Thirty-Seventh Congress beginning on July 4, 1861. Under Stevens's leadership, Congress committed four hundred million dollars to provide for an army of four hundred thousand men. Lovejoy

114   CHAPTER 8

was appointed chair of the House Agriculture Committee, a vital position that placed him among the chamber's core decision makers. He became a major floor leader as well as a leading voice on issues affecting slavery, particularly the "contrabands," a term coined by General Benjamin F. Butler to refer to former slaves who attached themselves to the Union Army. Such persons—considered "contraband of war"—would not be returned to their former masters. News of this policy spread quickly through the black community as well as political circles.[31] By July 9, Lovejoy had shepherded a resolution through the House of Representatives that proposed that the army would neither return nor capture runaway slaves. The measure passed by a ninety-three to fifty-five vote, a result that Lovejoy attributed to conservatives who were "timid and vexed" but nevertheless "had to vote right at last."[32] More radical abolitionists including Frederick Douglass and Gerrit Smith commended Lovejoy's proposal but sought more. Though they would temporarily accept that the primary purpose of the war was to perpetuate the Union, they insisted that winning would require emancipating the slaves and enlisting black troops in the Union Army.[33]

The first Battle of Bull Run, which took place on July 21 in northern Virginia, near Washington, D.C., was a shocking defeat for the Union Army, and Lovejoy was there. He and other civilians observed the battle from what they thought was a safe hill but soon found themselves caught up in the chaos of the retreating army. According to one report, Lovejoy offered his binoculars to General William T. Sherman, who exclaimed, "What in Goddamned hell are you doing here? Get out of my lines!"[34] An English reporter described the scene as one of hysteria and stupidity, but Lovejoy insisted that although the troops were exhausted and in disarray, they were lost rather than frightened or panicked. He blamed the officers for failing to rally the men at the proper time.[35]

Back in Bureau County, the local Democratic newspaper, *The Patriot*, charged that Lovejoy had failed to tell the recruits that the war's true purpose was to abolish slavery.[36] Though Lovejoy had never made any secret of his desire to end slavery, he firmly maintained that war had broken out only as a consequence of secession and that its sole purpose was to return the rebellious states to the Union, taking a moderate approach that fit the times. As Lovejoy's protégé, the Reverend David Todd, wrote in September 1861, "Does any sane person want [Lincoln] to come out & say he will free the slaves? I should like to see the slaves free but, as I desire that, I do not want Lincoln to say it now."[37]

The *Bureau County Republican*, too, rose to Lovejoy's defense, portraying the *Patriot*'s attacks as more of the same "falsehood, slander and backbiting [that] has been practiced on Lovejoy these twenty years and more." Nevertheless, some of his supporters began to fret that if a rally were planned for Lovejoy's return, the turnout would be small, indicating a decline in his popularity.[38] They need not have worried. When he arrived in Princeton on August 24, after the close of the special congressional session, three thousand supporters appeared at a reception for him, demonstrating his "deep and powerful roots among his constituents."[39]

Colonel Owen Lovejoy in Missouri

In the wake of the defeat at Bull Run, Lovejoy had resolved to address what he considered the biggest threat to Illinois—internal conflict between pro-slavery and antislavery forces in the border state of Missouri. If Missouri fell into rebel hands, he feared that Illinois would become the next battleground, and he was willing to do something about it. He had advocated a vigorous military defense of the Union since December 1860 and had rallied young men to go into battle. He informed secretary of war Simon Cameron of his desire to enlist, and in August 1861, he received orders to serve under General John C. Frémont in Missouri. When he arrived in St. Louis on September 27, he wrote home, "War is a terrible necessity at best. . . . All there is sacred in our government depends upon our maintaining its supremacy."[40] He wanted to observe the war zone and planned to use the knowledge gained from his three months of military duty as a basis for legislation and public policy.[41]

Lovejoy immediately realized that he had landed in the middle of a major political threat to the Lincoln administration. The commanding officer of the U.S. Army's Western Department, General Frémont, faced the problem of what to do with large numbers of runaway slaves who were crossing the Union Army lines. After consulting with members of his staff but not the president, Frémont had issued an August 30 pronouncement that any slaves crossing the lines in the Western Department would be considered free. This went beyond the Confiscation Act of August 6, which freed those slaves employed by rebel forces.[42] The president was in a bind: on one hand, Frémont's dismissal might demoralize the Western Army; on the other hand, if the proclamation were not rescinded, the arms that had been sent to Kentucky could be used against the Union. On September 11, Lincoln wrote to ask Frémont to modify the language of his proclamation: the president "understood that if the controversy became public, radical Republicans, whose loyalty was crucial to his governing coalition, might side with Frémont rather than with him." But the general refused, insisting that Lincoln make his request an order if he wanted it obeyed.[43]

After two months of back-and-forth with Frémont regarding this premature and unauthorized proclamation, Lincoln relieved the general of his command on November 2. The general left St. Louis two days later. Rumors claimed that Lovejoy had influenced Frémont's decision to issue the order, probably because it was known that Frémont had consulted his staff. But Lovejoy did not arrive until four weeks after Frémont's announcement. During these tense political and strategic maneuverings Lovejoy made no public comment.[44]

116 CHAPTER 8

In Missouri, Lovejoy served on a committee with Illinois's lieutenant governor, Gustave Koerner, and Congressman John Gurley of Cincinnati, a minister. The panel was charged with adjudicating which Missourians were loyal and which were secessionists, because only loyal citizens were entitled to reimbursement for property commandeered by the Union Army. According to Koerner, Lovejoy "was more prepared to allow claims than I."[45] Lovejoy's leniency would have been in keeping with U.S. military policy, which was at first relatively conciliatory but took on a "hard war" orientation as early as April 1863. Lincoln had initially hoped to avoid alienating southern citizens, but when this policy failed and it became clear that the rebellion would have to be crushed and the slaves freed, Lincoln played his other war card, seeking to destroy civilians' support of the war economy and to confiscate the property of the wealthy southerners who were driving the war.[46]

Lovejoy's Plan to Quell the Rebellion

On November 21, 1861, the *Bureau County Republican* announced that Lovejoy had returned from Missouri, where his experiences had given him new ideas regarding U.S. military policy. Shortly thereafter, he announced his new ideas to his constituents in a speech, "The Use of War Powers to Free the Slaves with the Help of Black Troops." Lovejoy began by declaring his overall support for Lincoln and his handling of the war, though he at times differed with the administration's actions. He disagreed with the removal of General Frémont from his command but added, "how far the President was justifiable in that removal, he could not say as doubtless the President had much more evidence in the premises than he had." He also stated that the Union's "organization and equipping of a citizen's army showed conclusively" that people were united on the question of "crushing out the treason that threatens our government. . . . But there is a difference of opinion on the slavery question." Both his dislike of slavery and his respect for the Constitution were well known, and based on those two pillars, he believed that four policy positions were necessary to accomplish the goal of ending slavery.[47]

First, Lincoln needed to employ the war powers that were implied in the president's status as commander in chief with the sworn "duty to crush out treason, insurrection and rebellion." Lovejoy believed that by virtue of having taken an oath to "preserve, protect and defend the Constitution," the president had the power to do whatever was necessary to achieve that end. Lovejoy based his arguments on ideas put forth by John Quincy Adams, James Monroe, and Theophilus Parsons, a noted law professor at Harvard who had claimed "that in time of war, if necessity demands it, we have a right to abolish slavery." According to Lovejoy, events on the battlefield had confirmed his opinion that there "was a long war before us and, if we do not destroy slavery, it will destroy us." "Slavery is the cause of the rebellion and we can have no permanent peace while it exists." He did not, however, specify when slavery needed to be eliminated.[48]

Second, Lovejoy supported the recruitment of black troops to hasten the rebellion's defeat. In his words, "The nation has the right to resort to such measures as will most speedily, and with least expense and loss of life, crush out this wicked rebellion, and the four million loyal blacks on the side of the Federal Government will enable us to settle the question." He continued, "If we proclaim freedom to these men, they will do nobly for us. I have seen a great many, and know how they feel. They are our natural allies, our natural friends." Lovejoy believed that white Americans were increasingly accepting of the idea that blacks were reliable persons who could assist in the war, a belief supported by Ira Berlin's contention that "by abandoning their owners, coming uninvited into Union lines, and offering their lives and labor in the Federal cause, slaves forced Federal soldiers at the lowest level to recognize their importance to the Union's success."[49]

Third, Lovejoy advocated the confiscation of enemy property. Lovejoy reminded his audience of the general acceptance of the idea that horses, mules, and wagons could be taken as property necessary for a war effort—precisely the process in which he had been involved in Missouri. By extension, since southern laws regarded slaves as property, they, too, were eligible for confiscation. Lovejoy understood that slaves belonging to loyal southerners, especially those in the border states, could not be confiscated via war powers, but he was now willing to offer compensation to loyal slaveholders who emancipated their slaves.[50]

Finally, Lovejoy believed that the United States should vigorously prosecute the war, with the goal of swiftly quelling the rebellion. Doing so would be painful and "take a generation to recover from . . . but it has to be done." He also believed that although the president had heretofore taken a tepid approach, he would soon be ready to take bolder steps: "President Lincoln is advancing step by step just as the cautious swimmer wades into the stream before taking a dive. President Lincoln will make a dive before long."[51] Six months into the war, therefore, Lovejoy remained a less than radical abolitionist. At least publicly, he still did not back full political rights for blacks or an immediate end to slavery in the South.

Some radicals in New England, among them Douglass, were ready to go further, organizing the Emancipation League to urge "upon the people and the government the emancipation of the Slaves as a measure of justice and military necessity."[52] He believed that in the wake of the attack on Fort Sumter, ordinary people were more willing to listen to his words.

For his part, Lincoln had begun quietly consulting with political leaders in Delaware on a plan to compensate slaveholders for freeing their slaves. Lincoln hoped that a negotiated settlement with representatives of slave owners in the smallest border state would set a precedent for how to proceed in the other slaveholding states that remained in the Union. His plan included gradual emancipation over a ten-year period and a five-hundred-dollar payment for each slave freed.[53] The compensation required to gain emancipation for all the slaves in the border states totaled only about one-third of the cost of supporting the war for one year.[54]

Lovejoy Returns to Congress

Soon after Thanksgiving, Lovejoy boarded a train for Washington, where the second session of the Thirty-Seventh Congress began in early December 1861. With the departure of the southern members, the House of Representatives included 108 Republicans, 28 Unionists, and 44 Democrats. As chair of the Agriculture Committee, Lovejoy continued to be part of Speaker Galusha A. Grow's inner circle. The atmosphere was alive with possibility. Lovejoy was committed to sustaining and supporting the administration, but Lincoln's caution and hesitation and especially his refusal to authorize a stronger confiscation policy were making the Republican Party's antislavery base uncomfortable.

As the Radical Republicans were speaking in higher decibels all over Washington and challenging establishment generals, the maneuverings of pro-slavery sympathizers in the military, the cabinet, and the administration became an issue. General Henry W. Halleck and District of Columbia sheriff Ward Hill Lamon were returning slaves to their rebel masters, a violation of the First Confiscation Act, devised by Lovejoy, but were not receiving censure from the administration.[55] Some Washingtonians were encouraging Cameron to make a public report supporting the confiscation of all "property" belonging to those fighting for the Confederacy as well as the emancipation and arming of slaves. The secretary of war prepared such a paper but did not consult with the president, and when Lincoln learned of the report on December 1, he immediately stopped its publication on the grounds that allowing African American troops to serve in the U.S. Army was the sole prerogative of the president.[56] He later explained that his "oath to preserve the constitution to the best of my ability, imposed upon me the duty of preserving, by every indispensable means, that government." In December 1861, he "did not yet think" that black Union soldiers were "an indispensable necessity."[57]

On December 2, the same day that the public learned of Lincoln's rebuke of Cameron, Washington hosted a celebration of the Republicans' new congressional power and social status. Lovejoy was chosen to introduce Senator James Lane, from the new state of Kansas, to a joyous audience. When the congressman entered the hall, the crowd applauded him. Just eight months earlier, according to the editor of the *Bureau County Republican*, "he might have been dragged from the stand and perhaps murdered." Much had changed. After commenting on the importance of the gathering and restating his commitment to abolition, Lovejoy seized the moment to air his differences with Lincoln. Lovejoy told his listeners of a tall king who "had by Divine command been told to destroy his enemies when he had his opportunity. The king refused to do so and he lost his crown." Lovejoy then paused before announcing that "he hoped that no one living now who resembled the king's height and station in life would follow his example or share his fate." After the audience laughed and cheered, Lovejoy "moved on to call for severe measures to crush the rebellion." After the program ended, Lovejoy, Ohio congressman John A. Bingham, and Vice President Hannibal Hamlin visited Cameron's home to thank him for bringing the issue of confiscation before the public.[58]

On December 3, Lincoln delivered his Annual Message to Congress, which had been postponed a day as a consequence of the Cameron incident. Lincoln's speech started out mild: "In the midst of unprecedented political troubles, we have cause of great gratitude to God for unusual good health and most abundant harvests."[59] After offering some modest practical ideas and suggesting that the time had come for the United States to recognize Haiti and Liberia, Lincoln turned to more controversial matters.

He referred to the secretary of war's report, offering his gratitude that more men had enlisted than he had called for. He then noted, "Obeying the dictates of prudence, as well as the obligations of law, instead of transcending, I have adhered to the act of Congress to confiscate property used for insurrectionary purposes. If a new law upon the same subject shall be proposed, its propriety will be duly considered." Lincoln was again on the same page as Lovejoy. Yet he also reminded Congress that freeing the slaves of disloyal rebels threatened loyal slaveholders in the border states: "The Union must be preserved, and hence, all indispensable means must be employed. We should not be in haste to determine that radical and extreme measures, which may reach the loyal as well as the disloyal, *are indispensable*." Lincoln concluded on a visionary note: "The struggle of today is not altogether for today—it is for a vast future also. With a reliance on Providence, all the more firm and earnest, let us proceed in the great task which events have devolved upon us."[60]

Lovejoy must have been pleased that Lincoln had openly declared support for further legislation on confiscation policy and his commitment to quell the rebellion, stated in religious terms. Lincoln had asserted his leadership as a radical. He had used the term *great task* in a divine moral context that involved ending the wrong of slavery. Other observers, however, were less quick than Lovejoy to understand the significance of what Lincoln had said.

Legislative Initiatives

Shortly after the address to Congress, Republicans caucused and unanimously endorsed the unconditional confiscation and emancipation of slaves held by disloyal masters. Lovejoy characteristically spoke on the importance of sustaining the administration.[61] On December 20, Lovejoy introduced a resolution directing the Judiciary Committee to draw up a confiscation bill, but he mistakenly tabled the resolution on a sixty-one to fifty-six vote. In keeping with Lincoln's admonition, some Republicans continued to fear that a stronger confiscation policy would threaten the loyalty of border state slave owners.[62]

Lovejoy and other radicals then worked with President Lincoln to persuade moderate Republicans that the time for emancipation was near and to persuade people in border states that they had nothing to fear. The president also continued to negotiate with representatives of those states regarding his plan to emancipate their slaves, a moderate effort that Lovejoy supported. However, with the border states refusing to accept Lincoln's offers of compensated, gradual emancipation, the declining military situation, and rising political pressure to end slavery, Lincoln realized that the time had come to change course.

On the first day of the new session of Congress, the House and the Senate passed a joint resolution presented by Lovejoy "tendering the thanks of Congress to Captain Wilkes, of the United States Navy . . . for his brave, adroit, and patriotic conduct in the arrest and detention of the traitors James M. Mason and John Slidell." On November 8, sailors under the command of Charles Wilkes had searched an English vessel, the *Trent*, near Bermuda and captured Mason and Slidell, two former members of Congress who were now commissioned envoys of the Confederacy and were on their way to solicit British military assistance for their cause. Though Wilkes was hailed as a hero in the United States, he had failed to follow the proper legal procedures allowing the civil courts to declare that his captives were contraband, and British authorities became outraged. Just prior to the introduction of Lovejoy's resolution, Senator Charles Sumner returned from England and told Lincoln that there was an "immense anti-American excitement in Great Britain because of Mason and Slidell." Lincoln began to meet almost daily with Sumner to assess the latest news and to consider the danger that this disagreement with the British might drift into conflict.[63]

On December 19, the British government threatened to declare war if the United States did not immediately release Mason and Slidell. Secretary of state Seward and Senator Sumner spent hours persuading the president that in the midst of one war, he could not afford another and that the Law of the Sea was vital to the British. Lincoln then quietly released Mason and Slidell. An angry Lovejoy saw the incident as a humiliating act of British interference in American affairs at a time when Britain should be supporting the Union.[64]

Holding Firmly to Their Promises

President Lincoln and Congressman Lovejoy were eager to pass legislation on projects proposed in the 1860 Republican Party platform. When Lincoln highlighted them in his annual message to Congress, Lovejoy was quick to introduce some of them in the House. On December 4, his position as chair of the Agricultural Committee gave him the privilege of reintroducing the Homestead Act that President Buchanan had vetoed in 1860. Lincoln had endorsed the measure and planned to sign it when it passed. On December 9, Lovejoy introduced a matter of particular concern for him: requiring the secretary of war to revoke General Halleck's order that barred fugitive slaves from entering U.S. Army lines. Whereas Frémont's proclamation had been premature and too radical, Halleck's order was too punitive and unrealistic; Lincoln, however, allowed it to stand. Lovejoy's resolution was considered impolite, so he introduced another resolution on December 11 that "respectfully requested" the commander in chief to "direct General Halleck to the recall order."[65] After a heated discussion of that resolution, Clement L. Vallandigham of Ohio moved to table Lovejoy's resolution, and the motion passed by a seventy-eight to sixty-four vote.[66]

The subject was reopened a few days later, and Lovejoy reiterated his view that the best way to put down the rebellion was to take away the rebels' "property" and liberate their slaves by permitting runaways to remain behind the Union lines: "Our battles should be fought so as to hurt slavery and enable the President to decree destruction of the mischievous institution." And, he added, "if the soldiers won't fight unless they are allowed to return fugitive slaves, then the Army is better off without them." He urged his colleagues to stop "coddling" the rebels and "stop supporting" Halleck's order.[67]

On December 11, Lovejoy had also introduced a resolution to establish diplomatic relations with Haiti and Liberia, a move Lincoln had requested.[68] For as long as half a century, African Americans and opponents of slavery, including Lovejoy, had been celebrating on August 1, the date in 1804 when the Haitians expelled the French and declared their independence. Liberia had been a sovereign nation since 1847, but although the American government was responsible for the new country's existence, the United States had refused to extend diplomatic recognition. Lovejoy's resolution stalled, with Douglass chiding Congress for its inaction, before finally passing the Senate on February 4, 1862. Lincoln signed it on June 5 and appointed the first U.S. diplomatic representative to Haiti the following month.[69]

As 1861 turned to 1862, the United States found itself in a precarious position, with its survival threatened not only by civil war but by factionalism and disagreements over what to do about slavery, precisely the issue that had caused the war. The split in the nation was mirrored at lower levels of society—states, religious denominations, and even families were divided. The national debt soared. Despite uncertainty and fear, Lincoln and Lovejoy were establishing a pattern: when

Lovejoy and the radicals had the votes to pass legislation for emancipation in the District of Columbia and for the nonextension of slavery in the territories, Lincoln would support them; when Lincoln initiated more moderate plans for compensated, gradual emancipation for the border states, Lovejoy would lead a pragmatic effort to support the president; and on more contentious issues such as undoing the Fugitive Slave Law, expanding confiscation policy, and recruiting black troops, they would wait for just the right moment to act. They would have to sustain that collaboration to navigate the treacherous path through the war to their shared radical principle of a free nation.

PART 3

Applying Political Power, 1862–1864

9 Restoring the Founding Purposes, 1862

"We must repent, and must proclaim liberty to the enslaved
of the land."
—Owen Lovejoy

Despite the military, political, social, and economic crises that beset the United States in 1862, national elected officials confronted an array of new opportunities. With the representatives of the slaveholding states having withdrawn from Congress, Republicans had clear majorities in both the House and the Senate. Abraham Lincoln in the White House and Owen Lovejoy in the House of Representatives were poised to start remaking the country in keeping with their vision. They saw themselves as working to hold together the Union while restoring the Founding Fathers' ideology as articulated in the Declaration of Independence.

Events leading up to and during the Civil War were influenced by both religion and tradition to a degree that Lincoln did not initially realize. Whereas the Declaration of Independence stated that God had created all men as equal, endowed them with certain inalienable rights, and established governments to protect those rights, the Confederacy's founders invoked "the favor and guidance of God" and took as their motto *Deo Vindice* (God will avenge). The difference would be settled on the battlefield. When the Confederate Army won the first Battle of Bull Run (Manassas), the Confederate people concluded that they had received a divine commission. By 1861, not only had the South adopted the northern practice of observing fast days, but ministers and other leaders had begun using services and sermons on these days to offer assurances that the cause of secession was righteous and that God was on their side.[1] Lovejoy had long argued that enslavement of and brutality toward human beings was not in keeping with the Bible, and he believed that God's purposes were likely to be more in accordance with the Union's founding principles. He had a suspicion that God willed "the perpetuity of the Union."[2] Lincoln recognized the importance of appealing to both patriotic tradition and religious belief in presenting a sustaining vision to his people.

CHAPTER 9

Conduct of the War

The first land battles in 1861 were military defeats for the Union Army—Bull Run in July, Wilson's Creek in August, and Ball's Bluff in October. Though only a small number of casualties were sustained at Ball's Bluff, the battle was significant because of the death of Colonel Edward D. Baker, an Oregon Republican who is the only U.S. senator ever to die in battle. Baker was a close friend of Lincoln as well as his mentor and early law partner; the president had named a son after Baker. Baker's death provided a wake-up call for the nation and its leaders. Some radical congressmen charged that Democratic generals were not sufficiently committed to the Union cause to engage the rebels in battle. The Joint Congressional Committee on the Conduct of the War had been established in December 1861 to investigate the absence of a vigorous prosecution of the war, and on January 6, 1862, the House of Representatives began debating the procedural details about who had the right to investigate whether generals had indeed been dallying. Many observers believed that Kentucky's John Crittenden and Charles Wickliffe were obfuscating matters by claiming that this issue did not fall under Congress's purview.[3]

Lovejoy was not a member of the committee, but he leapt into the debate, reminding Crittenden that the "Army is subject to the civil authority—if not in its minute details, certainly in its grand movements." He then clarified his concerns: "I do not think that the want of success in our military operations is owing so much to this general or that general. . . . I do not wish to blame any one or to discuss personal merits. . . . We are waiting in the hope—in my opinion a vain and fruitless hope—that this rebellion will put itself down; that if we do not hurt them these rebels will return to their allegiance." Lovejoy recognized "that the whole nation is waiting for the army to move forward. They have furnished the men and the money; and why does not the army move?" Well aware of his own limited knowledge of military affairs, he put to rest that excuse for not forming a Committee on the Conduct of War. "You may tell me I do not know how to make a coat. Very true; but I know when it is made, and know when it fits. And though I may not know how to conduct the details of military affairs, I know what results should be brought about. . . . I care very little about investigating these incidental facts."[4]

Lovejoy then placed the war into a moral context: "The great trouble is that this nation has failed, and is yet failing, rightly to interpret the providences of God. We are standing in front, not merely of rebels, but we are standing before an incensed God. . . . [W]e are standing in the presence of that divine Nemesis who has woven the threads of retribution into the web of national life no less than into that of individual life."[5]

The basic Old Testament theme that God "makes the nations prove the glories of His righteousness" was not a new concept. Isaac Watts had made it well known in the text of the eighteenth-century hymn "Joy to the World," which he adapted from Psalm 98.[6] And in 1862, Lovejoy argued, the nation was proving itself unworthy: "We must repent, and must proclaim liberty to the enslaved of the land."[7]

The remainder of Lovejoy's remarks turned into a heated exchange between defenders of slavery and the radical advocates of emancipation. Both groups included seasoned men of great skill, biblical literacy, and wit. Whenever Wickliffe spoke, Lovejoy's "brow was immediately darkened in token of the impending strife."[8] Lovejoy compared the biblical story of Jonah, whose crew threw him overboard to save their ship in a storm, to the idea that slavery needed to be thrown overboard to save the nation and asked Wickliffe whether slavery or the ship of state was more important. Wickliffe quickly replied, "I would prefer throwing the abolitionists overboard," to much laughter. Lovejoy took Wickliffe's retort to mean that he was more committed to slavery than to the Union and chided the Kentuckian for taking that position. Lovejoy, in contrast, was willing to die many times over to have the opportunity to rid the nation of the "accursed thing" of slavery: "I would lift myself up until I brought my heart in contact with the great heart of the eternal God, who loves the slave as well as he loves you or me; and say, as God lives, and my soul lives, the Union shall be preserved, the Constitution shall be saved, the accursed thing, which has destroyed both, shall be brought to the block."[9]

Lovejoy closed with another biblical reference, the Parable of the Wheat and the Tares from Matthew 13:24–30. He was no literalist, and he knew that the "'end of the world' can mean simply the end of an age—the end of the age of slavery."[10] "I wish to say that the harvest has already come, and that now is the time to separate the tares from the wheat . . . [T]hose slaveholders who are truly loyal will become abolitionists . . . and pro-slavery men will be secessionists. The Union men of Kentucky and the border states will thus be divided, the sheep and the goats."[11] Lovejoy was quite adept at the biblical parsing that was typical of both whites and blacks at that time.

Promoting the General Welfare

In his classic *Battle Cry of Freedom*, James M. McPherson calls the Thirty-Seventh Congress "one of the most productive in American history." In the midst of a time of national anguish, the legislators "enacted laws of far-reaching importance for the disposition of public lands, the future of higher education, and the building of transcontinental railroads." The "absence of southerners

128   CHAPTER 9

from Congress" made possible the passage of these measures, many of which had languished in Congress for years.[12]

The Homestead Act offered free land to expand the middle class. The newly created Bureau of Agriculture provided technical information and legislative support for the modernization of farming. The Morrill Act led to the establishment of federal land-grant colleges. And plans for the transcontinental railroad were approved. Lovejoy and his Agriculture Committee were in the thick of many of these formidable accomplishments. The Illinois congressman's influence in the House of Representatives was recognized by those who observed that his frequent parliamentary motions of procedure earned him the label the "bellwether of the House radicals."[13] After the second passage of the Homestead Act, the *Aurora Beacon* declared, "To me here, it looks like Lovejoy was a name of growing strength, of influence, of power."[14] The creation of the Department of Agriculture caused the *Bureau County Republican* to note, "The bill originated with Mr. Lovejoy, and was matured by him, and he secured its passage through the House. It is emphatically his measure, and to him are the farmers indebted for the first important movement by Congress looking directly to the interests of the man who cultivates the soil."[15]

When the Thirty-Seventh Congress took up the issue of the Pacific Railroad, Lovejoy recommended several changes to the proposed legislation. Speaking before the House on April 17, 1862, he likened the bill to the story of Jacob bestowing an extravagant coat of many colors on his favorite son, Joseph, to remind his colleagues of the need carefully to consider the ramifications of such a big, expensive project: "The road provided here is to pass over a region of country that has never been surveyed, and about which we know nothing; it is general in its terms, and yet we propose to give $67,000,000 to $100,000,000."[16] In the wake of his speech, the *Bureau County Republican* reported that "it is now conceded that [the bill] cannot pass until some important modifications and improvements are made."[17]

And the creation of the land-grant colleges reflected Lincoln and Lovejoy's shared and long-standing interest in public education and agricultural research. Jonathan Baldwin Turner of Jacksonville, Illinois, was a professor at Illinois College, a botanical researcher, and a longtime Lovejoy supporter. Turner came up with a plan under which the federal government would sell undeveloped lands and use the proceeds to permit states to establish institutions that would provide instruction in agriculture, home economics, mechanical arts, and related professions. In 1853, Turner encouraged Illinois legislators to call on their congressional delegation to push for a land-grant bill. Senator Lyman Trumbull thought it advisable to have the bill introduced by an easterner and asked Congressman Justin Morrill of Vermont to do so. Morrill was a friend of Lovejoy's who had visited with him in Princeton.[18] Introduced in 1857, the Morrill Act

Restoring the Founding Purposes 129

passed Congress in 1859 but was vetoed by President James Buchanan. After Lincoln's election, Morrill reintroduced the measure, both houses passed it, and President Lincoln signed it into law on July 2, 1862.[19] Plans for the University of Illinois and sister institutions in other states began soon thereafter.

Securing the Blessings of Liberty

In December 1861, when Senator Henry Wilson of Massachusetts introduced a bill to emancipate the slaves in the District of Columbia, Lincoln negotiated a concession that the slaveholders must be compensated. However, the measure would go into effect immediately, not gradually, and without the consent of the citizens of the District. When Wilson's bill passed the Senate, Thaddeus Stevens, the chair of the Ways and Means Committee, placed it ahead of other business, scheduling it to come to the floor for debate on March 5, 1862.[20]

Lincoln decided that the time had come to apply pressure to both the North and the border states by submitting an additional emancipation plan that neither side could reject without incurring significant political damage. On March 6, the president's proposal for gradual emancipation in the four border states was introduced in Congress.[21] The measure was a compromise: the impatient North would get emancipation, while the recalcitrant border states would have as long as thirty-eight years to free their slaves, would be able to devise their own methods of doing so, and would receive federal funds with which to compensate slaveholders. The political timing was exquisite: if the border states went along, Lincoln might be able to negotiate gradual emancipation in the District; if they refused, Lincoln could sign the D.C. Emancipation Act, signaling that he was serious about implementing emancipation.

Only a few northern leaders resisted Lincoln's suggestion for a joint resolution approving his plan. One was Stevens, whose present strategy for passing the D.C. Emancipation bill had suddenly been thwarted, and another was George Cheever of New York, an abolitionist minister in Manhattan and long-standing Lovejoy family friend who rejected compensating owners of slaves. Otherwise, Lincoln's plan found support in Congress and with the public. Even radical abolitionist Wendell Phillips of Boston thought the bill was a "thin wedge" that could be leveraged into a more universal emancipation process.[22] Lovejoy also disliked the idea of compensation (because it validated the idea that human beings could be legally considered property); however, if providing compensation would free the slaves, he "warmly support[ed] the proposition to pay for slaves out of the Treasury of the United States."[23] With his backing, the House approved the measure by an eighty-six to thirty-five vote on March 10. But representatives of the border states met on March 12 and refused to accept this "sugar-coated plan for emancipation."[24]

A few weeks later, Lovejoy stood before Congress and admonished the Kentucky representatives for voting against the proposal. He also discussed Lincoln's idea of coupling emancipation with colonization by supporting plans for resettling former slaves in Africa and South America. Radicals and African Americans were usually perceived as universally hostile to the idea of involuntary colonization, which would strip them of their right to citizenship. Lovejoy had strenuously objected to this idea since 1855.[25] However, he reluctantly accepted it if it was a supplement to an emancipation plan, offering relief for former slaves who did not wish to live in a racist society, or if it offered common ground. "And while I say that the slaves can take care of themselves, and that they should be let alone, [I do not] mean to preclude the idea of colonization that is not compulsory. The message of the President, therefore, presented ground where all might stand, the conservative and radical, and with common purpose and combined effort put forth their exertions for the beneficent object of universal emancipation accompanied by [voluntary] colonization, if just to the slave and best for the country."[26] Editor J. G. Hewitt of the *Bureau County Republican*, Lovejoy's hometown newspaper, shared his views. Though he found the president's proposal somewhat obscure, he still described it as an "Emancipation Proclamation": "Let no one belittle this great act of the President. . . . It is great in underlying principle. . . . Henceforth Mr. Lincoln is an historical figure."[27]

The D.C. Emancipation Bill languished in the House for another month. On March 24, Lincoln wrote to Horace Greeley of the *New York Tribune*, "I am a little uneasy about the abolishment of slavery in this District, not but I would be glad to see it abolished, but as to the time and manner of doing it. If some one or more of the border-states would move fast, I should greatly prefer it; but if this can not be in a reasonable time, I would like the bill to have the three main features—gradual—compensation—and vote of the people—I do not talk to members of Congress on the subject, except when they ask." Greeley responded by offering to use his paper to support Lincoln's position if the president desired and by relaying his understanding that the lack of vigorous prosecution of the war was causing opponents of slavery to feel that progress was not being made.[28]

On April 10, Stevens moved to circumvent the delaying tactics that Wickliffe, Clement L. Vallandigham, and Crittenden were using against the D.C. Emancipation Bill. After more debate, in which Lovejoy participated with his characteristic passion, the District of Columbia Emancipation Bill was passed, a result greeted with loud applause from the crowds of whites and sprinkling of blacks in the galleries. In the black churches near the Capitol, the District's African Americans expressed their joy and thanked not only God but also Owen Lovejoy, whom some called their liberator.[29] Though Lovejoy was ecstatic at the realization of one of his long-held goals, he did not rest on his laurels. By June 23, he had pushed through a bill to establish a board of trustees that would implement public schooling for the District's African American children.[30]

Lincoln publicly reacted ambivalently to the D.C. Emancipation Act, waiting five days before signing the bill. Rumors said that Wickliffe convinced Lincoln to delay so that the congressman could get some of his sick slaves out of Washington and back to his plantation—for their benefit. Lincoln told one Marylander that he had "come to the conclusion, after full consideration of the pros & cons, that he would do less mischief by approving than by rejecting it; and hoped the people of Maryland would see the difficulties of his position." Charles Sumner privately tried to hurry Lincoln by informing him that he had now become the largest slaveholder in the United States.[31] Just as important, the "thin wedge" was now firmly in place. Congressman Isaac Arnold assured his friends that the president "did not enter with reluctance upon the plan of emancipation, and in this statement I am corroborated by Lovejoy, and Sumner, and many others. If he did not act more promptly, it was because he knew he must not go faster than the people."[32] Lincoln remained hopeful that with more time, the border states could be convinced to consider his less radical plan. But he also was firmly committed to eventual emancipation.

On March 24, Arnold had introduced another emancipation bill—this one to free all slaves in the territories. New England abolitionist Lydia Maria Child and other activists claimed that although this measure would affect a relatively small area of land and relatively few slaves, the "effect it will produce is of more importance than the act itself."[33] Repeating traditional language taken from the 1843 Liberty Party platform, the bill stated that freedom was a national condition and that slavery was only a sectional condition. On May 9, Lovejoy introduced a broader substitute bill "to secure freedom to all persons within the exclusive jurisdiction of the Federal Government," a designation that included not only the territories but also vessels, forts, and arsenals. Southern sympathizers in Congress objected, saying that the proposed measure would violate state laws for granting land to the federal government for forts and arsenals. On May 12, Lovejoy yielded to the opposition and submitted a different substitute bill that prohibited slavery in all U.S. territories. It first passed the Senate before returning to the House on June 17. It then passed by a seventy-two to thirty-eight vote, and Lincoln signed it two days later.[34] Opponents of slavery had two major political victories that not only demonstrated a shift in public opinion but also showed that Lincoln and Lovejoy were not at odds but for the most part were working in tandem.

Increasing Their Friendship

Owen and Eunice Lovejoy received an invitation to the great ball to be held in the White House on February 5, 1862. Mary Todd Lincoln had devised the idea as a way to lift the spirits of the defenders of the Union who were working so hard in Washington. Eunice Lovejoy hesitated to go to such an event during a time of war, though she was quite well acquainted with official Washington, including Mary Lincoln. Owen Lovejoy wanted his wife to join him at the ball, and she finally agreed because it offered an opportunity to meet her husband's colleagues and their spouses.[35] However, soon after they arrived, they realized that the Lincolns were preoccupied because their sons were ill. In fact, eleven-year-old Willie died just over two weeks later. The Lovejoys had experienced the death of their infant son, Owen Glendower, in 1846, so Owen Lovejoy knew firsthand the pain of losing a child.[36] He later wrote home to his other children, "I have just been up to the White House to see the President. He feels very much the loss of his little boy Willie. . . . Father feels very thankful that one of his little boys is not taken away and hopes they may not be."[37]

On February 24, Lovejoy entered the East Room of the White House for the boy's funeral. The crowd included many officials, including the entire Illinois congressional delegation. Mary Lincoln was so overcome with grief that she could not attend the funeral and was confined to bed for weeks.[38] From his stay in Springfield in 1855, Owen understood how much she loved her children as well as her appreciation of literature and her deep interest in politics.[39] And as a pastor, he was accustomed to ministering to grief-stricken persons. He reached out to Mary and subsequently began to call on the Lincolns in a more personal way. Eunice Lovejoy later recalled that in the wake of Willie's death, "a very great change came over the relations of the two men."[40] Mary Lincoln later told the Lovejoys that she feared that Willie's death was a judgment against her for giving the fancy party during wartime. Indeed, Mary received a torrent of criticism for holding the ball that Eunice Lovejoy believed would have drowned her if Willie had not died.[41] On June 12, during a trip to New York City, Owen Lovejoy visited with and went for a carriage ride with Mary Lincoln, who had gone there seeking relief from her heartache, though both she and her husband were still in mourning.[42]

Clark E. Carr, a prominent resident of Galesburg, later recalled meeting Lovejoy on a Washington street and being invited to join the congressman on a visit to the White House, where the president was recovering from a mild case of smallpox. Lincoln "greeted Mr. Lovejoy, who had always stood by him, as his 'conservative' friend, which was a joke, as the latter was regarded as the most radical man in Congress. This elicited some remarks about the malcontents who were denouncing the President, for, as they thought, not going fast enough, which seemed to annoy him; and he probably showed this to us in a more marked degree than he would have done had he been well."[43] According to Arnold, "While the President, by his moderation, was seeking to hold the border states, and while his measures were severely criticized by many extreme abolitionists, he enjoyed, to the fullest extent, the confidence of Lovejoy and other radical members from Illinois. This old and *ultra* abolitionist [Lovejoy] perfectly understood and appreciated the motives of the Executive."[44]

The Turning Point on Confiscation Policy

Even thornier than the question of emancipation of slaves in areas controlled by the U.S. government was the matter of how to handle slaves in the eleven states that had seceded. Several bills on the subject had been presented in Congress in December 1861, but they had remained mired in the House Judiciary Committee as various Republican factions took different positions.[45] Committee members were pondering a number of constitutional issues. One was whether the constitutional provision of noninterference with southern laws protecting slavery still applied in time of war. Another was whether a legislative body could punish individuals without a trial during a time of rebellion. New York abolitionist Gerrit Smith considered the idea that the North had any constitutional obligation to the rebels to be a sign of insanity.[46]

On March 20, the committee finally reported on five bills.[47] The major one, introduced by Thomas Eliot of Massachusetts, authorized the president as commander in chief and the officers under him "to emancipate all persons held as slaves in any military district in a state of insurrection."[48] Other bills expanded this authority to include not only slaves employed by the Confederates but also slaves owned by masters who had not remained loyal to the United States and even to all slaves. The bills contained varying provisions regarding legal procedures for identifying traitors and for protecting emancipated former slaves.[49] One of the bills had been proposed by Lovejoy: it called for the "confiscation of all property of all citizens who shall be found to be engaged in rebellion against the government of the United States, and such as aid and abet such rebellion; also for the unconditional liberation of their slaves, and for the protection of such slaves from recapture from their rebel masters."[50]

On April 22, the House was slated to vote on the bills. But a group of conservative Republicans sought to weaken the bills, and Abram Olin of New York moved that they be sent to a select committee. Olin's action, along with a speech from Crittenden, "ignited violent attacks on the opponents of confiscation bills by various radical Republicans." Stevens exclaimed in consternation, "The Rebels have a majority in the house."[51]

The Rhetorical Climax
between Crittenden and Lovejoy

On April 23, a week after the president had signed the D.C. Emancipation Act and with the Republicans divided, Crittenden saw an opportunity to deliver what some observers saw as a plea for unity of purpose and avoidance of divisive issues and others saw as a defense of slavery.[52] According to Crittenden, the proposed emancipation bills would authorize the president not only "to take the property of rebels" but also "to take the property of every man who may own slaves. I do not stand here to discuss the question of the merits or demerits of slavery. . . . I look upon it as a matter settled and determined by the great compromise of the Constitution. If these compromises had not been entered into, the present Government would not have been established." Moreover, he argued, "The Constitution was designed for the protection of slave property and every other kind of property. The Constitution considers slaves property, and Congress under the Constitution has considered them property. . . . Questions of such momentous import ought to be seriously and dispassionately considered. . . . We have no constitutional power to do these things." And he concluded,

> I voted against Mr. Lincoln and opposed him honestly and sincerely; but Mr. Lincoln has won me to his side. There is a niche in the temple of fame, a niche near to Washington, which should be occupied by the statue of him who shall save this country. Mr. Lincoln has a mighty destiny. It is for him, if he will, to step in that niche. It is for him to be but a President of the people of the United States, and there will his statue be. But if he chooses to be, in these times, a mere sectarian and party man, that niche will be reserved for some future and better patriot. . . . Sir Mr. Lincoln is no coward. His not doing what the Constitution forbade him to do, and what all our institutions forbade him to do, is no proof of his cowardice.[53]

Incensed by Crittenden's speech, Lovejoy took to the floor to reply. However, he yielded to a call for adjournment by his fellow Republican, Francis P. Blair Jr.[54] The Republicans caucused that evening to formulate a response to Crittenden's challenge. With conservatives in Congress riding a wave of victory, the momentum for confiscation of property and emancipation of the slaves had slowed considerably. On April 24, the *New York Times*, a mouthpiece for the administration's moderates, claimed, "If the power of confiscation resides in Congress at all, and should be exercised, the time for its exertion has not yet arrived. . . . The feeling of the Northern people is strongly adverse to these premature, ill-considered and sweeping manifestations of resentment."[55] It was a pivotal moment.

The next morning, Lovejoy obtained the floor and began to address the House. He first noted that it was appropriate to allow those who supported rebellion to have a voice in government. Then he turned to refuting Crittenden's arguments:

> I deny in the presence of this House, I deny in the presence of the country, that slavery has any guarantee, any approving recognition, any sanction in the Constitution of these United States; none whatever. This claim is utterly false. . . .
> I wish gentlemen would point out the chapter and verse when they talk about the guarantees of the Constitution. . . . In what article, in what section, in what clause? Nowhere, in letter or syllable, or word or line, or section or article, can they be found, for they are not there. . . . Bold and reckless assertions will not do.[56]

Restoring the Founding Purposes 135

Next, Lovejoy chastised Crittenden for failing to support Lincoln's plan for gradual, compensated, emancipation.

> Sir, the friends of American slavery need not beslime the President with their praise. He is an anti-slavery man. He hates human bondage. The gentleman says he did not vote for him. . . . I did vote for the occupant of the executive chair, and labored for his election as I never labored for that of any other man. If the gentleman wants to sustain the President in his Administration in its stormy and perilous voyage, why did he not vote for his wise and patriotic message, hailed and approved, so far as I know, by the whole country, except slaveholders?[57]

Then Lovejoy arrived at the apex of his argument:

> I, too, have a niche for Abraham Lincoln; but it is in Freedom's holy fane [temple], and not in the blood-besmeared temple of human bondage; not surrounded by slaves, fetters, and chains, but with the symbols of freedom; not dark with bondage, but radiant with the light of liberty. In that niche he shall stand proudly, nobly, gloriously, with shattered fetters and broken chains and slave whips beneath his feet. If Abraham Lincoln pursues the path evidently pointed out for him in the providence of God, as I believe he will, then he will occupy the proud position I have indicated. That is a fame worth living for; ay, more, that is a fame worth dying for, though that death led through the blood of Gethsemane and the agony of the accursed tree. That is a fame which has glory and honor and immortality and eternal life. Let Abraham Lincoln make himself, as I trust he will, the emancipator, the liberator, as he has the opportunity of doing, and his name shall not only be enrolled in this earthly temple, but it will be traced on the living stones of that temple which rears itself amid the thrones and hierarchies of heaven, whose top stone is to be brought in with shouting of "Grace, grace unto it."[58]

Twenty-five thousand copies of the speech were printed.[59] According to Arnold, the speeches by Crittenden and Lovejoy, "the champions of slavery and freedom," were "read to Mr. Lincoln in his library at the White House to which he sometimes retired. He was moved by the picture Lovejoy drew. The tremendous responsibilities growing out of the slavery question; how he ought to treat these sons of 'unrequited toil,' were questions sinking deeper and deeper into his heart. With a purpose firmly to follow the path of duty, as God gave him to see his duty, he earnestly sought divine guidance."[60]

Crittenden had gone to the heart of the issue for Lincoln—his basic sense of fairness; his practical reverence for the law, especially the Constitution; and his desire to be esteemed by those he served. The Kentuckian had scored eloquently on all three points, compellingly arguing that the Founders had protected slavery where it existed to bring the South into the Union. Lovejoy, conversely, argued accurately that the word *slavery* did not appear in the Constitution and that if the argument against abolition was the taking of property without due

136 CHAPTER 9

process, then Lincoln's gradual plan for compensated emancipation overcame that obstacle. Both men appealed to Lincoln's desire to be esteemed. Slavery and emancipation were in a struggle for the soul not only of Abraham Lincoln but also of the nation.

The House Reconsiders Confiscation

On May 26, 1862, the House narrowly voted down HR 472, which provided that "any person held in service or labor in any state under the laws thereof . . . and such persons commonly called slaves are hereby declared forever discharged from such service."[61] On June 6, after the radicals had spent eleven days lobbying Republican swing voters, a vote to reconsider HR 472 passed. At that point, conservative Albert Porter of Indiana moved a substitute bill in place of the reconsidered bill, and the substitute was referred to another select committee.[62]

While the committee was considering the bill, Lovejoy was writing a major speech. He sensed that Lincoln was leaning toward a stronger exercise of his war powers but was waiting for the appropriate time. However, Union military successes threatened to lessen northern interest in the "punitive measures" of confiscation "now that Federal victories augured an early end to the war."[63] Moreover, the confiscation bill's fate remained in doubt, as did the extent of public support for freeing the slaves if the war ended soon. As he weighed these factors, Lovejoy became convinced that the time had come publicly to urge Lincoln to apply his presidential war powers.

William Cullen Bryant, editor of the *New York Evening Post* and president of New York's Emancipation League, had invited Lovejoy to address the League at Cooper Union on June 12. The congressman rose to the occasion, delivering what the moderate *New York Times* claimed was "one of the most successful efforts of the kind ever made."[64] Lovejoy assembled his most persuasive arguments to strengthen the president's hand, to reassure impatient radicals, to support members of Congress, to enlighten the public about the necessity of freeing the slaves to save the Union, and to provide confirmation that Lincoln was headed in the right direction.

Lovejoy began by telling his audience that emancipation had become "essential to the safety and perpetuity of the Republic"—a point that the *Times* omitted from its lengthy coverage of the speech. He then continued, "Freedom or Slavery, one or the other must perish; and if freedom falls, the Republic is lost; for what is the Union without freedom? . . . The equality of mankind . . . is the sun around which our political system revolves."[65]

Lovejoy pressed the radicals to have faith in Lincoln, explaining the "thin wedge" strategy and describing the president as driving a buggy with a gallant steed pulling forward and a weary nag, tied with a strap behind the buggy, holding it back:

Restoring the Founding Purposes 137

Now, the President knows that the horse Radical that he is driving can go ahead, for he has by him been taken in handsome style into the Executive Chair; but he is a little afraid that this mettlesome charger cannot be trusted going down hill, otherwise he would let go of the old rack-a-bones that hobbles along behind. Now, I do not propose to dash ahead so as to throw the President out or break the carriage, but to go so steadily that the Executive can be assured that he is safe with the Radical steed, down hill as well as up, and on level ground, and then he will drop the strap.[66]

With this image, Lovejoy literally depicted Lincoln in the driver's seat, a perspective that undercuts Eric Foner's argument that Lovejoy and other radicals saw themselves in charge.[67] Lovejoy's metaphor also undercuts Allen C. Guelzo's contention that the radicals were politically inept and demonstrates that the radicals understood Lincoln's pragmatism.[68]

Lovejoy then reassured his listeners that both he and the president remained committed to the cause of emancipation but used another metaphor to explain why caution was necessary: "I am for pouring on all the steam that the machinery will bear; but it is better to get into port a few hours later than to risk the explosion of the machinery. If the President does not believe all I do, I believe all he does. If he does not drive as fast as I would, he is on the same road, and it is a question of time."[69] Lovejoy explained that Lincoln needed the right time and place for emancipation and shared the president's plan for gradual, compensated, emancipation beginning with the border states. Then Lovejoy used Lincoln's revocation just three weeks earlier of General David Hunter's emancipation order to inform the audience that the president had said that it was his prerogative as commander in chief to decide when it had "become a necessity indispensable to the maintenance of the government" to declare the slaves free.[70]

Lovejoy told those assembled at Cooper Union that Lincoln advised "that if the slaveholders do not voluntarily break the yoke [of slavery] some one else must." Lovejoy quoted Lincoln addressing the South:

"You cannot," says he, "mistake the signs of the times. You have it in your power, in the Providence of God, to do a great work of beneficence, such as the world has rarely witnessed. I urge you to do it and to do it at once. The tide of events sweeps onward. I give you a few days more of grace. It is better for all that *you* should do it. . . . But if you will not, I will. I have the power. I have the right. It will be my duty, and I will do it. You must take the consequences of your neglect."[71]

Lovejoy then encouraged understanding of and sympathy for Lincoln's position on the grounds that "Never has a President, not even WASHINGTON, been beset with so many trials and difficulties as environ him. The wonder is not that he should make mistakes, but that he should make so few." He concluded by reiterating his support and that of the president for the goals of the Emancipation

138   CHAPTER 9

League: "I no more doubt his Anti-Slavery integrity, his ultimate Anti-Slavery action, than I do my own. . . . 'Long live the Republic! Let it be perpetual.' But American Slavery, which would blot out that Republic, let it *perish*! PERISH!! PERISH!!!"[72]

As the emancipation bill made its way through Congress, it was again amended, this time by radical Thomas Eliot of Massachusetts. It now limited the forfeiture of slave property to Confederate and military officials and provided legal guarantees for both loyal southerners and those slaves declared released from service. On June 18, the House of Representatives passed the bill by an eighty-two to fifty-four vote.[73]

After negotiations with the Senate to reconcile its version of the bill with that of the House, the Second Confiscation Act was sent to the president on July 12. It was a moderate bill in that it subjected only a small class of persons to confiscation of their slaves and required a rigorous legal process before any confiscations could occur. But it also provided stiff penalties for any person found guilty of treason against the United States—death, or at least five years in prison and a ten-thousand-dollar fine, and the confiscation of any slaves belonging to the traitor. Perhaps even more significantly, the act also authorized the enlistment of Negro troops.[74]

Substantial jockeying and managing had been necessary to secure passage of the Second Confiscation Act, and Lovejoy and Lincoln worked the situation from their different angles. Their efforts resulted in a political consensus for the legal justification of the confiscation of rebel property, a necessary precursor to the ultimate emancipation of all slaves. Congress occasionally moved beyond the president, and he occasionally moved ahead of the legislators. "Neither was ever in the lead for long, and they were never very far apart."[75] The Second Confiscation Act represented a significant turning point, although Lincoln remained unsure about whether Congress had the constitutional authority to emancipate the slaves, and he feared that the U.S. Supreme Court—still led by Chief Justice Roger B. Taney—would declare the new law unconstitutional.[76]

Republican Factions

The passage of the Second Confiscation Act exposed the existence of four subgroups of Republicans in the House of Representatives. The first comprised seven conservatives who first voted against emancipation and then did not vote on the motion to reconsider. Eight moderates did not vote the first time but voted for it on reconsideration. Seven more congressmen voted against the measure the first time and then switched and voted for it. And sixty-one radicals voted consistently for emancipation.[77]

Scholars have applied a wide spectrum of different definitions of the term *radical* in the context of abolition and the Civil War. Leonard Curry defines the

Restoring the Founding Purposes   139

radicals as those unwilling to compromise and willing to apply "coercion" by appealing to the war powers of the president as commander in chief in times of insurrection to free the slaves.[78] Hans Trefousse defines the radicals as "the pronounced antislavery faction within the Republican Party."[79] Even by Curry's narrow definition, Lincoln was a radical, since he advocated the presidential war powers. Conservative Republicans, in contrast, did not want to interfere with slavery in the South under any circumstances. And the moderates were willing to interfere with slavery in limited, constitutional ways but did not want to alienate the Unionist supporters throughout the South. The radical Republican core in the House was committed to passing emancipation measures and to enlisting contraband to end slavery. Members of this group were also highly motivated to take advantage of the southern rebellion to accomplish universal emancipation.[80] Listening to the moderates, Lincoln delayed action by Congress until hope that the border states would agree to a plan for gradual, compensated emancipation had been exhausted and the bill prohibiting slavery in the territories had passed.

In *The Congressman's Civil War*, Allan G. Bogue developed a scale of twenty-four key votes on slavery issues by Republicans in the Thirty-Seventh Congress. The scale assesses the voting patterns of groups according to the degree to which they supported antislavery legislation. Bogue concludes that "about one-third of the ninety-five Republicans demonstrated a distinct tendency to break from the radical position." Bogue's scale also indicates that fifty-one Radical Republicans voted antislavery on 90 percent of the key issues. His analysis demonstrates the complexity of the challenges of holding together both the country and the Republican Party. The many negotiations, debates, procedural motions, and reconsiderations testify to the existence of a vigorous and even rancorous democratic give-and-take.[81]

The House had a small leadership cadre of half a dozen respected, capable men who shared the conviction that slavery was wrong, who trusted each other, and who collaborated with each other and with the president at key points to abolish the legal foundations of the system of slavery. The team included the Speaker of the House, Galusha A. Grow, who had impressed Lincoln with his success in dealing with the Homestead Act in 1860. Other members of this core group included Stevens; Lovejoy; Elihu Washburne, chair of the Commerce Committee; John A. Bingham, chair of the Judiciary Committee; and James Ashley, chair of the Territorial Committee.[82]

The Refiner's Fire

Mid-July 1862 brought a new level of pressure to bear on Lincoln. On July 12, he met at the White House with the border state representatives and chided them, "If you all had voted for the resolution in the gradual emancipation message of last March, the war would now be substantially over."[83] The next day, amid reports of the tenuous military situation in the Peninsula Campaign, the president asked General George B. McClellan, "Returns show 23,500 killed, wounded, and missing. 'Have you any more perfect knowledge of this than I have?'"[84] Lincoln regularly visited the War Department, waiting for news from the front.

The same day, he confided his thoughts about emancipation to secretary of state William H. Seward and secretary of the navy Gideon Welles. The two men were surprised when Lincoln told them that he was considering "emancipating the slaves by proclamation in case the Rebels did not cease to persist in the war. . . . I have about come to the conclusion it is a military necessity absolutely essential for the salvation of the Union, that we must free the slaves or be ourselves subdued." Seward and Welles said that they would think about the idea.[85]

In the evening Lincoln retreated to his summer residence, Soldiers' Home, which was located away from downtown Washington. As the president tried to relax outside, Arnold and Lovejoy drove up in a carriage to visit. Lincoln was in anguish about whether to sign the Second Confiscation Act. According to Arnold, he told his visitors, "Oh, how I wish the border states would accept my proposition. Then you, Lovejoy, and you, Arnold, and all of us, would not have lived in vain! The labor of your life, Lovejoy, would be crowned with success. You would live to see the end of slavery."[86]

On July 14, Lincoln learned that twenty of the twenty-eight border state representatives had rejected his plan for gradual emancipation.[87] Conservative and moderate Republicans continued their intense pressure on the president to veto the Confiscation Act, but the knowledge that his attempt to find a moderate path had failed resulted in "an immediate radicalization of the Union war effort."[88]

The following day, his oldest political associate, U.S. senator Orville Browning, came to the White House, where he bluntly asked Lincoln "whether he was to control the abolitionists and radicals, or whether they were to control him."[89] Browning asserted that if Lincoln signed the Confiscation Act as it was written, terrible consequences would follow, but vetoing the bill "would raise a storm of enthusiasm for his Administration."[90] According to Browning, the president "looked very sad, and there was a cadence of deep sadness in his voice." Then, "in a very tender and touching tone," Lincoln said, "Browning, I must die sometime." The two men parted with tears in their eyes.[91]

Lincoln disregarded Browning's advice and instead chose to proceed cautiously. He informed Congress that he intended to veto the bill unless changes were made that assured slaveholders that their confiscated real estate would be returned to their heirs after a generation. Radicals initially challenged the president, but once they were persuaded that he was not bluffing, they passed the amended resolution. Some of the radicals then criticized Lincoln for unnecessarily provoking a large majority of Congress, but Sumner emphasized the positive: "Blacks are to be employed [as troops] and the slaves are free."[92] Lincoln signed the Second Confiscation Act into law on July 17. An anxious public was unsure about what would come next.

The Turning Point on Emancipation Policy

Before he informed his cabinet, the president confided in his trusted friend, Owen Lovejoy, sharing with him the news that he believed that it was now necessary to invoke the war powers of the commander in chief to free the slaves.[93] On July 22, Lincoln announced to his cabinet that he had prepared a draft of a document that would free the slaves. The decision "was settled in his mind," and "the responsibility of the measure was his."[94] According to historian Douglas L. Wilson, the ideas Lincoln presented were "only a germ of what would become the Emancipation Proclamation"; nonetheless, the president had settled on the way forward.[95]

By September 22, Lincoln had worked out the details, and he announced his plan to the country. If the slave states did not free the slaves by January 1, 1863, he would do it. By issuing this preliminary proclamation, he presented voters with a clear decision to be made in the November midterm congressional elections. In the 1860 campaign, Lincoln had committed himself to preventing the spread of slavery by legal means, putting it on a course to extinction. He had not campaigned on the platform of legally ending slavery. His respect for the consent of the governed required him to take the emancipation issue before the American voters. If the people chose not to elect representatives who favored this dramatic step, another way would have to be found. But if the South rejected his offer and the majority of the people voted their confidence in the Republican administration, Lincoln would have a mandate for emancipation. Lincoln had reframed the political debate. On September 24, he told a large crowd outside the White House, "What I did, I did after very full deliberation, and under a very heavy and solemn sense of responsibility. I can only trust in God I have made no mistake."[96]

The 1862 Campaign

Lovejoy returned home to a newly drawn Fifth Congressional District. It included only Bureau County and Putnam County from his old Fourth Congressional District and added new counties to the west—strongly Democratic Peoria County and Republican-oriented Henry County. On September 19, the *Chicago Daily Tribune* announced Lovejoy's nomination and predicted a comfortable win for him, but as the House's leading voice against slavery, he encountered unexpectedly strong opposition.[97]

142   CHAPTER 9

The Democrats nominated an ambitious and conservative army officer, Colonel Thomas J. Henderson, a former friend of Lincoln and a Republican member of the state senate from Stark County between 1856 and 1860, to run against Lovejoy on a so-called Union ticket. Henderson attracted support not only from Stephen A. Douglas and his party but also from the conservative former Whigs led by T. Lyle Dickey and Copperheads who backed the Confederacy. In addition, some Republicans felt that Lovejoy had not provided enough patronage, and some voters who had lost loved ones in the war heeded the Peace Democrats' calls to end the war and let the South have its slaves. The stakes were high: the *Geneseo Union Advocate* claimed that a Lovejoy electoral victory would be equivalent to a Union battle victory that resulted in a loss of fifty thousand rebels.[98]

After a bitter campaign that saw Lovejoy embark "on a tour of almost daily speech-making," he squeaked out a narrow victory made possible by his strong backing from the antislavery areas around Galesburg, Geneseo, Princeton, and Granville. In particular, William Allan and the Republican editors of the major papers in Geneseo, Princeton, Peoria, and Chicago played key roles. Also vital was the work of his "most efficient" "supporters in the field . . . including many young men, some of them not old enough to vote."[99]

Lincoln as Radical

Lincoln's decision to issue the Emancipation Proclamation prevented the Henderson campaign from trying to win over voters with the argument that Lovejoy was too much of a radical. As the *Peoria Daily Transcript* noted about a month before the election, "It is useless to charge Lovejoy with being radical—The President of the United States has issued a proclamation as radical as anything Mr. Lovejoy has uttered."[100] Lovejoy had advocated an Emancipation Proclamation for months before Lincoln made his announcement, and the congressman had worked to strengthen the president's hand before he took that step. The proclamation, in turn, strengthened Lovejoy's congressional campaign. Once again, the two men had established a symbiotic relationship that benefited both of them. Lovejoy's reelection was a powerful symbolic victory for the antislavery cause.

However, the Republicans would control only 46.2 percent of the new House. They could establish a governing coalition with sixteen pro-Union Democrats and pro-emancipation members of the Unconditional Union Party in the border states, but it was hardly the mandate for emancipation for which Lincoln had hoped.[101] Nevertheless, the administration's emancipation plan had indeed received the consent of the governed.

10 Assuring That the Nation Would Long Endure, 1863

> "Our fathers brought forth on this continent, a new nation, conceived in Liberty, and dedicated to the proposition that all men are created equal. Now we are engaged in a great civil war, testing whether that nation, or any nation so conceived and so dedicated, can long endure."
>
> —Abraham Lincoln

On New Year's Eve, across the nation, diverse constituencies were gearing up to express their responses to the signing of the Emancipation Proclamation. Some shared the anxiety held by Senator Orville Browning, who predicted that white officers would resign and white soldiers would not reenlist if black recruits joined the Union Army.[1] A newly enlisted white officer wrote from the front, "The president's proclamation is of course received with universal disgust, particularly the part which enjoins officers to see that it is carried out. You may be sure that we shan't see to any thing of the kind, having decidedly too much reverence for the constitution."[2] Owen Lovejoy wrote to his apprehensive hometown friend, Cyrus Bryant, that "some of our people are alarmed about the movements in the North of the Copperhead Democracy which seem to be productive.... But I still have faith in the loyalty and Unionism of the masses of the people."[3] But emancipation brought no major revolts in the army. According to Allen C. Guelzo, "If anything, the Proclamation forced officers and generals . . . to get off their fences and embrace both emancipation and black enlistment."[4]

The proclamation did increase the desperation felt by slaveholders in areas close to the invading armies. "Nothing in their previous experience had prepared them for the speed with which slaves were now asserting their freedom," writes Armstead L. Robinson. "As northern armies plunged further into the southern heartland, many slaves believed emancipation imminent. With hiring of competent slave managers virtually impossible on many plantations, planters begged Richmond to exempt experienced overseers from compulsory military service."[5]

144   CHAPTER 10

The role of resisting and escaping slaves in the emancipation process is now well documented. They emboldened the political process for emancipation, and the Emancipation Proclamation emboldened more resistance to slave masters and more cooperation in the Union's war efforts. Lovejoy's experience in the Missouri campaign and with black churches and District of Columbia reforms made him well aware of both the former resistance and the present cooperation.

Signing the Proclamation

Knowing that the proclamation would be signed the next day, both black and white attendees at December 31, 1862, Watch Night services at Methodist and African American churches offered religious reflections. It was the perfect venue, since these services focused on learning from the imperfect past and resolving for a better future. George E. Stephens, a free black Philadelphian working in a military camp near Fredericksburg, Virginia, evaluated himself in his journal: "As the annual watch-night approaches, thinks I to myself . . . Is devotion to the cause of God and my fellow-man more firm? Am I prepared to brave the storms and conflicts of the hour, or willing to sacrifice interests, home, comfort, or life if need be for God and liberty?" Then he charged himself and others to renew their dedication to end slavery.[6] Many other religious people shared such thoughts that night. The radical proclamation demanded deep reflection, repentance, and rededication.

Lincoln received religious counsel that night from Lovejoy's friend Joseph Medill, the publisher of the *Chicago Daily Tribune*; Dr. Nathan Brown, editor of the *American Baptist*; and outspoken abolitionist and Congregational preacher George B. Cheever. According to Medill, "The Pro-Slavery Committee had entered the White House before us. . . . But as they passed out, we passed in, after 9 o'clock, and remained till a late hour."[7]

At Boston's Tremont Temple, the antislavery crowd waited impatiently. Suddenly someone shouted that the proclamation was coming—"It is on the wires!" Frederick Douglass then led the three thousand audience members in singing, "Blow Ye the Trumpet."[8] Douglass had feared that the southern states would accept Lincoln's offer of gradual abolition, but now his hopes grew. Douglass had urged the arming of Negro troops since the beginning of the war, and Lincoln's decision to do so galvanized Douglass. He spent months traveling to recruit black soldiers; in late February, he issued a call, "Men of Color, to Arms." Douglass believed that "to be free [African Americans] must themselves strike the blow. Now they could prove their manhood, demonstrate their equality with the white man in fighting prowess and in love of country."[9]

On January 29, Thaddeus Stevens and Lovejoy set in motion the passage of a bill to create Negro regiments. To opponents who circulated racist innuendo and contended that blacks could not be officers, Lovejoy retorted, "And now, in regard to 'general Sambo,' 'colonel Sambo,' or 'captain Sambo.' Why, sir, I do not advocate putting white men under black officers. Nobody else does or ever did. But, as God is my judge, I would rather follow the black man than a slaveholder as an officer, for I would expect that the one would betray me, whatever his ability, while I am sure the other would be loyal and true, and fight it out."[10]

Massachusetts and Connecticut began recruiting black volunteers and white officers for black regiments at the start of 1863. By May, the president had authorized the War Department to establish the Bureau of the U.S. Colored Troops, making the Stevens-Lovejoy bill unnecessary. Though it passed the House, it stalled in the Senate over the insistence that white officers must command black troops. Kentucky's representatives in Congress and the conservative New York papers attacked Lincoln, limiting his support for black officers as well as for equal pay for black soldiers.[11]

By August, however, Lincoln was less reluctant to alienate the racists. When General Ulysses S. Grant sent him an unequivocal letter of support for African American troops, Lincoln passed on the news in a public letter: "Some of the commanders of our armies in the field who have given us our most important successes, believe the emancipation policy, and the use of colored troops, constitute the heaviest blow yet dealt to the rebellion; and that at least one of those important successes, could not have been achieved when it was, but for the black soldiers." Then he rebuked those with opposing views: "You say you will not fight to free negroes. Some of them seem willing to fight for you."[12]

On December 14, Lovejoy introduced a bill "to place all regularly enlisted soldiers on the same footing as to pay, without distinction of color." However, in the face of opposition to his measure, he compromised, announcing, "I prefer the resolution as it now stands, still I am willing to yield to the request of my friends and modify it so that it will instruct the committee to inquire into the expediency of doing what is proposed."[13] The bill ultimately passed in March 1865.

Reconstruction Policy

At the same time that they were managing the war and emancipation, Lincoln, Lovejoy, Stevens, and Senators Charles Sumner and Henry Wilson debated how to reintegrate the southern states back into the Union once the war had ended.

In 1862, Lincoln had tried to deal leniently with residents of seceded states who remained loyal to the Union, with little success. Radicals became irritated with loyalists in western Virginia, eastern Tennessee, coastal North Carolina, and Louisiana.[14] Lincoln believed that compromises—sometimes ugly—were necessary to maintain order in militarily defeated areas. Most radicals, however,

146   CHAPTER 10

saw no reason to show compassion toward those they saw as responsible for the war. For example, in December 1862, at the beginning of the third session of the Thirty-Seventh Congress, Lincoln was furious when Congress initially refused to seat two recently elected loyal congressmen from Louisiana.[15]

In January 1863, when the House began to debate reconstruction policy, antislavery leaders consequently could not agree on the best way to proceed. Stevens presented his "conquered provinces" theory. Under his plan, Confederate states would be required to go through a lengthy process to return to the Union since they had lost all their rights except those conferred under international law.[16] Sumner had a less harsh "state suicide" plan that claimed that the seceded areas remained part of the Union but had lost their statehood status and were to be considered territories under the jurisdiction of the federal government.[17] Lovejoy's approach resembled Lincoln's: the southern states that had participated in the rebellion remained states but needed to reestablish constitutional governments through elected representatives and by demonstrating loyalty to the Union. The federal government would provide aid to the states as they went through that process.[18]

Lovejoy and Stevens sparred good-naturedly on the House floor, but their inability to reach a consensus had long-term negative consequences for the eventual reconstruction of the southern states.[19] At base, the problem was that the president and Lovejoy had confidence that the Unionists in the rebellious states could restore their own governance, while the radicals believed that the state structures would have to be rebuilt by congressional action to protect the rights of the former slaves.[20] Lovejoy supported a policy that between 25 percent and 33 percent of the population of a rebel state had to take an oath of allegiance before a new state constitution could be written and the state could reenter the Union.[21] The more lenient Lincoln believed that 10 percent was sufficient. The two men also differed on the role that the federal military should take in policing the states during the transition, on the constitutionality of the sequestration of land for development by former slaves, and on how the federal government could best protect African American rights.

Lovejoy's Health

In mid-February 1863, Lovejoy became seriously ill, possibly with smallpox. His wife, Eunice, had not joined him in Washington for the February social season because the congressional session was to end early, but she rushed there to care for him. Although he was dangerously ill for many weeks, he continued to work, and people continued to visit his apartment and to demand his attention. On February 3, H. Ford Douglas, a black abolitionist from Illinois and a junior colleague of Frederick Douglass and John Jones, wrote to Lovejoy to request a transfer to an all-black South Carolina military unit that was "in the course of formation." Lovejoy attended to the matter, helping Douglas become one of the few black officers to serve during the war.[22] Lovejoy also pursued a request from the Reverend Henry McNeal Turner, the African American minister of one of the churches Lovejoy attended, for a commission as the first black chaplain.[23]

Congress left town on March 3, but Lovejoy remained too unwell to travel home. On March 17, the *Peoria Daily Transcript* said, "Mr. Lovejoy has been quite ill for some time past in Washington. He is now convalescent." On April 8, the *Transcript* reprinted a *Chicago Journal* report that "Mr. Lovejoy is still lying very ill at his boardinghouse. . . . The President called upon him yesterday, and was admitted to his room. He was thought to be better for the hopeful, cheerful [manner] his visitor carried with him, but the hopes o[ver] his recovery are not very strong."[24]

By the middle of April, however, Lovejoy was well enough to travel back to Princeton on the train. Being at home with his children improved his physical and mental states, and he wrote that he was a "*might* weak, but *terrible* comfortable."[25] Though doctors in Washington had told Lovejoy to refrain from speaking engagements through the summer, the National Union League of America was meeting in Cleveland on May 20, and he could not stay away.[26]

The Union League had been formed in Pekin, Illinois, in 1862 by Enoch Emery, the young editor of the *Peoria Daily Transcript* who had been instrumental in Lovejoy's 1862 reelection. The League sought to bring together members of all parties who were committed to a vigorous prosecution of the war and opposed to the efforts of Copperhead southern sympathizers and had quickly grown into a large national movement. However, the League's ultra-antislavery wing, led by Senator James H. Lane of Kansas, was now appealing to the old abolitionists to move against the administration. Lane wanted a special committee to demand that Lincoln recall the unpopular General John Schofield. By 1863, Missouri was near anarchy as a consequence of its long-standing divisions over slavery, and Schofield was accused of failing to protect Union loyalists and of supporting the disloyal.[27] Lovejoy could not let such a narrow interest hamper the League's broad purpose.

John Howard Bryant agreed to accompany Lovejoy to Cleveland as part of a twenty-three-man Illinois delegation led by Medill. At the meeting, Lane gave an "eloquent and bitter indictment of the administration in general and the President in particular."[28] An obviously weak Lovejoy was called on to speak. He told his audience that he disagreed with the position of his old radical friends who were criticizing the administration. Patriots and government supporters should put aside these minor differences, and "the President should be sustained in any measure he might deem it necessary to employ."[29]

Lovejoy then returned to Washington. In June, he went with the president to visit hospitalized soldiers. Private William Laing of Dixon, Illinois, and the others in his ward were astounded when they saw the two tall men standing in

148 CHAPTER 10

the doorway. He was even more astounded when Lovejoy shouted, "Are there any Illinois boys here?" Laing eagerly announced, "Over here, sir." And, then, as he wrote to his parents, "The President and Mr. Lovejoy came and stayed with me for considerable time."[30]

Lovejoy gained strength into the summer, aided by leisurely travel and by optimistic news from the front, including the Union's July 4 victories at Gettysburg and Vicksburg. However, he also learned of the death of his nephew, Eddie Wiswall. Lovejoy's ill health prevented him from attending Wiswall's funeral.[31]

Supporting the War Effort

Despite the Union's military success, administration opponents in both the North and South continued to try to convince the public that the war was foolish and unnecessary, that their loved ones had died under false pretenses, and that the conflict had been stirred up by extreme abolitionists and was directed by a tyrant. Republicans sought to smoke out the Copperheads and take the sting out of their bite, an endeavor frequently spearheaded by the state chapters of the Union League of America. James C. Conkling, a close friend of Lincoln's, had become president of the Union League in their home state, where Governor Richard Yates, saddled with a pesky Democratic state legislature, was also actively involved in the effort. The Illinois Union League met in Springfield in September 1863 to address the issue. Both Lincoln and Lovejoy were invited to attend.[32]

Lovejoy was too weak to appear and sent a letter to be read:

> I should love to address an assemblage made up of those, whatever their antecedents, who now love their country in sincerity and truth. This is a platform broad enough to afford a place for every loyal citizen. Those who cannot occupy such a position ought, logically, to be with the Copperheads, or with the rebels, which is indeed very much the same thing. To maintain the Union, is, in my judgment, under the present circumstances, the same thing as to sustain the Administration. To profess an attachment to the former, while opposing the latter, if not insincere, is certainly illogical.
>
> The fact is worthy of being recalled, that Aaron Burr, a Copperhead of the olden time, used substantially the same language in speaking of George Washington, that the Copperheads of the present day employ in speaking of Abraham Lincoln.

Lovejoy also told those in attendance that he knew they would "give three hearty, deep-toned cheers for Abraham Lincoln, who is not only honestly, but ably, under God, leading the nation through the terrible wilderness of this rebellion into the Canaan of Union, peace and immortal freedom."[33]

Assuring That the Nation Would Long Endure

Lincoln also did not attend the Springfield meeting and sent a letter to be read. Conkling read it slowly, as Lincoln had instructed.

> There are those who are dissatisfied with me. To such I would say: You desire peace; and you blame me that we do not have it. But how can we attain it? There are but three conceivable ways. First, to suppress the rebellion by force of arms. This, I am trying to do. Are you for it? If you are, so far we are agreed. If you are not for it, a second way is, to give up the Union. I am against this. Are you for it? If you are, you should say so plainly. If you are not for *force*, nor yet for *dissolution*, there only remains some imaginable *compromise*. I do not believe any compromise, embracing the maintenance of the Union, is now possible.

Lincoln then denied the accusation that he had rejected official terms of compromise from the Confederacy. He would consider any such proposal because he was a servant of the people according to the U.S. Constitution and consequently was responsible to them.

> But to be plain, you are dissatisfied with me about the negro. Quite likely there is a difference of opinion between you and myself upon that subject. I certainly wish that all men could be free, while I suppose you do not. . . .
>
> You dislike the emancipation proclamation; and perhaps would have it retracted. You think it is unconstitutional. I think differently.
>
> Peace does not appear so distant as it did. I hope it will come soon, and come to stay; and so come as to be worth the keeping in all future time.

Lincoln concluded, "Let us diligently apply the means, never doubting that a just God, in his own good time, will give us the rightful result."[34]

During the first week of September, Lovejoy returned to Washington, telling a friend that he had traveled there "to thank the President for his letter to the Springfield Convention." Lovejoy had little doubt that Lincoln held the "highest place among living statesmen—a claim which history will triumphantly vindicate."[35]

In October, while again recuperating at home in Princeton, Lovejoy learned that the off-year elections in five states had supported the administration. As a result of the good news, he felt up to making another speech. He told his listeners,

> I can say that my soul doth magnify the Lord. I am exalted. I am joyous. I am jubilant and elevated. I look upon these victories, upon the result of the election in Maine, in California and more recently in Pennsylvania, Ohio, and Iowa as the most important victories, or victory if we group them together, that we have had since the breaking out of the rebellion. I think that the result of the election in these States, so overwhelmingly for the Union, is a heavier blow to the armed treason and traitors of this country than has been dealt to them since the opening

of the war. I think that they will feel it more—will feel greater discouragement than they did at Gettysburg, Vicksburg, New Orleans, or any other place, where victory has crowned our arms.[36]

Sustaining Each Other

Mary A. Livermore and Jane Hoge were tireless promoters who organized the North Western Sanitary Commission to provide aid to Union soldiers. On November 5, 1863, at the Metropolitan Hall in Chicago, they opened a two-week-long North Western Sanitary Fair, which would collect goods and money to be distributed to the troops through the U.S. Sanitary Commission. Livermore had the idea of obtaining a copy of the Emancipation Proclamation from Lincoln and selling it at the fair.[37] She sought Lovejoy's help, and on October 14, he wrote to the president and asked for the document: "If you do not deposit it in the Archives of the Nation, it seems to me that Illinois would be a very suitable resting place for a document that ought to be laid away in some holy place like the ancient Jewish symbols."[38]

Livermore and Hoge also invited Lovejoy to speak at the fair, and he used the opportunity to give his "cordial, unselfish and unstinted support to the administration." He reminded the audience, "I am radical—that is antislavery from the crown of my head to the sole of my foot." Nevertheless, he was "not prepared to denounce the President as wrong and unrighteous in his decisions, because he does not act as I think I would act, when, perhaps, if I knew all the facts and could look over the whole field, I should not differ from him." Lovejoy went on to warn the radicals that if they continued to criticize the president, justifying their actions as "wounds from the faithful," they could be assured that the presidential "scepter would not pass into what they might deem abler hands, but would be grasped by some quasi traitor."[39] Contrary to those who believe that the radicals pulled the president into emancipation, Lovejoy's speech illustrates that some were complicating Lincoln's job at a critical time. But Lovejoy and the president persisted in pursuing their radical agenda.

Seeking God's Favor

Unlike most Americans, Lincoln was not comfortable with public assertions about the will of God, questioning both the motives and ability of human beings to make such authoritative claims. One of the striking features of American evangelicalism in the nineteenth century was that virtually every believer, regardless of position, thought he or she could discern the will of God in a providential reading of events. Lovejoy, however, became cautious at times about claiming God's will. In August 1862 at a huge Chicago meeting to recruit troops, he admitted, "I don't know what God wills, but I have a shrewd suspicion that He wills what *we* will. The maintenance of the Government and the perpetuity of the Union are a necessity."[40] He and Lincoln were thus closer on this subject than might be expected.

Lincoln did not, however, hesitate to seek divine help in guiding and healing his nation and in urging his people to repent their sins. On July 15, 1863, after the Union victories at Gettysburg and Vicksburg, Lincoln issued a Thanksgiving Proclamation designating August 6 "a day for National Thanksgiving, Praise and Prayer." He sought to "invoke the influence of His Holy Spirit to subdue the anger, which has produced, and so long sustained a needless and cruel rebellion, to change the hearts of the insurgents, to guide the counsels of the Government with wisdom adequate to so great a national emergency . . . and finally to lead the whole nation through the paths of *repentance* and submission to Divine Will."[41] On October 3, he issued another proclamation, this one establishing the fourth Thursday of November as a national day of thanksgiving. He declared the country's "humble *penitence* for our national perverseness and disobedience" and asked God to "commend to His tender care all those who have become widows, orphans, mourners or sufferers."[42] Also, at the request of "a joint Committee of both Houses of Congress," the president proclaimed "a day of public humiliation, prayer and fasting" on August 12, 1861, and the Senate made a similar request on March 30, 1863.[43]

Lovejoy, too, asked the American people to repent. At his home church in Princeton on the nation's first Thanksgiving, November 26, 1863, he prayed, "We have, our Father, to lament that we have not fully obeyed the great principles which we avowed to be self-evident. We feel that we are called upon in accordance with the sentiments of the chief magistrate, to acknowledge our sins and to humble ourselves before thee. We have been guilty in that we have oppressed our fellow man, in that we have robbed the slave of his wages, and his most valuable and sacred right." He continued by thanking God for Lincoln's leadership and asking for guidance so that the president would "see the truth in regard to the claims of *all* to liberty and their rights."[44]

Southerners, too, saw God's hand as visible in daily events. The battlefield defeats suffered by the Confederacy in 1863 led to intense soul-searching. Writing in his diary, John Beauchamp Jones asked the ultimate question occupying southern minds: "Is Providence frowning upon us for our sins, or upon our cause?"[45] Southern newspapers, politicians, and ministers responded overwhelmingly that "the Confederacy's cause was just and God's punishment was purification for sin." Men were accused of "card playing, profanity, usury, and drinking," while women were thought to be guilty of "covetousness, pride, excessive attachment to worldly apparel, gossip, and loose talking."[46] However, according to historian Mitchell Snay, "The breaking of the Sabbath was perhaps the sin

152   CHAPTER 10

most often cited in the litany."[47] Southerners could not bear to think that they were suffering because God looked with disfavor on their cause.

Lovejoy, in contrast, believed that people needed to repent for their society's collective wrongdoings rather than for individual sins. The people and the government officials were guilty for the injustice of their policies. God judged not only people but nations. And key to this repentance was freeing the slaves. Both radical and pragmatic evangelicals commonly believed that God allowed suffering as a consequence of the neglect of moral duty, and Lincoln came to employ this idea to great effect.

On November 19, 1863, the president consecrated the battlefield at Gettysburg with a speech that perfectly encapsulated his simultaneously pragmatic and radical approach to both politics and religion. He began by putting the speech in the context of the Declaration of Independence as the foundation of the republic presented "four score and seven years ago." Lincoln repeated the radical understanding that the nation was "conceived in Liberty, and dedicated to the proposition that all men are created equal." He described the root issue before the people—whether such a "nation so conceived and so dedicated, can long endure"—and challenged them to a noble future by being "dedicated here to the unfinished work which they who fought here have thus far so nobly advanced." In religious language, Lincoln encouraged the people "to be here dedicated to the great task remaining before us—that from these honored dead we take increased devotion to that cause for which they gave the last full measure of devotion." He concluded with a resolve that this "nation under God, shall have a new birth of freedom," appealing to his audience's awareness that divine regeneration was thickly woven into the fabric of the nation's life.[48]

After Lincoln returned to Washington, he faced the issue of one desperate Copperhead who was threatening to disrupt the Thirty-Eighth Congress, which was to begin shortly. Clerk of the House Emerson Etheridge had enacted a requirement that all congressmen's official certificates of election must use specific and complex wording. Etheridge planned to invoke this technical requirement to prevent Republicans from being seated. If his scheme succeeded, the Democrats could hold the majority and elect the Speaker.[49] Lincoln and his staff learned of the scheme and alerted Republicans. On December 6, the day before the opening session, Lincoln met with key Republicans, including Schuyler Colfax, the leading candidate for Speaker, and Lovejoy, who had been contemplating running against Colfax but could not do so because of his poor health.[50] They devised a plan to outmaneuver Etheridge, and when Congress opened, Colfax became the Speaker. He then appointed Lovejoy to chair the Committee for the District of Columbia.[51]

With Congress organized, Lincoln announced that he would not resist any legal effort to end slavery throughout the nation. Lovejoy may have had an inkling that such a statement was forthcoming, because just five days later, on December 14, he introduced the first bill to secure a constitutional right to freedom "for the formerly enslaved people of color"—that is, universal emancipation. His bill was based on the Declaration of Independence's idea of the inalienable right to liberty and the constitutional provision that "no person shall be deprived of liberty without due process of law." The measure declared that "all persons heretofore held in slavery . . . are declared freed men" and that keeping someone in involuntary servitude or bondage would be a high misdemeanor, punishable by at least one year in prison and a one-thousand-dollar fine.[52]

Lovejoy's bill was referred to the Judiciary Committee. Lincoln as well as many of Lovejoy's colleagues feared that any emancipation law could be repealed by a succeeding Congress or overruled by the Supreme Court, so they preferred to free the slaves via a constitutional amendment. That strategy ultimately won out, leading to the ratification of the Thirteenth Amendment on December 6, 1865. However, Congress never enacted the necessary enforcement legislation, resulting in immense suffering, as Douglas A. Blackmon details in *Slavery by Another Name*.[53]

As 1863 drew to a close, many of Lovejoy's long-sought goals finally appeared to be coming within reach. The war was going favorably for the North, and Lincoln had finally agreed to universal emancipation. And as head of the District of Columbia Committee, Lovejoy was positioned to bring great benefits to the District's African American residents.

11 Binding Up the Nation's Wounds, 1864

"I am hoping . . . for a revival of religion, pure and undefiled, which
will be eminently practical . . . giving eyes to the blind, ears to the
deaf and charity to all."
—Owen Lovejoy

Owen Lovejoy's opportunity to assist in shaping Abraham Lincoln's legacy came unexpectedly in December 1863, when well-known painter Francis Carpenter invited Lovejoy to visit his studio in New York City. Carpenter asked for Lovejoy's assistance in encouraging Lincoln to sit for a composite portrait depicting the moment when Lincoln read the preliminary Emancipation Proclamation to his cabinet.[1] Lovejoy eagerly supported Carpenter's endeavor, believing that the life-size portrait would convey tremendous symbolism and would help cement Lincoln's reputation as the Great Emancipator. On February 5, Carpenter went to the Lovejoy residence and found him feeble but optimistic: he told the painter, "I am gaining very slowly.—It is hard work drawing the sled up-hill." Nevertheless, Lovejoy willingly dictated an introductory note, and when Carpenter presented the note to the president, Lincoln said, "Well Mr. C——, we will turn you in loose [*sic*] here, and try to give you a good chance to work out your idea."[2] Carpenter ultimately produced not only an iconic painting that today hangs in the U.S. Capitol but also an 1866 book, *Six Months at the White House with Abraham Lincoln*, that is still read for its insights into Lincoln.

The book provides evidence of the intimate relationship between Lincoln and Lovejoy. According to Carpenter, "Lovejoy had much more of the agitator, the reformer, in his nature, but both drew the inspiration of their lives from the same source, and it was founded in sterling honesty."[3] Carpenter also observed some of Lincoln's other basic character traits: "Though kind-hearted almost to a fault, nevertheless Mr. Lincoln always endeavored to be just." On one occasion, Carpenter overheard a man complain that "the trouble with" Lincoln was "that he is so afraid of doing something wrong." Lincoln had said the same thing to Joshua Speed in 1855.[4]

Binding Up the Nation's Wounds

Carpenter visited Lovejoy again near the end of February and found him "nearly well again and in fine spirits." When Carpenter noted that "many of the extreme anti-slavery men appeared to distrust the President," Lovejoy responded indignantly, "'I tell you,' said he, 'Mr. Lincoln is at heart as strong an anti-slavery man as any of them, but he is compelled to *feel* his way. He has a responsibility in this matter which many men do not seem to be able to comprehend. I say to you frankly, that I believe his course to be right. His mind acts slowly, but when he moves, it is *forward*. You will never find him receding from a position once taken.'"[5]

On March 9, Lincoln invited Lovejoy to the small ceremony at which Ulysses S. Grant was sworn in as lieutenant general of the Armies of the Republic. The only other politicians present were the president and his cabinet.[6] Three of the four great spokesmen for the large constituencies that ended slavery were in the room; only Frederick Douglass was absent.

Owen Lovejoy died less than three weeks later, on March 25, 1864, while on his way to the South Carolina Sea Islands.[7] Slaveholders had abandoned plantations in that area as Union forces invaded, and some ex-slaves were permitted to purchase small tracts of the vacated land. The Sea Islands thus became an experiment in land sequestration for African Americans, and Lovejoy was undoubtedly eager to observe firsthand whether this form of reconstruction could be replicated throughout the South after the war was over.[8] Abraham Lincoln, of course, lived less than thirteen months longer than Lovejoy. For the last ten years of their lives, the two men had relied on each other, working in tandem to bring together the divergent factions in the Illinois Republican Party, to keep the Republican Party united in Congress, and finally to convince moderate and radical members of Congress to pass emancipation legislation. James McPherson claims that the slaves were freed by Lincoln's decisions to resist compromise, supply Fort Sumter, and call the Union Army into being. Owen Lovejoy provided crucial support for all of those decisions.[9]

Lovejoy's death brought tributes from many of the people whose lives his activities had touched. John L. Lee, a black leader in the District of Columbia, asked, "What, sir have been the fruits of the labors of this great man?" and then answered his own question:

> Why it has hurried into the earth the law of slavery, which said that a free and respectable colored person shall not walk after 10 o'clock at night, without being provided with a pass; it has enabled us to testify in all legal courts of justice, in any and all cases that come under our notice; the shouldering of the musket is also allowed, and free schools for the education of our children, are commenced to be strewed in profusion throughout our city and I expect soon, to be seen walking to the polls of the 7th ward, handing in my little piece of paper with a name of candidate.[10]

156   CHAPTER 11

Before he met Lovejoy, New York congressman Thomas T. Davis had

> supposed . . . that he had not only an ardent but a vindictive temper; that he was
> rough and savage in his nature. . . . It was only when we came together in our
> committee-room, when the formalities which prevail here are laid aside, and in
> frank intercourse men express their sentiments, that we found that the highest
> intellect was combined with a childlike simplicity of character. . . . He was ever
> amiable and gentle, always ready to do full and ample justice, to listen patiently
> to those who sought redress of wrong.[11]

Sounding a more personal note, Mary Todd Lincoln, whom Lovejoy had be-
friended and counseled as she mourned the loss of her child, wrote to Charles
Sumner, "Our friend, whom we all so loved and esteemed, has so suddenly
and unexpectedly passed away—Mr. Lovejoy! An all-wise power directs these
dispensations. Yet it appears in our weak and oftentimes erring judgments, 'he
should have died hereafter.'"[12]

Radical Lincoln, Pragmatic Lovejoy

A month before his death, Lovejoy wrote to William Lloyd Garrison expressing
appreciation for his support for Lincoln's reelection. Although Lincoln was not
perfect, Lovejoy was "satisfied, as the old theologians used to say in regard to
the world, that if he is not the best conceivable President, he is the best possible.
I have known something of the facts inside during his administration, and I
know that he has been just as radical as any of his Cabinet."[13] Seventeenth-
century philosopher Gottfried Wilhelm Leibnitz had famously argued that this
world is not "the best of all imaginable worlds but only the best of all possible
worlds."[14] Earlier in his career, Garrison had acted from a perspective of the best
of imagined worlds (a radical vision); at midcentury, Lovejoy and Lincoln had
acted from the perspectives of both the best imaginable worlds (radical justice)
and the best possible worlds (pragmatic action). These remarks on the relation
between the ideal and the practical provide the foundational assumptions for
interpreting the relationship between the radical and the pragmatic. Today's
philosophical thinking has moved beyond reflecting on the "mutually exclusive
features of reality" to the consideration of the "mutually implicative features"
of reality. In "this method of dipolar relation it is explicitly recognized that the
definition of one principle requires reference to its counter principle."[15] From
this perspective, the understanding of governance requires the exploration of
the interactive relationship between the radical and the pragmatic.

The need for a radical vision of what should be imagined is encapsulated in
Proverbs 29:18: "Without a vision the people perish." Don E. Fehrenbacher suggests that Lincoln was challenged to "articulate a vision for the new antislavery

republic being born."[16] Eric Foner recognizes that the abolitionists' vision prepared the public to support antislavery measures. But Lovejoy's oft-repeated and persuasive contention that Lincoln was a radical challenges one of the standard assessments of Lincoln—that radical politicians were mainly leading the way to end slavery without the support of the executive.[17] At the same time, Lovejoy's argument also challenges Allen C. Guelzo's assessment that the abolitionists, including antislavery political abolitionists, were troublemakers who hindered Lincoln's task of freeing the slaves.[18] In a sense, the question about Lincoln and Lovejoy has shifted. We no longer ask who was more radical and who was more pragmatic; rather, we question how these two radicals collaborated pragmatically to make major and lasting contributions to the process of emancipation.

An examination of these two men that goes deeper than their apparent superficial differences reveals many commonalities. The practical ways that Lovejoy applied the levers of power on behalf of the people resembled the way Lincoln listened to the common people who constantly came into his office. Both cared for people as well as policy, and keeping in touch with their constituents was a source of their political strength. Lovejoy excelled at using biblical references to support arguments about contemporary matters, a skill that Lincoln developed until he became quite expert at it. This common religious approach enhanced their mutual trust and respect as well as their ability to collaborate, and according to John Lovejoy Elliott, "On Sundays Mr. Lovejoy would take his Bible to the White House and read passages to the President."[19]

In this light, as Carpenter wrote, "It is not strange that they should have been bosom friends. . . . The president repeatedly called to see him during his illness; and it was on one of these occasions that he confided to Lovejoy, 'This war is eating my life out; I have a strong impression that I shall not live to see the end.'"[20] Carl Sandburg claimed, "They came to cling to each other."[21] And as Lincoln himself recalled, their relationship "was quite intimate, and every step in it has been one of increasing respect and esteem, ending, with his life in no less than affection on my part."[22]

The Source of Their Radicalism and Pragmatism

Writing to his close friend, Governor John Andrew of Massachusetts, on February 22, 1864, Lovejoy expressed his hope that when slavery had been swept away, religion would experience a revival, "that instead of expending its energies on theologies and creeds and rubrics it shall go around like its divine author healing the sick, cleansing lepers, giving eyes to the blind, ears to the deaf and charity to all."[23] A year later, Lincoln uttered words that have since become famous: "With malice toward none; with charity for all; with firmness in the right, as God gives us to see the right, let us strive to bind up the nation's wounds."[24] It

158   CHAPTER 11

is not a matter of who influenced whom; rather, both men came to appreciate how much they shared sentiments, goals, and values.

In their trusting relationship, Lincoln and Lovejoy came to recognize that trusting only in regenerative love was dangerous. At times, it was also necessary to trust the power of retributive justice. Lovejoy frequently reminded the public of the need to repent not only for personal sins but also for sins committed by larger communities—specifically, a town that allowed its elite to kill an antislavery editor and a nation that perpetuated a system that enslaved more than four million people. Most radically, however, Lovejoy reminded the people that the Divine Presence "has woven the threads of retribution into the web of national life no less than into that of individual life."[25] In November 1863, as the war dragged on and black and white soldiers died by the thousands, he prayed, "We feel that thy judgments are upon us, and justly we are suffering for disregarding thy commands."[26]

Lincoln was just as radically concerned with divine retributive justice and had on several occasions called the whole nation to repentance. In a letter written shortly after Lovejoy's death, he explained his reasons for issuing the Emancipation Proclamation: "If God now wills the removal of a great wrong, and wills also that we of the North as well as you of the South, shall pay fairly for our complicity in that wrong, impartial history will find therein new cause to attest and revere the justice and goodness of God."[27] And in his Second Inaugural Address, he applied the Scripture and appealed to the faithful: "If we shall suppose [that God] gives to both North and South, this terrible war, as the woe due to those by whom the offence came, shall we discern therein any departure from those divine attributes which the believers in a Living God always ascribe to Him?"[28]

Both men had the courage to speak truthfully to powerful officials and the even more powerful citizens of the republic. Though both felt their lives ebbing, their radical vision carried them forward. The remarkable nature of their relationship and its accomplishments deserves a greater appreciation than historians have generally afforded, though their colleagues and associates were more perceptive. On January 31, 1865, the day the House of Representatives passed what would become the Thirteenth Amendment, the leaders bestowed the honor of dismissing that historic meeting to recently sworn-in congressman Ebon Ingersoll. He said, "Mr. Speaker, in honor of this immortal and sublime event, I move that the House now adjourn."[29] Newcomer Ingersoll had taken Lovejoy's seat.

Appendix

Lincoln's Major Radical Risk-Taking Steps toward Emancipation

1837	Calling slavery unjust
	Opposing an anti-abolitionist resolution in the Illinois House of Representatives
1846	Considering introducing a bill in the U.S. House of Representatives to abolish slavery in the District of Columbia
	Casting a decisive vote against a resolution setting a federal precedent that slaves were property
1854	Calling for repeal of the Kansas-Nebraska Act, agreeing with the abolitionists when they do the same, writing Codding to ask if he misunderstood the radicals
1855	Making a deal with radical leaders of the Illinois House of Representatives to support the nonextension of slavery
	Writing the radical Lovejoy that he was as anxious as Lovejoy to stop the spread of slavery
1856	Helping plan a political convention to unite all anti-Nebraska factions, including the radicals
	Attending a political rally in Lovejoy's hometown
	Telling his conservative friends not to oppose Lovejoy
	Admitting that he was in company of abolitionists in Kalamazoo
	Ending those remarks with "So sure as God lives, the victory shall be yours"
1857	Charging that the Dred Scott decision wrecked the "glorious Declaration"
	Mocking Senator Douglas's claim that "all men are equal" referred solely to white Britons
1858	Warning Lovejoy that slavery sympathizers could be scheming against his renomination
	Risking alienating conservatives by giving indirect support to Lovejoy behind the scenes
	Accepting a plan for the "ultimate extinction of slavery" by stopping its spread

160 Appendix

Entrusting the cause of stopping the spread of slavery "to those whose hearts are in the matter"

Calling Lovejoy his friend in the first debate with Douglas

1859 Announcing unequivocally in Ohio speeches that Republicans claimed that slavery was wrong

Agreeing with Chicago leaders that the idea of slavery as nonnegotiable should come to an end

Saying that slavery was responsible for John Brown's raid

1860 Declaring at Cooper Union the duty to prevent slavery from overrunning the free states

Adhering to the Republican platform's resistance to extending slavery into any U.S. territory and to its insistence that there is no property right to own a person

Allowing Lovejoy to be his most effective campaign surrogate

1861 Refusing to compromise regarding the extension of slavery to the territories

Declaring war on the South when it violently defended its right to spread and keep slavery

Signing the First Confiscation Act, even with passive resistance of nonenforcement

Stating his willingness to sign another confiscation act in his Annual Message to Congress

1862 Supporting bills for emancipation in the District of Columbia and the nonextension of slavery in the territories

Advocating a gradual, compensated emancipation plan

Recognizing the military necessity of freeing the slaves to save the Union

Issuing the preliminary Emancipation Proclamation

1863 Signing the Emancipation Proclamation

Approving the deployment of black combat regiments

Defending the Emancipation Proclamation in an open letter to the Springfield Union League

Describing the war as having given the nation under God a new birth of freedom

Announcing that he would not resist any legal effort to end slavery throughout the country

1864 Appointing Ulysses S. Grant as lieutenant general of the Armies of the Republic

Lovejoy's Major Pragmatic Activities in Obtaining, Maintaining, and Utilizing Political Power

1838 Writing Elijah Lovejoy's *Memoir* with the leaders of the American Antislavery Society

1840 Establishing the West's first Liberty Party organization in Bureau County, Illinois

1842 Participating in Underground Railroad on religious grounds, energizing the antislavery political base

Helping to establish the Illinois State Liberty Party, committed to eliminating slavery only through constitutional means

Appendix

	Helping to establish the *Western Citizen* antislavery newspaper
1843	Inspiring and serving on the platform committee at the Buffalo Liberty Party Convention
1846	Running as a Liberty Party candidate for a seat in the U.S. House of Representatives
1848	Expanding his promise to end slavery constitutionally by adopting wider Free Soil Party policies
	Running as a Free Soil Party candidate for a seat in the U.S. House of Representatives
1851	Helping organize national, state, and local Free Democratic Party conventions
1854	Helping organize Republican/anti-Nebraska state and congressional district conventions
	Winning election to the Illinois General Assembly
1855	Making a deal with Lincoln to pass nonextension legislation in Illinois House of Representatives
	Keeping antislavery and black rights issue on the agenda
	Helping to pass an Illinois public education bill
	Reaching out to Lincoln, Lyman Trumbull, and Archibald Williams
	Recognizing the political liability of fanatical abolitionist label
1856	Resigning as pastor in Princeton
	Taking a leading role at the first national Republican Planning Convention
	Clarifying at the Bloomington Convention that he was committed only to nonextension
	Maneuvering for Republican congressional nomination
	Taking a leading role in June at the first national Republican Nominating Convention
	Winning a seat in the U.S. Congress by openly stating that slavery was wrong
1857	Preparing to become a lawyer
	Securing his financial status
	Challenging the Buchanan administration during his first month in Congress
1858	Condemning in Congress the doctrine that human beings are property, energizing voters
	Preparing his associates with a letter concerning his renomination process
	Foiling conservative scheme to eliminate mutual support with Lincoln
	Endorsing Lincoln as unseduced by ambition and unintimidated by power
	Campaigning and winning reelection
	Maneuvering diplomatically to help elect a Republican Speaker
1859	Shifting the stigma with a speech in Congress on the "Fanaticism of the Democratic Party"
	Interpreting the John Brown affair as leading to the question, "Is slaveholding right?"
1860	Becoming part of the Republican leadership as chair of the Committee on Public Lands
	Exposing the religious, political, and social aspects of the "Barbarism of Slavery"
	Urging southern leaders to free their slaves, even gradually

162 *Appendix*

Supporting any Republican presidential nominee firmly committed to non-extension

Delivering about one hundred speeches to huge audiences on behalf of Lincoln's presidential campaign

Making speeches appealing to Henry Clay's principles, supporting the Homestead Act

Initiating a resolution stating that the president has a duty to protect and defend U.S. property

1861　Resisting efforts to compromise with disunionists by allowing slavery to expand

Cooperating with Illinois Lincoln supporters to assure his safe arrival in Washington

Encouraging Lincoln to vigorously prosecute the war

Initiating the First Confiscation Act

Recruiting troops by assuring them that the rebel revolt had no cause

Enlisting as a colonel in the Missouri Campaign, learning firsthand about escaping slaves

Encouraging support of the president even when he fired Frémont for freeing slaves

Becoming an active floor manager and introducing legislation in the Thirty-Seventh Congress

1862　Calling for repentance because the war is a result of the U.S. failure to free the slaves

Agreeing with the president's request for compensation to the slaveholders in the District of Columbia

Overseeing passage of a bill prohibiting slavery in the territories

Supporting Lincoln's bill for compensated, gradual emancipation in the border states

Reminding radicals to trust Lincoln

Establishing relationships with African Americans

Reaching out personally and pastorally to Abraham and Mary Lincoln

1863　Defending the president when radicals considered abandoning him

Encouraging members of the public to avoid letting anything deter them from supporting the administration

Initiating universal emancipation

1864　Listening to the president's feelings and struggles

Encouraging his friends to have confidence in the president

Hoping for an eminently practical religion with charity for all

Notes

Abbreviations

AIC	Edward Magdol, *Owen Lovejoy: Abolitionist in Congress*. New Brunswick, N.J.: Rutgers University Press, 1967.
ALAL	Michael Burlingame. *Abraham Lincoln: A Life*. Baltimore: Johns Hopkins University Press, 2008.
ALP	Abraham Lincoln Papers, Library of Congress, Washington, D.C.
ALPL	Abraham Lincoln Presidential Library, Springfield, Ill.
BCR	*Bureau County Republican*
CW	Roy P. Basler, ed. *The Collected Works of Abraham Lincoln*. 8 vols. New Brunswick, N.J.: Rutgers University Press, 1953–55.
FJ	*Freeport Journal*
HBB	Owen Lovejoy. *His Brother's Blood: Speeches and Writings of Owen Lovejoy, 1838–64*. Ed. William F. Moore and Jane Ann Moore. Urbana: University of Illinois Press, 2004.
Lovejoy Papers, BCHS	Lovejoy Papers, Bureau County Historical Society, Princeton, Ill.
Lovejoy Papers, Clements	Owen Lovejoy Papers, 1829–1943, William L. Clements Library, University of Michigan, Ann Arbor
Lovejoy Society Papers	Lovejoy Society Papers, Illinois Historical Survey, University of Illinois at Urbana-Champaign

Introduction

1. *HBB*, 411.

2. Ibid., 160.

3. Carl Sandburg, *Abraham Lincoln: The Prairie Years and the War Years* (New York: Harcourt, Brace, 1954), 64.

4. T. Harry Williams, *Lincoln and the Radicals* (Madison: University of Wisconsin Press, 2005), title page.

164   *Notes to Introduction*

5. Ibid., 5.

6. Ibid., xiii.

7. Ibid., 1.

8. *HBB*, 346.

9. James G. Randall, *Lincoln the President* (New York: Dodd, Mead, 1945–55).

10. Charles A. Beard and Mary Beard, *The Rise of American Civilization* (New York: Macmillan, 1927).

11. John Ashworth, "The Republican Triumph," in *A Companion to the Civil War and Reconstruction*, ed. Lacy K Ford (Sussex, Eng.: Blackwell, 2011), 167.

12. Merton L. Dillon, "Gilbert H. Barnes and Dwight L. Dumond: A Reappraisal," *Reviews in American History* 21 (1993): 539–52.

13. Kenneth M. Stampp, *And the War Came: The North and the Secession Crisis, 1860–1861* (Baton Rouge: Louisiana State University Press, 1950).

14. John Hope Franklin, *From Slavery to Freedom: History of Negro Americans*, 8th ed. (New York: Knopf Doubleday, 2000), 233.

15. *AIC*, viii.

16. Hans L. Trefousse, *The Radical Republicans: Lincoln's Vanguard for Racial Justice* (New York: Knopf, 1969); Eric Foner, *Free Soil, Free Labor, Free Men: The Ideology of the Republican Party before the Civil War* (New York: Oxford University Press, 1970); Frederick Blue, *The Free Soilers: Third Party Politics, 1848–54* (Urbana: University of Illinois Press, 1973); James M. McPherson, *Struggle for Equality: Abolitionists and the Negro in the Civil War and Reconstruction* (Princeton: Princeton University Press, 1964); James Brewer Stewart, *Holy Warriors: The Abolitionists and American Slavery* (New York: Hill and Wang, 1976).

17. Mark E. Neely Jr., *The Last Best Hope of Earth: Abraham Lincoln and the Promise of America* (Cambridge: Harvard University Press, 1993), front flap.

18. Allen C. Guelzo, *Abraham Lincoln: Redeemer President* (Grand Rapids, Mich.: Eerdmans, 1999), 463.

19. David Herbert Donald, *Lincoln* (New York: Simon and Schuster, 1997), back flap, 14.

20. Ibid., 333.

21. David Herbert Donald, *"We Are Lincoln Men": Abraham Lincoln and His Friends* (New York: Simon and Schuster, 2003), xvi.

22. Matthew Pinsker, "Lincoln Theme 2.0," *Journal of American History* 96 (September 2009): 9.

23. Stewart Winger, *Lincoln, Religion, and Romantic Cultural Politics* (DeKalb: Northern Illinois University Press, 2003), 11.

24. Ibid., 182.

25. Pinsker, "Lincoln Theme 2.0," 9.

26. William Lee Miller, *Lincoln's Virtues: An Ethical Biography* (New York: Knopf, 2002), 225, 438.

27. Richard J. Carwardine, *Lincoln* (Harlow, Eng.: Pearson/Longman, 2003), 306; Pinsker, "Lincoln Theme 2.0," 9.

28. Allen C. Guelzo, *Lincoln's Emancipation Proclamation: The End of Slavery in America* (New York: Simon and Schuster, 2004), 3, 7, 17, 26.

29. Eric Foner, *The Fiery Trial: Abraham Lincoln and American Slavery* (New York: Norton, 2010), xix.

Notes to Introduction and Chapter 1

30. Ibid., 89, xvii–xviii.

31. Guelzo, *Abraham Lincoln*, 207.

32. Guelzo, *Lincoln's Emancipation Proclamation*, 5.

33. Eric Foner, *Fiery Trial*, xx.

34. Guelzo, *Lincoln's Emancipation Proclamation*, 4.

35. Ibid., 5, 66.

36. Ibid., 6, 7.

37. Eric Foner, *Fiery Trial*, xix.

38. Ibid., xx, xix.

39. Ibid., 35.

40. Milton Meltzer, *Thaddeus Stevens and the Fight for Negro Rights* (New York: Crowell, 1967), 159.

41. *AIC*, viii.

Chapter 1. Hating the Zeal to Spread Slavery, 1854

1. Donald, *Lincoln*, 173.

2. Eric Foner, *Fiery Trial*, 64.

3. *CW*, 2:255.

4. Isaac N. Arnold in *Addresses on the Death of Hon. Owen Lovejoy, Delivered in the Senate and House of Representatives, on Monday, March 28, 29, 1864* (Washington, D.C.: U.S. Government Printing Office, 1864); *HBB*, 66, 24.

5. *CW*, 2:248.

6. Ibid., 255.

7. Ibid.

8. Ibid., 256.

9. Ibid., 272.

10. Ibid., 264.

11. Ibid., 4:271.

12. Ibid., 2:275.

13. Ibid., 273. These words do not appear in the newspaper accounts of the October 5 speech, but they are included in the written text of the basically same speech delivered on October 16 in Bloomington.

14. *Free West*, September 7, 1854.

15. Benjamin P. Thomas, *Abraham Lincoln: A Biography* (New York: Barnes and Noble, 1952), 152.

16. Kerck Kelsey, *Israel Washburn Jr.: Maine's Little-Known Giant of the Civil War* (Rockport Me.: Picton, 2004), 68; *FJ*, October 12, 1854.

17. Paul Selby, "Republican State Convention, Springfield, Ill., October 4–5, 1854," in *Transactions of the McLean County Historical Society*, vol. 3, ed. Ezra M. Prince (Bloomington, Ill.: Pantagraph, 1900), 44.

18. Douglas L. Wilson, "Terrific in Denunciation: Taking a New Look at Lincoln the Lawyer," *Humanities* 29 (January–February 2008), http://www.neh.gov/news/humanities/2008-01/Lincoln_the_lawyer.html.

19. *AIC*, 113, 130; *FJ*, October 12, 1854.

20. *FJ*, October 12, 1854.

166   *Notes to Chapter 1*

21. Merton L. Dillon, *Antislavery Movement in Illinois: 1809–1844* (Ann Arbor: University Microfilms International, 1951), 353.

22. *FJ*, October 12, 1854.

23. Ibid.

24. Selby, "Republican State Convention," 46.

25. *AIC*, 113.

26. Victor B. Howard, "The Illinois Republican Party, Part I: A Party Organizer for the Republicans in 1854," *Illinois State Historical Journal* 64 (Summer 1971): 145; *Chicago Weekly Democrat*, November 10, 1860.

27. Selby, "Republican State Convention," 44.

28. *Illinois State Journal*, October 7, 1854.

29. *Illinois State Register*, October 7, 8, 1854.

30. *FJ*, October 12, 1854.

31. *Illinois State Register*, October 6, 1854.

32. Thomas, *Abraham Lincoln*, 152.

33. *Dictionary of American Biography* (New York: Scribner's, 1946), 2:435.

34. Victor B. Howard, "The Illinois Republican Party, Part II: The Party Became Conservative, 1855–1856," *Illinois State Historical Journal* 64 (Autumn 1971): 285.

35. Arthur Charles Cole, *The Centennial History of Illinois*, vol. 3, *The Era of the Civil War* (Chicago: McClurg, 1922), 129.

36. Don E. Fehrenbacher, *Prelude to Greatness: Lincoln in the 1850s* (Stanford, Calif.: Stanford University Press, 1962), 35.

37. William E. Gienapp, *The Origins of the Republican Party, 1852–1856* (Oxford: Oxford University Press, 1987), 124.

38. Donald, *Lincoln*, 189.

39. Guelzo, *Abraham Lincoln*, 201.

40. Eric Foner, *Fiery Trial*, 89.

41. See the *Transactions of the McLean County Historical Society* 3 (1900); Howard, "Illinois Republican Party, Part I"; Howard, "Illinois Republican Party, Part II"; *AIC*.

42. Matthew Pinsker, "Senator Abraham Lincoln," *Journal of the Abraham Lincoln Association* 14 (Summer 1993): 12. Pinsker refers to a "List of the Members Composing the Nineteenth General Assembly of the State of Illinois," printed by the State Register Office, 1855, ALPL.

43. *Dixon Telegraph*, September 14, 1854.

44. Owen Lovejoy to Joshua Giddings, November 10, 1854, Giddings Papers, Ohio Historical Society, Columbus.

45. "Mr. Lincoln's First Senate Bid," http://www.nps.gov/liho/planyourvisit/upload/First%20Senate%20Bid%20Front%20and%20Back.pdf; *CW*, 2:296 includes Lincoln's worksheets.

46. Howard, "Illinois Republican Party, Part II," 306; Howard, "Illinois Republican Party, Part I," 155–60.

47. *CW*, 2:288, Abraham Lincoln to Ichabod Codding, November 27, 1854, 3:228–29, from Lincoln's rebuttal at the Galesburg Debate; Charles C. Patton, comp., *A Manuscript Collection of the Letters of Charles H. Lanphier* (Springfield, Ill.: Frye-Williamson, 1973), 105.

48. *CW*, 2:323, Abraham Lincoln to Joshua F. Speed, August 24, 1855.

Notes to Chapter 2

Chapter 2. Traversing Uneven Political Ground, 1855

1. William F. Moore, "Owen Lovejoy's Method of Political Success: Challenging the Fugitive Slave Laws with the Bible and the Underground Railroad," Baylor Institute for Faith and Learning, 2004 Pruitt Memorial Symposium, Lovejoy Society Papers.

2. *CW*, 1:8, *Sanagamo Journal*, March 9, 1832.

3. Thomas, *Abraham Lincoln*, 35.

4. Ibid., 41–42.

5. *CW*, 1:316, "Address to the People of Illinois" (coauthored with Stephen T. Logan and A. T. Bledsoe).

6. Paul Findley, *A. Lincoln: The Crucible of Congress* (New York: Crown, 1979), 22–32.

7. *AIC*, 77; *Western Citizen*, June 23, 1846.

8. *Cyclopædia of Political Science, Political Economy, and the Political History of the United States*, "Kansas-Nebraska Bill," II.227.7, http://www.econlib.org/library/YPD-Books/Lalor/llCy618.html.

9. Robert Pierce Forbes, *The Missouri Compromise and Its Aftermath* (Chapel Hill: University of North Carolina Press, 2007), 67.

10. Austin Willey, *History of the Antislavery Cause in State and Nation* (New York: Negro Universities Press, 1970), 42; Calvin Montague Clark, *American Slavery and Maine Congregationalists* (Bangor, Me.: the author, 1940), 15; Forbes, *Missouri Compromise*, 61–68. The people of Maine were humiliated at the prospect of selling themselves in this manner to the Slave Power even though they had worked for their own statehood for twenty years.

11. Joseph C. Lovejoy and Owen Lovejoy, *Memoir of the Rev. Elijah P. Lovejoy Who Was Murdered in Defence of the Liberty of the Press, at Alton, Illinois, Nov. 7, 1837* (New York: Taylor, 1838), 344.

12. Paul Simon, *Freedom's Champion: Elijah Lovejoy* (Carbondale: Southern Illinois University Press, 1994), 138.

13. Ibid., 101, 102, 104.

14. *CW*, 1:112.

15. Simon, *Freedom's Champion*, 139; Mark E. Neely Jr., *The Abraham Lincoln Encyclopedia* (New York: McGraw-Hill, 1982), 193.

16. *Emancipator*, December 7, 1837.

17. Owen Lovejoy to *Emancipator*, December 28, 1837.

18. Lovejoy and Lovejoy, *Memoir*, 247.

19. *Liberator*, November 24, 1837.

20. Owen Lovejoy to *Emancipator*, December 28, 1837.

21. *AIC*, 78.

22. Ibid., 98.

23. Elihu Washburne to Abraham Lincoln, December 26, 1854, ALP. The letters are part of the extensive collection of Lincoln Papers donated by Robert Todd Lincoln to the Library of Congress and not opened to the public until July 26, 1947. The letters are now available online at the ALP, transcribed by the Lincoln Studies Center, Knox College, Galesburg, Ill.

24. Abraham Lincoln to Elihu Washburne, January 6, 1855, ALP.

25. Elihu Washburne to Abraham Lincoln, January 17, 1855, ALP.

168   *Notes to Chapter 2*

26. Ibid., January 20, 1855.

27. These letters are now available online at http://memory.loc.gov/ammem/alhtml/malhome.html.

28. *AIC*, 120.

29. *ALAL*, 396, Jesse O. Norton to Abraham Lincoln, December 20, 1854.

30. Ibid., January 20, 1855.

31. Ibid., Abraham Lincoln to Jesse O. Norton, February 16, 1855.

32. *Journal of the House of Representatives of the Nineteenth General Assembly of the State of Illinois, 1855*, 284.

33. Thomas J. Turner to Abraham Lincoln, December 10, 1854, ALP.

34. Abraham Lincoln to Elihu Washburne, December 11, 1854, ALP.

35. *ALAL*, 1:394; Anson S. Miller to Elihu Washburne, December 18, 1854, Elihu B. Washburne Papers, Library of Congress, Washington, D.C.

36. Robert Walker Johannsen, *Lincoln, the South, and Slavery* (Baton Rouge: Louisiana State University Press, 1993), 43.

37. *Free West*, November 30, 1854.

38. Ibid., December 20, 1854.

39. Ibid., November 30, 1854.

40. *ALAL*, 1:394; Elihu Washburne to Zebina Eastman, December 19, 1854, Zebina Eastman Papers, Chicago Historical Society Museum, Chicago.

41. Jay Monaghan, *The Man Who Elected Lincoln* (New York: Bobbs-Merrill, 1956), 45.

42. *ALAL*, 1:395; Charles H. Ray to Elihu B. Washburne, December 16, 1854, Washburne Papers.

43. *ALAL*, 1:395–96; Charles H. Ray to Elihu B. Washburne January 12, 1855, Washburne Papers.

44. Willard L. King, *Lincoln's Manager: David Davis* (Cambridge: Harvard University Press, 1960), 107.

45. Douglas L. Wilson and Rodney O. Davis, eds., *Herndon's Informants: Letters, Interviews, and Statements about Abraham Lincoln* (Urbana: University of Illinois Press, 1998), 467.

46. *Journal of the House of Representatives of the Nineteenth General Assembly of the State of Illinois, 1855*, 306.

47. Ibid., 307, 308.

48. *Journal of the Senate of the Nineteenth General Assembly of the State of Illinois, 1855*, 242–45.

49. *ALAL*, 401, 402; Donald, *Lincoln*, 184.

50. *AIC*, 120.

51. *Journal of the House of Representatives of the Nineteenth General Assembly of the State of Illinois, 1855*, 307. All quotations from Lovejoy's speech are taken from the text as it appeared in the *Free West*, April 5, 1855.

52. *CW*, 2:248.

53. Ibid., 242–43.

54. *HBB*, 108, 110.

55. *CW*, 2:266.

Notes to Chapter 2

56. *HBB*, 111.

57. *CW*, 2:272.

58. *HBB*, 114.

59. *CW*, 2:245, 264.

60. *HBB*, 113–14.

61. *CW*, 2:278.

62. *HBB*, 114.

63. *CW*, 2:546.

64. Carwardine, *Lincoln*, 37, xiii.

65. William W. Brown, comp., *The Anti-Slavery Harp* (Boston: Marsh, 1848), 18.

66. William Lloyd Garrison, *Liberator*, January 1, 1831.

67. Russell B. Nye, *Fettered Freedom: A Discussion of Civil Liberties and the Slavery Controversy in the United States, 1830 to 1860* (East Lansing: Michigan State College Press, 1949), esp. 3–31.

68. *Proceedings of the Antislavery Convention Assembled at Philadelphia Dec. 4, 5, & 6, 1833* (New York: Door and Butterfield, 1833).

69. Betty Fladeland, *Men and Brothers: Anglo-American Antislavery Cooperation* (Urbana: University of Illinois Press, 1972), xii.

70. Lawrence J. Friedman, *Gregarious Saints: Self and Community in American Abolitionism, 1830–1870* (Cambridge: Cambridge University Press, 1982), 1.

71. Benjamin F. Shaw, "Owen Lovejoy, Constitutional Abolitionists, and the Republican Party," in *Transactions*, ed. Prince, 64.

72. *CW*, 2:255.

73. Ibid., 1:75.

74. *American Anti-Slavery Society Minutes*, 1838, Boston Public Library Archives, Boston.

75. Gilbert Hobbs Barnes, *Anti-Slavery Impulse, 1830–44*, intro. William G. McLoughlin (New York: Harcourt, Brace, and World, 1974), viii.

76. Ibid.

77. Guelzo, *Lincoln's Emancipation Proclamation*, 26.

78. *CW*, 2:273.

79. *ALAL*, 1:380, 381.

80. *CW*, 2:256.

81. *FJ*, October 12, 1854.

82. *HBB*, 118.

83. H. C. Bradsby, ed., *History of Bureau County, Illinois* (Chicago: World, 1885), 332.

84. *HBB*, 117.

85. *CW*, 1:112.

86. Howard, "Illinois Republican Party, Part II," 288.

87. Ibid., 306.

88. Elwell Crissey, *Lincoln's Lost Speech* (New York: Hawthorn, 1967), 339.

89. *Quincy Whig*, July 31, 1855.

90. Howard, "Illinois Republican Party, Part II," 291.

91. *Aurora Guardian*, October 4, 1855.

170 Notes to Chapters 2 and 3

92. *Illinois State Historical Journal*, July 17, 1855.

93. Lyman Trumbull to Owen Lovejoy, August 23, 1855, ALPL.

94. Owen Lovejoy to Archibald Williams, August 6, 1855, Lilly Library Manuscript Collections, African American Related Collections, University of Indiana, Bloomington.

95. *CW*, 2:316.

96. Ibid.

97. Ibid., 322–23.

98. Horace White, "Abraham Lincoln in 1854," *Illinois State Historical Society Journal*, January 1908, 6.

Chapter 3. Standing Together Nobly, 1856

1. Howard, "Illinois Republican Party, Part II," 291–330.

2. *AIC*, 128; *Joliet Signal*, September 18, 1855.

3. *The Compact Edition of the Oxford English Dictionary* (Oxford: Oxford University Press, 1971), 1:240. In the mid-nineteenth century, when logs needed to be transported from the forest to a river or public road, lumbermen frequently used two short bobsleds rather than one long sled for increased maneuverability.

4. *AIC*, 137.

5. *Proceedings of the First Three Republican National Conventions of 1856, 1860, and 1864: Including Proceedings of the Antecedent National Convention Held at Pittsburg, in February, 1856* (Minneapolis: Harrison and Smith, 1893), 7.

6. Ibid., 7; *HBB*, 123–24; *Princeton Post*, March 6, 1856.

7. *Proceedings of the First Three Republican National Conventions*, 8; *New York Times*, February 22, 23, 1856.

8. *HBB*, 123; *Proceedings of the First Three Republican National Conventions*, 29.

9. *AIC*, 140; George Washington Julian, *Political Recollections, 1840 to 1872* (Chicago: Jansen, McClurg, 1884), 320.

10. Paul Selby, "The Editorial Convention, February 22, 1856," in *Transactions*, ed. Prince, 38.

11. Ibid.

12. Ibid., 41.

13. *Chicago Tribune*, May 17, 1856.

14. *AIC*, 143.

15. For the full report, see Selby, "Editorial Convention," 30–43.

16. Crissey, *Lincoln's Lost Speech*, 297; Neely, *Abraham Lincoln Encyclopedia*, 38.

17. Crissey, *Lincoln's Lost Speech*, 142.

18. *Chicago Democrat*, June 7, 1856, in *Transactions*, ed. Prince, 174.

19. "Official Record of Convention," in *Transactions*, ed. Prince, 164.

20. Ibid., 174.

21. Crissey, *Lincoln's Lost Speech*, 121.

22. Ibid., 217.

23. Ibid., 206.

24. Crissey, *Lincoln's Lost Speech*, 206–7; *Bloomington Weekly Pantagraph*, June 1856.

25. Monaghan, *Man Who Elected Lincoln*, 77.

26. "Official Record," 156.

Notes to Chapter 3

27. *Proceedings of First Three Republican National Conventions,* 29–30.

28. Ibid., 57.

29. Ibid., 53.

30. Albert J. Beveridge, *Abraham Lincoln, 1809–1858* (Boston: Houghton Mifflin, 1928), 2:396.

31. Donald, *Lincoln,* 192; *ALAL,* 422.

32. *Proceedings of the First Three Republican National Conventions,* 64.

33. Crissey, *Lincoln's Lost Speech,* 314.

34. Parker Earle to General Elliott, January 9, 1908, Lovejoy Papers, BCHS. The *Ottawa Republican,* July 6, 1856, reported the three close tallies of the fifty-four official delegates, substantiating Earle's claim.

35. Abraham Lincoln to David Davis, July 7, 1856, David Davis Papers, Chicago Historical Society, Chicago.

36. *Tiskilwa Independent,* July 11, 1856.

37. *CW,* 2:347; Abraham Lincoln to David Davis, July 7, 1856, Davis Papers.

38. *AIC,* 166; *Bloomington Daily Pantagraph,* November 17, 1856.

39. Donald, *Lincoln,* 193.

40. Julia M. Fenster, *The Case of Abraham Lincoln* (New York: Palgrave Macmillan, 2007), 153, 154, 161.

41. Ibid., 163; *Springfield Register,* July 16, 1856.

42. Fenster, *Case of Abraham Lincoln,* 151–52; *Missouri Republican,* June 25, 1856.

43. "The Lincoln Log: A Daily Chronology of the Life of Abraham Lincoln," http://www.thelincolnlog.org/.

44. Owen Lovejoy to Gerrit Smith, November 18, 1856, Gerrit Smith Papers, Special Collections Research Center, Syracuse University, Syracuse, N.Y.

45. *Bloomington Pantagraph,* July 9, 1856; *HBB,* 133; Ezra M. Prince and John H. Burnham, eds. *Encyclopedia of Illinois, and History of McLean County* (Chicago: Munsell, 1908), 2:829–30; *AIC,* 157–63.

46. Parker Earle to General Elliott, January 9, 1908, Lovejoy Papers, BCHS.

47. *Bloomington Pantagraph,* June 11, 1856.

48. *HBB,* 130.

49. Parker Earle to General Elliott, January 9, 1908, Lovejoy Papers, BCHS.

50. *Bloomington Pantagraph,* July 23, 1856, November 17, 1907; *HBB,* 130; Philip Atkinson, "Anecdotes of Owen Lovejoy," Lovejoy Papers, BCHS.

51. *AIC,* 158.

52. Owen Lovejoy to Jesse Fell, October 25, 1856, Jesse W. Fell Papers, Library of Congress, Washington, D.C.

53. T. L. Dickey to Owen Lovejoy, July 30, 1856, Owen Lovejoy to T. L. Dickey, n.d., both in Lovejoy Papers, BCHS.

54. King, *Lincoln's Manager,* 114.

55. Douglas L. Wilson and Davis, *Herndon's Informants,* 504.

56. J. A. McClun to Abraham Lincoln, July 21, 1856, Davis Papers.

57. *Bloomington Weekly National Flag,* November 7, 1856.

58. *HBB,* 160.

59. *CW,* 2:366.

172   *Notes to Chapters 3 and 4*

60. *FJ*, October 12, 1854.

61. Owen Lovejoy to Gerrit Smith, November 18, 1856, Smith Papers; *AIC*, 166.

62. King, *Lincoln's Manager*, 114; David Davis to T. L. Dickey, July 18, 1856, Davis Papers.

63. Fehrenbacher, *Prelude to Greatness*, 41.

64. *CW*, 2:358.

65. N. Dwight Harris, History of Negro Servitude in Illinois (Chicago: McClurg, 1904), 204–5.

66. *Chicago Democratic Press*, December 11, 1856.

Chapter 4. Disputing the Supreme Court Decision, 1857

1. Leonard L. Richards, *The Slave Power: The Free North and Southern Domination, 1780–1860* (Baton Rouge: Louisiana State University Press, 2000), 14.

2. *AIC*, 44.

3. Ibid.

4. N. Dwight Harris, *History of Negro Servitude*, 112.

5. Ibid., 113.

6. Paul Finkelman, *An Imperfect Union: Slavery, Federalism, and Comity* (Union, N.J.: Lawbook Exchange, 2000), 99; N. Dwight Harris, *History of Negro Servitude*, 114.

7. Carl Adams, "Lincoln's First Freed Slave," *Journal of the Illinois State Historical Society* 101 (Fall–Winter 2008): 101.

8. *ALAL*, 1:251.

9. *Journal of the House of Representatives of the United States, 1848–1849*, December 21, 1848, 134.

10. Findley, *A. Lincoln*, 139.

11. Ibid.

12. George Washington Julian, *The Life of Joshua R. Giddings* (Chicago: McClurg, 1892), 262.

13. Ibid., 263; James Brewer Stewart, *Joshua R. Giddings and the Tactics of Radical Politics* (Cleveland: Press of Case Western Reserve University, 1970), 49.

14. Eric Foner, *Fiery Trial*, 59.

15. Julian, *Life of Joshua R. Giddings*, 264.

16. *Congressional Globe*, 30th Cong., 2nd sess., xx, 174–77.

17. Julian, *Life of Joshua R. Giddings*, 264.

18. *Congressional Globe*, 30th Cong., 2nd sess., 276.

19. Eric Foner, *Fiery Trial*, 59.

20. Carwardine, *Lincoln*, 82–83.

21. Guelzo, *Lincoln's Emancipation Proclamation*, 201.

22. Ibid.

23. *CW*, 1:279, 271, 272; Winger, Lincoln, 185–92.

24. *CW*, 2:289.

25. Winger, *Lincoln*, 186.

26. *CW*, 2:274.

27. Winger, *Lincoln*, 186.

Notes to Chapters 4 and 5

28. *CW*, 1:272.

29. Ibid., 273.

30. Ibid.

31. *HBB*, 33, 43.

32. Henry D. Kingsbury and S. L. Deyo, "Town of Albion," in *Illustrated History of Kennebec County, Maine* (New York: Blake, 1892), chapter 45; Ruby Crosby Wiggins, *Albion on the Narrow Gage* (Auburn, Me.: Little Guy, 1964), 173.

33. *HBB*, 34.

34. Ibid.

35. Ibid., 36.

36. Ibid. See also Howard Jones, *Mutiny on the Amistad: The Saga of a Slave Revolt and Its Impact on American Abolition, Law, and Diplomacy* (New York: Oxford University Press, 1987).

37. *HBB*, 38, 39–40.

38. Ibid., 40, 43.

39. Ibid., 42.

40. National Abolition Hall of Fame and Museum, "William Lloyd Garrison (1805–1879)," http://www.nationalabolitionhalloffameandmuseum.org/wgarrison.html.

41. Edward Magdol, "New Look at Abolitionists" (review of Aileen S. Kraditor, *Means and Ends in American Abolitionism*), *Nation*, February 17, 1969, 214; Carwardine, *Lincoln*, 82.

42. *CW*, 1:112.

43. Donald, *Lincoln*, 201.

44. *CW*, 2:401.

45. Ibid., 3:358.

46. Ibid., 2:398–409.

47. Ibid., 405, 408.

48. Ibid., 403.

49. Ibid., 404.

50. Ibid., 404, 407.

51. Ibid., 409.

52. *HBB*, 145.

53. Ibid., 145, 146.

54. Ibid., 149, 151, 146, 152.

55. Ibid., 151.

56. *CW*, 1:247.

57. Ella W. Harrison, "Lovejoy, the Pastor," 5, Lovejoy Papers, BCHS.

Chapter 5. Trusting Those Who Care for the Results, 1858

1. *CW*, 2:435–36.

2. Ibid.

3. No copy of this letter has been located to date.

4. Isabel Wallace, *Life and Letters of General W. H. L. Wallace* (Chicago: Donnelley, 1909), 83 (Josh Whitmore to W. H. L. Wallace, June 5, 1858).

174   Notes to Chapter 5

5. Ibid., 83–84.

6. *AIC*, 206–7.

7. Henry Clay Whitney to Abraham Lincoln, July 31, 1858, ALP. See PBS History Detectives, "Lincoln Letter Episode," August 27, 2007, http://www.pbs.org/opb/historydetectives/investigation/lincoln-letter/.

8. *CW*, 2:532–33.

9. Owen Lovejoy to Abraham Lincoln, August 4, 1858, ALP.

10. Robert Walker Johannsen, *Stephen A. Douglas* (Urbana: University of Illinois Press, 1997), 613.

11. Ibid., 632.

12. Lyman Trumbull to Abraham Lincoln, January 3, 1858, ALP.

13. Johannsen, *Stephen A. Douglas*, 632; Abraham Lincoln to Lyman Trumbull, December 27, 1857, *CW*, 2:430.

14. Johannsen, *Stephen A. Douglas*, 633; William Herndon to Elihu Washburne, April 10, 1858, Washburne Papers.

15. *Springfield Journal*, July 15, 1858.

16. *BCR*, June 17, 1858.

17. *Chicago Tribune*, June 15, 1858.

18. *Ottawa Free Trader*, July 24, 1858. We are grateful to Michael Burlingame for sharing this newspaper clipping on Lovejoy.

19. Cole, *Centennial History*, 3:169.

20. *CW*, 2:131.

21. *HBB*, 145.

22. *CW*, 2:461.

23. Ibid.

24. Ibid., 461, 468.

25. Eric Foner, *Fiery Trial*, 102.

26. *CW*, 2:471, Abraham Lincoln to John L. Scripps, June 23, 1858.

27. Allen C. Guelzo, *Lincoln and Douglas: The Debates That Defined America* (New York: Simon and Schuster, 2008), 63.

28. Ibid., 223.

29. Eric Foner, *Fiery Trial*, 109.

30. Ibid., 101.

31. Guelzo, *Lincoln and Douglas*, 110–11.

32. Eric Foner, *Fiery Trial*, 108.

33. Ibid., 63.

34. *AIC*, 201; Robert H. Browne, *Abraham Lincoln and the Men of His Time* (Cincinnati: Jennings and Pye, 1901), 2:211.

35. *HBB*, 159–60.

36. *CW*, 2:459.

37. *HBB*, 160.

38. Ibid., 161.

39. Envelope addressed to Lincoln from Lovejoy and a copy of the Joliet speech from the *BCR*, July 8, 1858, ALPL.

Notes to Chapters 5 and 6

40. Owen Lovejoy to Abraham Lincoln, August 4, 1858, ALP.

41. *HBB*, 193; George R. Price and James Brewer Stewart, *To Heal the Scourge of Prejudice: The Life of Hosea Easton* (Amherst: University of Massachusetts Press, 1999), 87.

42. *AIC*, 99.

43. *Bloomington Daily Pantagraph*, August 13, 1856.

44. Owen Lovejoy to Abraham Lincoln, August 4, 1858, ALP.

45. *CW*, vol. 3, at http://quod.lib.umich.edu/l/lincoln/lincoln3?type=simple&rgn=full +text&q1=lovejoy&submit=Go.

46. *CW*, 3:10.

47. Ibid.; *Chicago Press and Tribune*, August 26, 1858.

48. *CW*, 3:13.

49. Charles H. Lanphier, *Glory to God and the Sucker Democracy: A Manuscript Collection of the Letters of Charles H. Lanphier*, comp. Charles C. Patton (Springfield, Ill.: Frye-Williamson, 1973), 104.

50. *CW*, 3:13.

51. Ibid.

52. Paul Angle, ed., *The Lincoln Reader* (New Brunswick, N.J.: Rutgers University Press, 1947), 254.

53. Charles W. Marsh, *Recollections, 1837–1910* (Chicago: Farm Implement News, 1910), 75.

54. *Chicago Press and Tribune*, August 26, 1858.

55. Shaw, "Owen Lovejoy," 71.

56. *CW*, 3:40–41.

57. Shaw, "Owen Lovejoy," 72.

58. William F. Moore, "Owen Lovejoy's Role in the Election of Abraham Lincoln," Conference on Illinois History, October 4, 2002, Lovejoy Society Papers.

59. *CW*, 3:298.

60. Ibid., 312.

61. Ibid., 313.

62. Timothy S. Good, *The Lincoln-Douglas Debates and the Making of a President* (Jefferson, N.C.: McFarland, 2007), 175–76.

63. Donald, *Lincoln*, 228.

64. Allen C. Guelzo, "Houses Divided: Lincoln, Douglas, and the Political Landscape of 1858," *Journal of American History* 94 (September 2007): 391–417.

65. Guelzo, *Lincoln and Douglas*, 284, 288; Johannsen, *Stephen A. Douglas*, 653; Douglas L. Wilson and Davis, *Herndon's Informants*, 643.

66. *CW*, 3:339.

67. Browne, *Abraham Lincoln*, 2:253.

68. Ibid.

Chapter 6. Remaining Steadfast to the Right, 1859

1. Donald, *Lincoln*, 235.

2. Michael Burlingame, *The Inner World of Abraham Lincoln* (Urbana: University of Illinois Press, 1994), xvii.

176 — Notes to Chapter 6

3. Donald, *Lincoln*, 237.

4. Tony Stoneburner, "Illinois Methodists and Antislavery Activity: Through a Literary Lens," Lovejoy Society Symposium, March 18, 2000, Lovejoy Society Papers.

5. In an 1844 meeting in Farmington, the General Association of the Illinois Congregational Churches agreed that all ministers must "rank slaveholding with other heinous sins" (Matthew Spinka, ed., *A History of Illinois Congregational and Christian Churches* [Chicago: Congregational and Christian Conference of Illinois, 1944], 94).

6. Donald, *Lincoln*, 232.

7. *CW*, 3:365–70.

8. Ibid., 436.

9. Ibid., 425.

10. Ibid., 426.

11. Ibid., 435.

12. Ibid., 370.

13. Gail Hamilton, postfuneral article in the *Congregationalist*, April 1864.

14. William W. Freehling, *The Road to Disunion*, vol. 2, *Secessionists Triumphant, 1854–1861* (New York: Oxford University Press, 2007), 283; *Charleston Mercury*, July 18, 1859.

15. *HBB*, 158.

16. Ibid., 301.

17. Gretchen A. Adams, *The Specter of Salem: Remembering the Witch Trials in Nineteenth-Century America* (Chicago: University of Chicago Press, 2008), chapter 4.

18. Ibid., 118.

19. *HBB*, 115.

20. *CW*, 3:550.

21. *HBB*, 173, 168.

22. *AIC*, 224.

23. *BCR*, March 3, 1859.

24. *New York Tribune* quoted in ibid.

25. *HBB*, 166, 169, 172–73.

26. Ibid., 176. See also Randall Kennedy, *Nigger: The Strange Career of a Troublesome Word* (New York: Random House, 2002), 109. Mark Twain's *Huckleberry Finn* has often been misinterpreted because readers are unaware of the play of irony in the story. According to Kennedy, "Twain is not willfully buttressing racism here; he is seeking ruthlessly to unveil and ridicule it. By putting *nigger* in white characters' mouths, the author is not branding blacks, but rather branding the whites."

27. *HBB*, 178.

28. Ibid., 166.

29. J. C. Lovejoy to Owen Lovejoy, March 16, 1859, in *Washington Union*, March 20, 1859. The letter was subsequently reprinted as a pamphlet, *The North and the South!: Letter from J. C. Lovejoy, Esq., to His Brother, Hon. Owen Lovejoy, M.C.: With Remarks by the Editor of the Washington Union* (n.p., 1859).

30. Owen Lovejoy to Lucy Denham, November 30, 1859, Lovejoy Papers, Clements.

31. Douglas L. Wilson and Davis, *Herndon's Informants*, 643; *CW*, 3:335.

32. J. C. Lovejoy to Owen Lovejoy, March 16, 1859, in *Washington Union*, March 20, 1859.

33. *Valley Spirit*, March 30, 1859.

Notes to Chapters 6 and 7

34. William McKee Evans, *Open Wound: The Long View of Race in America* (Urbana: University of Illinois Press, 2009), 107–8.

35. John W. Blassingame, ed., *The Frederick Douglass Papers*, ser. 1, Speeches, Debates, Interviews, vol. 3, 1855–1863 (New Haven: Yale University Press, 1986), Itinerary of Speeches, xxix–xxx.

36. Owen W. Muelder, *The Underground Railroad in Western Illinois* (Jefferson, N.C.: McFarland, 2008), 133.

37. *ALAL*, 1:575; *CW*, 3:496.

38. *CW*, 3:503.

39. *ALAL*, 1:575.

40. *HBB*, 193.

41. *ALAL*, 576.

42. *HBB*, 204; *Congressional Globe*, 36th Cong., 1st sess., 202–6; *BCR*, April 19, 1860, September 14, 1972.

43. *HBB*, 204.

44. Ibid. In the Old Testament, Numbers 22–24, Balak, the King of Moab, urged Balaam to curse the Israelites for invading Moab, but Yahweh required Balaam to bless the Israelites rather than curse them. This became known as one of the saving acts of Yahweh for the people of Israel.

45. Ibid., 204.

46. Ibid. Here, Lovejoy was referring to Governor Henry A. Wise of Virginia, who had John Brown hanged.

47. Ibid.

48 James Oakes, *The Radical and the Republican: Frederick Douglass, Abraham Lincoln and the Triumph of Antislavery Politics* (New York: Norton, 2007), 105.

49. William Wordsworth, *Ecclesiastical Sonnets* (Ann Arbor: University of Michigan Library, 2009), 2:17; *HBB*, 204.

50. *HBB*, 205.

51. Freehling, *Road to Disunion*, 265.

52. *AIC*, 230; *Congressional Globe*, 36th Cong., 1st sess., 16.

53. *HBB*, 189.

54. Owen Lovejoy, *An Agricultural Poem* (Princeton, Ill.: Bureau County Republican Book and Job Print, 1862), iv. In October 1859, Lovejoy read the poem to the Bureau County Agricultural Society.

55. Donald, *Lincoln*, 244; Norman Judd to Abraham Lincoln, December 12, 1859, ALP.

56. Owen Lovejoy to O. M. Hatch, October 31, 1859, O. M. Hatch Papers, box 1, folder 6, ALPL.

57. *AIC*, 227–28; Owen Lovejoy to Charles Sumner, November 23, 1859, Harvard University Library, Cambridge, Mass.; Edward L. Pierce, ed., *Memoirs and Letters of Charles Sumner* (Boston: Roberts, 1877–93), 602.

Chapter 7. Disenchanting the Nation of Slavery, 1860

1. Debby Applegate, *The Most Famous Man in America: The Biography of Henry Ward Beecher* (New York: Three Leaves, 2006), 341–44.

2. Ibid., 6.

178   *Notes to Chapter 7*

3. Applegate, *Most Famous Man*, 322; Doris Kearns Goodwin, *Team of Rivals* (New York: Simon and Schuster, 2005), 230.

4. Ibid., 323.

5. *CW*, 3:535.

6. Ibid., 536, 542.

7. Ibid., 547.

8. Ibid., 547, 550.

9. Goodwin, *Team of Rivals*, 232.

10. Harold Holzer, *Lincoln at Cooper Union* (New York: Simon and Schuster, 2004), 206.

11. *ALAL*, 587.

12. Applegate, *Most Famous Man*, 323.

13. George V. Bohman, "Owen Lovejoy on 'The Barbarism of Slavery,' April 5, 1860," in J. Jeffery Auer, *Antislavery and Disunion, 1858–1861: Studies in the Rhetoric of Compromise and Conflict* (New York: Harper and Row, 1963), 114–32. Bohman provides a full accounting and interpretation of the speech.

14. *HBB*, 192; *Congressional Globe*, 36th Cong., 1st sess., 202–6.

15. *HBB*, 192–93.

16. Ibid., 193.

17. Freehling, *Road to Disunion*, 288; *AIC*, 233–43.

18. Kelsey, *Israel Washburn Jr.*, 97–98.

19. Owen Lovejoy to Eunice Lovejoy, April 6, 1860, Lovejoy Papers, Clements.

20. *HBB*, 198. Lovejoy had heard Frederick Douglass use similar words at the 1852 Free Democratic Convention in Pittsburgh, where he described "a ravenous wolf in the act of throttling an infant" (Philip Foner, *Life and Writings of Frederick Douglass* [New York: International, 1952], 2:44).

21. *HBB*, 207–8.

22. Ibid., 207.

23. Bohman, "Owen Lovejoy."

24. Henry Wilson, *History of Antislavery Measures of the Thirty-Seventh and Thirty-Eighth Congresses, 1861–1864* (Boston: Walter, Wise, 1864), 2:671.

25. Owen Lovejoy to Eunice Lovejoy, April 6, 1860, Lovejoy Papers, Clements.

26. Donald, *Lincoln*, 242.

27. Murat Halstead, *Three against Lincoln: Murat Halstead Reports the Caucuses of 1860*, ed. and intro. William B. Hesseltine (Baton Rouge: Louisiana State University Press, 1960), 156–57.

28. Julian, *Life of Joshua R. Giddings*, 173, 174.

29. Donald, *Lincoln*, 244–46.

30. Owen Lovejoy to Abraham Lincoln, June 10, 1860, ALP.

31. *AIC*, 248.

32. Neely, *Abraham Lincoln Encyclopedia*, 77.

33. *AIC*, 248.

34. *CW*, Frist Supplement, 32.

35. Owen Lovejoy to Jesse Fell, June 27, 1860, in *Bloomington Daily Telegraph*, May 29, 1900.

Notes to Chapter 7

36. *AIC*, 252.

37. Ibid., 254.

38. Donald. *Lincoln*, 253.

39. *Congressional Globe*, 38th Cong., 1st sess., 1334.

40. Jon Grinspan, "'Young Men for War': The Wide Awakes and Lincoln's 1860 Presidential Campaign," *Journal of American History* 96 (September 2009): 4, 5.

41. Ibid., 1–22.

42. Ibid., 3, 4.

43. *HBB*, 244.

44. *BCR*, November 1, 1860.

45. Donald, *Lincoln*, 253.

46. *Freeport Bulletin*, September 20, 1860; *Salem Advocate*, October 25, 1860. Dates and locations have been documented for forty-two of Lovejoy's speeches (William F. Moore, "Owen Lovejoy's Role in the Election of Abraham Lincoln in 1860," Lovejoy Society Papers). The texts of two of Lovejoy's complete speeches survive: one delivered at Freeport on September 12 (*FJ*, September 26, 1860) and the other delivered at the Chicago Wigwam on October 15 (*Chicago Press and Tribune*, October 18, 1860).

47. *Salem Advocate*, September 25, 1860.

48. Halstead, *Three against Lincoln*, 156–57.

49. *HBB*, 231–32.

50. Ibid., 217.

51. Shaw, "Owen Lovejoy," 71.

52. *HBB*, 42; *Chicago Press and Tribune*, October 18, 1860.

53. *Pike County Democrat*, October 25, 1860; Monaghan, *Man Who Elected Lincoln*, 179.

54. *Freeport Bulletin*, July 5, 1860.

55. David Davis to Abraham Lincoln, October 5, 1860, ALP.

56. *HBB*, 220, 221.

57. Ibid., 218, 222.

58. *Alton Courier*, July 23, 1860.

59. Howard W. Allen and Vincent A. Lacey, eds., *Illinois Elections, 1818–1900* (Carbondale: Southern Illinois University Press, 1992), 137, 145.

60. *FJ*, September 26, 1860.

61. *Chicago Press and Tribune*, October 18, 1860.

62. *FJ*, September 26, 1860.

63. Carl Schurz to Abraham Lincoln, August 22, 1860, ALP.

64. Owen Lovejoy to Jesse Fell, July 21, 1860, in *Bloomington Daily Telegraph*, May 28, 1900.

65. Owen Lovejoy to O. M. Hatch, October 31, 1859, Hatch Papers, box 1, folder 6.

66. Owen Lovejoy to Jesse Fell, July 21, 1860, in *Bloomington Daily Telegraph*, May 28, 1900.

67. Edward Dewitt Jones, *Lincoln and the Preachers* (New York: Harper, 1948), 65.

68. *HBB*, 245.

69. Ibid., 320; *Geneseo Republic*, November 19, 1862, republished in *Lovejoy Society Newsletter* 1, no. 3 (December 1996).

180   *Notes to Chapters 7 and 8*

70. Moore, "Owen Lovejoy's Role."

71. William E. Gienapp, "Who Voted for Lincoln," in *Abraham Lincoln and the American Political Tradition*, ed. John L. Thomas (Amherst: University of Massachusetts Press, 1986), 76–77.

72. Ibid., 81, as interpreted by Dr. Robert Suchner.

73. *HBB*, 245.

Chapter 8. Holding Firmly to Their Promises, 1861

1. Goodwin, *Team of Rivals*, 278.

2. Donald, *Lincoln*, 261.

3. Freehling, *Road to Disunion*, 405.

4. *ALAL*, 1:692.

5. Ibid.

6. Freehling, *Road to Disunion*, 422; see chapter 25, "The Triumph."

7. William Lee Miller, *Lincoln's Virtues: An Ethical Biography* (New York: Knopf, 2002), 431.

8. Ibid., 433.

9. Bertram Wyatt-Brown, "Honor, Secession, and Civil War," 2004 James Pinckney Harrison Lectures in History, 4, http://www.humiliationstudies.org/documents/Wyatt-BrownSecession.pdf.

10. Ibid., 2.

11. *CW*, 1:273.

12. Ibid., 8:356.

13. *HBB*, 411; *BCR*, June 9, 1864.

14. Goodwin, *Team of Rivals*, 298–99.

15. Eric Foner, *Fiery Trial*, 148.

16. Miller, *Lincoln's Virtues*, 428.

17. *ALAL*, 1:707.

18. *CW*, 4:157.

19. James M. McPherson, "Who Freed the Slaves?," in *Drawn with the Sword: Reflections on the American Civil War*, ed. James M. McPherson (New York: Oxford University Press, 1996), reprinted in Michael Vorenberg, *The Emancipation Proclamation: A Brief History with Documents* (Boston: Bedford/St. Martin's, 2010), 133.

20. Trefousse, *Radical Republicans*, 143–44; Miller, *Lincoln's Virtues*, 434, 435.

21. *HBB*, 256.

22. Ibid., 258.

23. *AIC*, 270, 273.

24. *CW*, 4:190.

25. *HBB*, 158.

26. Envelope addressed to Lincoln from Lovejoy and a copy of the Joliet Speech from the *BCR*, July 8, 1858, ALPL.

27. Donald, *Lincoln*, 283–84.

28. Browne, *Abraham Lincoln*, 2:593, 598–613. Browne's book must be used with caution. It contains Browne's recollections of events related to him by Lovejoy four

Notes to Chapter 8

decades before its publication at the turn of the twentieth century. It is also idealistic and flattering and written in a mixture of stilted and dramatic language. Nonetheless, it provides some interesting clues about the nature of Lovejoy and Lincoln's personal relationship.

29. James Sesley Jr. to Owen Lovejoy, July 31, 1861, Lovejoy Collection.

30. *BCR*, April 25, 1861; *HBB*, 264.

31. *AIC*, 279, 280–81.

32. *HBB*, 27; *Congressional Globe*, 37th Cong., 1st sess., 32; *AIC*, 282.

33. *AIC*, 283.

34. Stephen Oates, *The Whirlwind of War: Voices of the Storm, 1861–1865* (New York: Harper Collins, 1998), 47–48.

35. *AIC*, 289.

36. Ibid., 290.

37. David Todd to John Todd, September 12, 1861, David Todd Papers, Illinois Historical Survey, University of Illinois at Urbana-Champaign.

38. *BCR*, August 1, 1861.

39. *AIC*, 290.

40. Ibid., 292.

41. *HBB*, 271–80.

42. Philip S. Foner, *Life and Writings*, 3:17; Goodwin, *Team of Rivals*, 390–93; *CW*, 4:518.

43. *ALAL*, 208; Goodwin, *Team of Rivals*, 390, 392; *CW*, 4:518.

44. *AIC*, 296; Catherine Coffin Phillips, *Jessie Benton Frémont: A Woman Who Made History* (Lincoln: University of Nebraska Press, 1995), 244. Phillips claims that on August 28, Frémont asked for the opinions of his staff officers, including Lovejoy and the Reverend John A. Gurley, a Universalist minister, on the proposed proclamation; all responded "that no other course was possible in Missouri under existing conditions." However, another Frémont biographer, Pamela Herr (*Jessie Benton Frémont: A Biography* [New York: Franklin Watts, 1987], 332–33) makes no mention of Lovejoy and reports that Quaker abolitionist Edward M. Davis encouraged Frémont to make the proclamation.

45. *AIC*, 295; Gustave Koerner, *Memoir of Gustave Koerner, 1809–1896*, ed. Thomas J. McCormack (Cedar Rapids, Iowa: Torch, 1909), 2:182.

46. Mark Grimsley, *The Hard Hand of War: Union Military Policy toward Southern Civilians, 1861–1865* (Cambridge: Cambridge University Press, 1995), 3, 4.

47. Ibid., 272–73.

48. Ibid., 274–75; Guelzo, *Lincoln's Emancipation Proclamation*, 112–14. For more on the debate on Lincoln and war powers, see *ALAL*, 2:362.

49. *HBB*, 274–75; Ira Berlin, "Who Freed the Slaves?: Emancipation and Its Meaning," in *Union and Emancipation: Essays on Politics in the Civil War*, ed. David W. Blight and Brooks D. Simpson (Kent, Ohio: Kent State University Press, 1997), reprinted in Vorenberg, *Emancipation Proclamation*, 141.

50. *HBB*, 276, 277.

51. Ibid., 276.

52. Philip S. Foner, *Life and Writings*, 3:20.

Notes to Chapters 8 and 9

53. *CW*, 5:29.

54. *ALAL*, 2:229–30.

55. Ibid., 237.

56. Ibid., 238.

57. Goodwin, *Team of Rivals*, 405; *CW*, 7:281–82, Abraham Lincoln to Albert G. Hodges, April 4, 1864.

58. *BCR*, December 12, 1861; *AIC*, 303, 304.

59. *CW*, 5:35.

60. Ibid., 48–49, 53.

61. *AIC*, 304; *ALAL*, 2:237.

62. *HBB*, 280.

63. *Congressional Globe*, 37th Cong., 2nd sess., 5; Isaac N. Arnold, *The Life of Abraham Lincoln* (Lincoln: University of Nebraska Press, 1994), 234–36; Donald, *Lincoln*, 322–23.

64. Arnold, *Life of Abraham Lincoln*, 236; *HBB*, 295–97.

65. *Congressional Globe*, 37th Cong., 2nd sess., 57.

66. Ibid., 58.

67. Ibid., 58–59; *AIC*, 311, 312.

68. *HBB*, 281.

69. Oakes, *Radical and the Republican*, 157.

Chapter 9. Restoring the Founding Purposes, 1862

1. Harry S. Stout and Christopher Grasso, "Civil War, Religion, and Communications: The Case of Richmond," in *Religion and the American Civil War*, ed. Randall M. Miller, Harry S. Stout, and Charles Reagan Wilson (New York: Oxford University Press, 1998), 321, 322, 323, 320.

2. *HBB*, 350.

3. *Congressional Globe*, 37th Cong., 2nd sess., 194–97.

4. *HBB*, 283, 284.

5. Ibid., 285.

6. Kristen L. Forman, ed., *The New Century Hymnal Companion: A Guide to the Hymns* (Cleveland: Pilgrim, 1998), 277.

7. *HBB*, 285.

8. Julian, *Political Recollections*, 366.

9. *HBB*, 288, 289.

10. Glenn Meeter, "Biblical Analogies for Slavery, the War, and the Union: Owen Lovejoy's January 1862 Speech on Prosecuting the Civil War," Lovejoy Society Papers.

11. *HBB*, 293.

12. James M. McPherson, *Battle Cry of Freedom: The Civil War Era* (Oxford: Oxford University Press, 1988), 450.

13. Leonard P. Curry, *Blueprint for Modern America: Nonmilitary Legislation of the First Civil War Congress* (Nashville: Vanderbilt University Press, 1968), 72.

14. *AIC*, 355; *Aurora Beacon* article reprinted in *BCR*, June 12, 1862.

15. *BCR*, May 15, 1862.

16. *HBB*, 307.

17. *BCR*, April 24, 1862.

Notes to Chapter 9   183

18. Justin Morrill, *Congressional Globe*, 38th Cong., 1st sess., 1329.

19. Library of Congress, "Primary Documents in American History: Morrill Act," http://www.loc.gov/rr/program/bib/ourdocs/Morrill.html.

20. See Henry Wilson, *History of the Antislavery Measures in the Thirty-Seventh and Thirty-Eighth Congresses, 1861–64* (Boston: Walker, Wise, 1864), chapter 5.

21. *CW*, 5:144–46.

22. *ALAL*, 2:337.

23. *AIC*, 323–24.

24. *ALAL*, 2:343.

25. *Free West*, January 11, 1855; Jane Ann Moore, "Chipping away at Racism in the 1855 Illinois Legislature," Illinois Historical Survey, University of Illinois at Urbana-Champaign.

26. *HBB*, 320.

27. *BCR*, March 20, 1862.

28. *ALAL*, 2:343; *CW*, 5:169.

29. Benjamin Quarles, *The Negro in the Civil War* (Amherst: Little, Brown, 1953), 141.

30. Henry Wilson, *History of the Antislavery Measures*, 187.

31. *ALAL*, 2:344.

32. Isaac N. Arnold, *Sketch of the Life of Abraham Lincoln* (New York: Bachelder, 1869), 70.

33. *ALAL*, 2:345.

34. *HBB*, 327, 328–29.

35. David Todd to John Todd, June 11, 1862, Todd Papers.

36. Clarence Earle Lovejoy, *Lovejoy Genealogy* (New York: Lovejoy, 1930), 172.

37. Owen Lovejoy to sons, February 23, 1862, Lovejoy Papers, Clements.

38. Donald, *Lincoln*, 337.

39. Owen Lovejoy to Abraham Lincoln, June 10, 1860, ALP.

40. David Todd to John Todd, June 11, 1862, Todd Papers.

41. Jennifer Fleischner, *Mrs. Lincoln and Mrs. Keckley: The Remarkable Story of the Friendship between a First Lady and a Former Slave* (New York: Broadway, 2003), 231; John Lovejoy Elliott, "Owen Lovejoy," *Cornell Magazine*, January 15, 1890.

42. Fleischner, *Mrs. Lincoln and Mrs. Keckley*, 243, 245; Owen Lovejoy to Sarah Lovejoy, June 12, 1862, Lovejoy Papers, BCHS.

43. Clark E. Carr, *My Day and Generation* (Chicago: McClurg, 1908), 251–53. Though Carr recalls the incident as taking place in the winter of 1862, Lincoln had smallpox at the time of the Gettysburg Address, in November 1863.

44. Arnold, *Sketch*, 229.

45. Guelzo, *Lincoln's Emancipation Proclamation*, 64.

46. *ALAL*, 2:358.

47. Curry, *Blueprint for Modern America*, 85.

48. Horace Greeley, *The American Conflict: A History of the Great Rebellion of the United States of America, 1860–1865* (Hartford, Conn.: Case, 1866), 2:263.

49. Guelzo, *Lincoln's Emancipation Proclamation*, 63–64.

50. *HBB*, 279–80.

51. Curry, *Blueprint for Modern America*, 85.

52. Ibid., 86.

53. *Congressional Globe*, 37th Cong., 2nd sess., 1803, 1805.

54. Ibid.

55. Curry, *Blueprint for Modern America*, 86.

56. *HBB*, 312.

57. Ibid., 320–21.

58. Ibid.

59. *AIC*, 329.

60. Isaac N. Arnold, *The History of Abraham Lincoln, and the Overthrow of Slavery* (Chicago: Clark, 1867), 276.

61. *Congressional Globe*, 37th Cong., 2nd sess., 2363.

62. Curry, *Blueprint for Modern America*, 68.

63. Grimsley, *Hard Hand of War*, 70.

64. *New York Times*, June 13, 1862.

65. *HBB*, 331–32.

66. Ibid., 346.

67. Eric Foner, *Fiery Trial*, xix; Stewart Winger, Associate Professor of History, Illinois State University, Comment, January 14, 2013.

68. Guelzo, *Lincoln's Emancipation Proclamation*, 66.

69. *HBB*, 346.

70. Ibid., 347.

71. Ibid., 346–47.

72. Ibid., 348.

73. Curry, *Blueprint for Modern America*, 70; *Congressional Globe*, 37th Cong., 2nd sess., 2793.

74. Curry, *Blueprint for Modern America*, 94.

75. James Oakes, *Freedom National: The Destruction of Slavery in the United States, 1861–1865* (New York: Norton, 2013), xviii.

76. Guelzo, *Lincoln's Emancipation Proclamation*, 116, 117.

77. Allan G. Bogue, *The Congressman's Civil War* (Cambridge: Cambridge University Press. 1989), 138, 139; *Congressional Globe*, 37th Cong., 2nd sess., 2561. The June 6 vote to reconsider passed by a margin of eighty-four to sixty-six, with a few Unionists and Democrats also shifting or adding their votes.

78. Curry, *Blueprint for Modern America*, 14.

79. Trefousse, *Radical Republicans*, 21.

80. Bogue, *Congressman's Civil War*, 139. On December 20, 1861, Lovejoy's confiscation bill was tabled by a vote of sixty-one to fifty-six (*Congressional Globe*, 37th Cong., 2nd sess., 159).

81. Bogue, *Congressman's Civil War*, 136, 139.

82. Ibid., 24–30.

83. *CW*, 5:317.

84. Ibid., 322, Abraham Lincoln to George B. McClellan, July 13, 1862.

85. Goodwin, *Team of Rivals,* 463, from Gideon Welles's diary; *ALAL* 2:360.

86. Matthew Pinsker, *Lincoln's Sanctuary: Abraham Lincoln and the Soldiers' Home* (New York: Oxford University Press, 2003), 40; Arnold, *Sketch*, 251.

Notes to Chapters 9 and 10

87. *ALAL*, 2:356.

88. Armstead L. Robinson, *Bitter Fruits of Bondage: The Demise of Slavery and the Collapse of the Confederacy, 1861–1865* (Charlottesville: University of Virginia Press, 2005), 176.

89. *ALAL*, 2:357.

90. Ibid.

91. Ibid., 356.

92. Ibid., 359.

93. Gideon Welles, "Administration of Abraham Lincoln," *The Galaxy* 24 (October 1877): 448; *HBB*, 408.

94. Guelzo, *Lincoln's Emancipation Proclamation*, 118.

95. Douglas L. Wilson, *Lincoln's Sword: The Presidency and the Power of Words* (New York: Vintage, 2007), 124.

96. "Lincoln Log"; *Washington Star*, September 24, 1862.

97. *Chicago Daily Tribune*, September 19, 1862.

98. *Geneseo Union Advocate*, October 31, 1862; Allen and Lacey, *Illinois Elections*, 150–51.

99. Allen and Lacey, *Illinois Elections*, 147–49; *AIC*, 369. See also William F. Moore, "The Nasty Election Campaign of 1862," paper presented at the Illinois Historical Society Symposium, December 6, 2002, Lovejoy Society Papers.

100. *AIC*, 369.

101. James M. McPherson, *Ordeal by Fire: The Civil War and Reconstruction* (New York: Knopf, 1982), 297.

Chapter 10. Assuring That the Nation Would Long Endure, 1863

1. Guelzo, *Lincoln's Emancipation Proclamation*, 222.

2. Louis Menand, *The Metaphysical Club: A Story of Ideas in America* (New York: Farrar, Straus, and Giroux, 2001), 40.

3. Owen Lovejoy to Cyrus Bryant, February 16, 1863, ALPL.

4. Guelzo, *Lincoln's Emancipation Proclamation*, 222.

5. Robinson, *Bitter Fruits of Bondage*, 182.

6. George E. Stephens, *A Voice of Thunder: The Civil War Letters of George E. Stephens*, ed. Donald Yacovone (Urbana: University of Illinois Press, 1997), 217.

7. *Chicago Daily Tribune*, June 12, 1874; Victor Howard, *Religion and the Radical Republican Movement, 1860–1870* (Lexington: University Press of Kentucky, 1990), 49.

8. Philip S. Foner, *Life and Writings*, 3:28.

9. Ibid., 31.

10. *HBB*, 375.

11. Robert L. Harris, "H. Ford Douglas: Afro-American Antislavery Emigrationist," *Journal of Negro History* 62 (July 1977): 229.

12. *CW*, 6:409.

13. *HBB*, 403; *Congressional Globe*, 38th Cong., 1st sess., 20.

14. *ALAL*, 2:582–83.

15. Ibid., 588.

16. Hans L. Trefousse, *Thaddeus Stevens: Nineteenth-Century Egalitarian* (Chapel Hill: University of North Carolina Press, 1997), 139–40.

Notes to Chapter 10

17. *ALAL*, 2:662.

18. *HBB*, 401.

19. For Lovejoy and Stevens's remarkably jocular exchange, see ibid., 368–69.

20. William C. Harris, *With Charity for All* (Lexington: University Press of Kentucky, 1997), 5–6.

21. *HBB*, 368.

22. Robert L. Harris, "H. Ford Douglas," 229.

23. Stephen Ward Angell, *Bishop Henry McNeal Turner* (Knoxville: University of Tennessee Press, 1992), 51.

24. *Peoria Daily Transcript*, March 17, April 8, 1863.

25. *AIC*, 384.

26. Ibid.; *BCR*, March 12, 1863.

27. *ALAL*, 2:551.

28. Frank L. Klement, *Dark Lanterns: Secret Political Societies, Conspiracies, and Treason Trials in the Civil War* (Baton Rouge: Louisiana State University Press, 1984), 58.

29. *Cleveland Morning Leader*, May 21, 1863; *AIC*, 386.

30. William Laing to parents, June 4, 1863, Dixon Public Library, Dixon, Ill.

31. Julian E. Bryant to Owen Lovejoy, July 28, 1863, Austin Wiswall Papers, 1863–1912, Southwest Collection/Special Collections Library, Texas Tech University, Lubbock.

32. *CW*, 6:406.

33. *HBB*, 380, 381.

34. *CW*, 6:406–10.

35. *AIC*, 388; *Chicago Tribune*, September 7, 1863.

36. *HBB*, 382.

37. Mary A. Livermore, *My Story of the War* (New York: Da Capo, 1972), 411–12.

38. Owen Lovejoy to Abraham Lincoln, October 14, 1863, ALP; Guelzo, *Lincoln's Emancipation Proclamation*, 258. The copy of the Emancipation Proclamation was purchased by the Chicago Historical Society but was destroyed in the 1871 Great Chicago Fire.

39. *HBB*, 387.

40. Ibid., 350.

41. *CW*, 6:332.

42. Ibid., 496.

43. *CW*, 4:482, 6:155.

44. *HBB*, 394.

45. John Beauchamp Jones, *Rebel War Clerk's Diary at the Confederate States Capital* (Philadelphia: Lippincott, 1866), 1:390.

46. Miller, Stout, and Wilson, *Religion and the American Civil War*, 326.

47. Mitchell Snay, *Gospel of Disunion: Religion and Separatism in the Antebellum South* (Chapel Hill: University of North Carolina Press, 1993), 168.

48. *CW*, 7:18–19.

49. *AIC*, 395.

50. Owen Lovejoy to Sarah Moody, December 6, 1863, Lovejoy Papers, Clements.

51. *AIC*, 395; *Congressional Globe*, 38th Cong., 1st sess., 4, 6; Robert V. Remini, *The House: The History of the House of Representatives* (New York: Smithsonian Books in association with HarperCollins, 2006), 180–83.

Notes to Chapters 10 and 11

52. *HBB*, 403.

53. Douglas A. Blackmon, *Slavery by Another Name* (New York: Doubleday, 2008), 175.

Chapter 11. Binding Up the Nation's Wounds, 1864

1. Francis B. Carpenter, *Six Months at the White House with Abraham Lincoln* (New York: Hurd and Houghton, 1866), 14–15.

2. Ibid., 15, 17, 19, 20.

3. Ibid., 17.

4. *CW*, 2:316.

5. Carpenter, *Six Months at the White House*, 47.

6. Ibid., 57.

7. Owen Lovejoy to Mary Denham, March 13, 1864, Lovejoy Papers, Clements.

8. Willie Lee Rose, *Rehearsal for Reconstruction: The Port Royal Experiment* (Indianapolis: Bobbs-Merrill, 1964), 201, 214.

9. McPherson, "Who Freed the Slaves?," 133.

10. *Christian Recorder*, April 30, 1864.

11. Thomas T. Davis in *Addresses on the Death of Owen Lovejoy*, 35. Sixteen colleagues, among them the key leaders of Congress, presented speeches in tribute to Lovejoy's personal and professional qualities. The University of Illinois has made them available at books.google.com/books?id=dqvhAAAAMAAJ.

12. Ruth Painter Randall, *Mary Lincoln: Biography of a Marriage* (Boston: Little, Brown, 1953), 356.

13. *HBB*, 408.

14. Daniel J. Bronstein and Harold M. Schulweis, eds., *Approaches to the Philosophy of Religion: A Book of Readings* (New York: Prentice-Hall, 1954), 234n.

15. Michael Epperson, "Mission Statement," 2008, http://www.csus.edu/cpns/about.html.

16. Don E. Fehrenbacher and Ward M. McAfee, *The Slaveholding Republic: An Account of the United States Government's Relations to Slavery* (Oxford: Oxford University Press, 2001), 311.

17. Eric Foner, *Fiery Trial*, xviii, xix.

18. Guelzo, *Lincoln's Emancipation Proclamation*, 26.

19. Elliott, "Owen Lovejoy"; Rose, *Rehearsal for Reconstruction*, 234.

20. Carpenter, *Six Months at the White House*, 17.

21. Sandburg, *Abraham Lincoln*, 64.

22. *HBB*, 411.

23. Owen Lovejoy to John Andrew, February 22, 1864, in *BCR*, May 5, 1864.

24. *CW*, 8:333.

25. *HBB*, 285.

26. Ibid., 394.

27. *CW*, 7:282, Abraham Lincoln to Albert G. Hodges, April 4, 1864.

28. Ibid., 8:333.

29. *Congressional Globe*, 38th Cong. 2nd sess., 531.

Index

abolitionists: antislavery, 13–14, 29–32, 38–39, 49; changed, 12, 29, 77, 159; critics of, 15, 30, 36, 40, 58; as denouncers of the South, 108; as fanatics, 2, 3, 38, 81; historians on, 6–7; immediatists, 28, 30; Lincoln supports, 77; as political extremists, 79, 132, 140; as radical, 99; religious, 30, 32, 79; as supporters of Lovejoy, 38, 64, 67, 114; as unworthy of respect, 127, 157; worrisome, 1, 40, 55. *See also* antislavery movement

African Americans: attitudes toward, 7, 24, 30, 51, 85, 86, 93, 117; August first celebrations, 121; and black churches, 130, 144, 147; causes of inequality of, 72; as equals, 12, 30, 60, 69, 71–72, 86, 99, 100; leaders, 51, 146, 147, 155; legal rights of, 14, 23, 30, 60, 72; as liberators, 117; and Lovejoy, 81, 117, 127, 130; positions of, on slavery, 51, 121, 144, 155–56; proposed resettling of, in Africa, 130; and reconstruction, 155; as soldiers, 4, 117, 118, 141, 144, 145; Whig view of, 12. *See also* amalgamation, racial; slavery: blacks' position on

African slave trade, 78, 80

Agnes (runaway slave), 52

Agricultural Department, 114, 118, 121, 128

Alton, Ill.: Lincoln condemns murder, 22; Lincoln-Douglas debate, 75; murder of Elijah P. Lovejoy, 2, 75, 90; residence of Owen Lovejoy, 29; Trumbull home, 14, 35; Usher Linder, 21, 22

Alton Observer, 22

amalgamation, racial, 60, 71, 81

American Anti-Slavery Society, 22, 29, 30, 32

American Colonization Society, 21

American Party. *See* Know-Nothings (American Party)

Amistad (ship), 58

Andrew, John, 157

Anti-Nebraska Party: Bloomington (1856), 40–43, 161; Democrats in, 14, 35, 36, 38, 49; Springfield convention (1854), 15, 25, 40, 48, 73. *See also* Republican Party

antislavery newspapers: *Alton Observer*, 22; *Emancipator*, 22; *Free West*, 16, 25; *Liberator*, 22, 29; *Western Citizen*, 161

antislavery movement: in campaigns, 69, 79; in Illinois, 2, 16, 19, 21–22, 25; Lincoln and, 13, 24, 26; Joseph Lovejoy and, 83–84; national, 4, 15, 30, 32; religion in, 19, 30, 32, 79. *See also* abolitionists

Arnold, Isaac, 35, 131; and Lincoln-Lovejoy relationship, 132, 135, 140

Ashley, John, 139

Aurora Guardian, 35

Bailey, David, 53

Bailey, Gamaliel, 80, 81

Baptists, 102

Barnes, Gilbert Hobbs, 31

battles: Ball's Bluff and Wilson's Creek, 126; Bull Run, 114, 115, 125, 126; Peninsula campaign, 140

Beard, Charles and Mary, 3, 4

Beecher, Rev. Edward, 90

Beecher, Rev. Henry Ward, 89–91

Bell, John, 102

Index

Bible: Esther, 94; Jonah, 127; Matthew 12:25, 68, Matthew 13:24–30, 127; Matthew 25:34–37, 47, 102; Micah 6:8, 92; Proverbs 29:18. 156, Psalm 98:6, 127; Timothy 2:28, 57
Bill of Rights, 21, 100
Bingham, John A., 119, 139
Bissell, William, 25, 35
blacks. *See* African Americans
Blanchard, Rev. Jonathan, 59
Blodgett, Henry, 34
Bloomington, Ill.: Anti-Nebraska Party convention (1856), 40–43, 161; Bolters' convention, 44–46; congressional district convention (1854), 13; meeting to endorse Lovejoy, 47
Bloomington Pantagraph, 96
Bloomington Weekly National Flag, 48
Blue, Frederick, 1, 4
bobsleds strategy: description of, 170n3; difficulty with, 46: and uneven political ground, 19, 36, 39, 40
Bolters, 44, 48; convention, 44–46
border states and slavery: congressmen on, 127, 129–30, 134–35; plans regarding, 131, 139
Bowen, Henry, 91
Breckenridge John C., 102, 109
Brown, John: Lovejoy's "wounded lion" speech, 84–86, 87, 160; punishment by hanging, 94, 177n45
Browne, Robert, 112
Browning, Orville: as Emancipation Proclamation opponent, 140, 143; as Illinois Whig leader, 34, 41; as Lincoln's friend, 41, 95, 97, 112
Bryant, Cyrus, 143
Bryant, Jane (former slave), 53
Bryant, John Howard: and Lincoln, xi, 44, 96, 108; supports Lovejoy, 35, 39, 44, 46, 96, 147
Bryant, William Cullen, 44, 92, 136
Buchanan, James, 61; and Dred Scott case, 61, 69; Homestead bill vetoed by, 88, 121; and Kansas statehood, 66, 75, 81; and northern Democrats, 78, 129; South supplied by, 109, 111
Bureau County Republican: defends Lovejoy, 114, 116, 128, 130; Lovejoy material, 71, 82, 119; Lincoln letter, xi
Butler, Gen. Benjamin F., 114

Calvinism, 3, 59
Cameron, Simon, 95, 115, 118–19
Carwardine, Richard: on Lincoln and evangelical Protestantism, 6, 29; position on Lincoln, 1, 55

Caton, John D. (judge), 52
Chase, Salmon, 92, 96
Cheever, Rev. George B., 129, 144
Chicago Daily Tribune, 141, 144
Chicago Democrat, 100
Chicago Press and Tribune, 96, 109
Chicago Tribune, 16, 34, 38, 40, 41
Child, Lydia Maria, 131
Christ, Lovejoy's views of, 93, 101, 136
Christianity, Lincoln's, 5, 7, 56. *See also* religion
Cinque (leader of Mendi Africans), 58
Civil War, slavery as cause of, 113–14, 121. *See also* war
Clay, Henry: as candidate for President, 44, 96; commitment to nonextension of slavery, 75, 100, 162; Illinois devotees of, 42; as Lincoln's idol, 17, 68; and Missouri Compromise, 17, 34, 68, 75, 100
Codding, Ichabod: critics of, 16; and Lincoln, 17; and Lovejoy, 15; as organizer in 1854 campaign, 13, 16, 25, 26, 159; as organizer in 1855 campaign, 19, 23, 34–36, 37; as organizer in 1860 campaign, 97; as speaker in 1856 campaign, 39
Colfax, Schuyler, 87, 89, 152
confiscation bills, 117, 118, 120, 133–35, 140, 158
Congregationalists: clergy, 90, 114, 144; General Association of Illinois Congregational Churches, 79, 90, 176n5; Hampshire Colony Church, 62, 79; Lovejoy as, 2, 19, 20, 102
Conkling, James C., 148–49
Conkling, Roscoe, 111
Cook, Burton C.: as anti-Nebraska Democrat, 35, 49; as Lovejoy backer, 44, 50, 65
Cooper Union, 81, 90–91, 136–37, 160
Copperhead plot, 152
Cowper, William (poet), 52, 58
Crissey, Elwell, 41
Crittenden, John: as friend of T. Lyle Dickey, 44, 83; offers compromise after Lincoln's election, 109; opposes Lincoln, 71, 76, 83; opposes Lovejoy's policies, 126, 133–35, 150
Cromwell, William, 53
Cunningham, J. O., 40
Cushman, Rev. Joshua, 20

Davis, David: as judge, 32; on Kansas, 48–49; as Lincoln's political associate, 26, 44, 64, 65, 95, 100; and Lovejoy's election, 47, 96
Davis, Jefferson, 112
Decatur, Ill.: editors' convention, 39–41; Lincoln and Lovejoy share platform (1856), 46; State Republican Presidential Nominating Convention (1860), 88

Index

191

Declaration of Independence: as basis of antislavery political parties, 2; as basis of Lincoln's political position, 45, 60, 61 79, 125; as basis of Lovejoy's political position, 28, 42, 47, 62, 90; and endowed rights, 54, 125, 152, 153, 159; reinterpretations of, 61, 62; in Republican Platform (1860), 95

democracy vs. despotism, Lovejoy on, 93

Democratic Party: and campaign of 1858, northern, 62, 64–67, 73, 78; and campaign of 1860, 98–100; and campaign of 1862, 141, 148; characterizations of, 82; and Dred Scott decision, 62, 78, 82; generals of, 126; and Kansas, 11, 66, 68; southern, 87, 102, 109

Democrats' views of slavery: northern, 38, 48, 65, 79–80, 83–84; southern, 68, 79–82, 84–85, 108;

depression, Lincoln's, 45, 76

Dickey, T. Lyle: and Eight Judicial Circuit, 24, 32; and Lincoln, 45, 65, 76, 83; and Lovejoy, 46, 47, 142; withdrawal of candidacy, 47, 48

District of Columbia, 152; emancipation in, 122, 129–31

Dodge, Mary Abigail (Gail Hamilton), 81

Donald, David Herbert, 5; on Lincoln, 59, 94, 95; on Lovejoy, 15

Douglas, Stephen A.: defeated in 1860, 102; followers support Lovejoy's opponent in 1862, 142; and Kansas-Nebraska Act, 11, 12, 14, 35; and Kansas statehood, 66; and Lincoln, 42, 59, 73–77, 79–80, 90, 110; Lovejoy warns against, 28, 42; supported by Republicans, 66, 67

Douglass, Frederick, 59, 87, 144; and black recruitment and promotion, 114, 146; on Stephen A. Douglas, 69; on emancipation, 114, 117; historic role of, 7, 84, 155; in Illinois antislavery movement, 59

Dred Scott decision: Buchanan's support of, 61; dissent of, 60; Douglas's response to, 62, 66, 159; effect upon elections, 78, 80–81; Lincoln and Lovejoy opposition to, 51–62, 66; northerners' outrage at, 68

Dubois, Jesse, 35, 88, 95

Dumond, Dwight, 30

Earle, Parker, 44, 46

Eastman, Zebina, 16, 34; distrust of Lincoln, 25; as organizer, 19, 23, 35

Easton, Rev. Hosea, 72

education, public. See public education

Edwards, Cyrus, 21

Eels, Rev. Richard, 52

Elliott, John Lovejoy, 157

emancipation: bill in House, 138–39, 142; constitutional debate over, 134–35, 138, 141; in D.C., 129–31; and escaping slaves, 144; gradual, 54, 118, 129, 135, 136, 137, 140; history of, 12, 30, 31, 54; humanity of, 68, 136; immediate, 68, 100; Lincoln and Lovejoy collaborating on, 1, 8, 130, 137, 150, 155–57; Lincoln's plans to achieve, 56, 69, 118, 120, 129, 141–42; Lovejoy's plans to achieve, 103, 122, 127, 135, 153; military necessity of, 117, 136, 145; in territories, 131; universal, 152. *See also appendix*

Emancipation Proclamation, 4–5, 158; celebration of, 143; effect of, 144, 149, 150; preliminary, 140–41; timing of, 140, 144

Emancipator (newspaper), 22

Emery, Enoch, 147

encroachment on northern rights, 21, 51, 53, 68

equality: Stephen A. Douglas on, 60, 69; Frederick Douglass on, 144; Hosea Easton on, 72; Garrisonians on, 12; Lincoln on, 61, 69, 71; Lovejoy on, 4, 71–72, 93, 99–101, 136. *See also* African Americans: as equals

Etheridge, Emerson, 152

evangelical Protestantism, 16, 29, 30–32, 55, 69, 152

Fehrenbacher, Don E., 15, 49, 156

Fell, Jesse, 46–48, 96, 102

Fillmore, Millard, 49

fire-eaters, 3, 78–79, 81, 84

Fladeland, Betty, 30

Franklin, John Hope, 4

Free Democratic Party: antislavery faction in political fusion, 25, 34, 35, 67; Illinois formation of, 2, Illinois leaders of, 35; Lovejoy and, 16, 23, 40; national, 23, 40, 52; neglect of, 16

freedom of religion, 21, 86, 100

Free Soil Party: leaders, 23; and Liberty Party, 30; Lovejoy and, 2, 23, 40, 88

Free Soil sentiment: as common ground, 14, 24, 25; influence of, 88, 95

Frémont, John: campaign for presidency, 43–46; Millard Fillmore and, 49; Lincoln and, 48; Lovejoy and, 116, 162, 181n45; in Missouri, 115

Fugitive Slave Act of 1850: Lincoln and Lovejoy disagree on, 32, 33, 43; Lincoln's position characterized, 73, 110; Lovejoy's resolution for repeal, 25, 27; modification of, 14, 24

Fugitive Slave laws: Lovejoy and, 2, 114, 120, 167n1; Lincoln and, 2, 14, 33, 34

Funk, Isaac, 44, 48

192 *Index*

Garrison, William Lloyd, 29–32, 55, 59; Lovejoy letter to, 156
Garrisonians, 30–32, 70, 79
General Association of Illinois Congregational churches, 79, 90, 176n5
German Americans, 41, 42, 97, 101
Giddings, Joshua, 54, 72, 95; and John Brown, 85–87; and Lincoln, 15, 16, 23–24, 54–55
God's truth, 69, 100
God's will, 150–51
Grant, Ulysses S., 7, 145, 155, 160
Gridley, Asahel, 44, 46
Grow, Galusha, 118, 139
Guelzo, Allen C., 6; on Lincoln's Christianity, 5, 7, 56; on Lincoln's defeat in 1858, 76; on Lincoln's prudence, 5–6, 55, 143; on radicals, 6, 7, 15, 32, 137, 157
Gurley, Rev. John A., 116, 181n45

Haiti, 119, 121
Halleck Order No. 3, 121
Halleck, Henry W., 118, 121
Hamlin, Hannibal, 119
Hammond, James Henry, 107, 108
Hardin, John J., 20
Hampshire Colony Congregational Church (Princeton, Ill.), 62, 79
Harris, N. Dwight, 38, 49
Hatch, Ozias, 35, 88, 95
Helper, Hinton R., 87
Henderson, Thomas, 142
Herndon, William, 66, 76
Hogan, Rev. John, 21
Hoge, Jane, 150
Holly, Myron, 14
homestead bill, 88, 121, 128
honor: appeals to, 42, 113; Lovejoy's, 82; southern, 108;
Howard, Victor, 34

Illinois, slaves in, 52
Illinois General Assembly, 2, 16, 19, 161; Lovejoy in, 16–18, 23–27
Illinois Republican Party: at Bloomington Anti-Nebraska convention (1856), 34, 40, 42, 45; in Bureau County (1856), 44, 67; factions of, 8, 15, 18, 26, 34–36; Lincoln and, 36, 38, 42, 43, 49; nominating convention (1858), 67; in Springfield (1854), 14–15, 25, 33, 35, 40, 45, 73
Illinois State Antislavery Society, 21–22
Illinois Supreme Court, on slave transit law, 51–52
Illinois Union League, 148–49

Ingersoll, Ebon, 158

Jefferson, Thomas, 89
Joliet, Ill., 46
Joliet Signal, 38
Jones, John, 146
Judd, Norman, 43, 49, 88, 94, 95

Kansas: David Davis on, 48–49; Stephen Douglas on statehood policy, 66–67, 75; effect on election and platform, 81, 95; Lincoln speaks in, 85
Kansas-Nebraska Act: Stephen Douglas's claims, 28, 67; efforts for repeal, 11, 35, 159; opposition to, 17, 19, 27, 38, 68; passage of, 11, 13, 20; slavery issue agitated, 65
Kellogg, William, 110
Kelsey, Charles L., 44
Know-Nothings (American Party): campaign of 1860, 95, 101, 103; characteristics of, 35; Lincoln and, 17, 34–36, 88, 95, 103; Lovejoy and, 34–36, 41, 42, 101
Koerner, Gustave: as German American leader, 35, 95; as surrogate campaigner for Lincoln, 97; in Union Army, 116

Lacon, Ill., 46
Laing, William, 147
Lamon, Ward, 24, 32, 70; slaves returned to masters by, 118
Lane, James, 118, 147
language, religious: Lincoln's use of, 6, 29, 48, 55; Lincoln's use of biblical, 68, 69, 157; Lincoln's use of romantic, 56–59
Lanphier, Charles, 17, 27
law, higher, 2, 33, 55, 160
Leavitt, Joshua, 22, 32
Legins-Costly, Nance (indentured servant), 53
Leibnitz, Gottfried Wilhelm, 156
Liberator, 22, 29
Liberia, 119, 121
Liberty Party: David Davis's disdain of, 96; Illinois founding of, 2, 14, 23, 160;; Lovejoy and, 2, 20, 23, 40, 96; policies of, 14, 28, 30, 55, 131; national founding of, 32, remnants of, 35
Lincoln, Abraham:
—candidacy for U.S. Senate (1855): deal with republicans, 26–27; strategy for, 16, 17, 23–26
—candidacy for U.S. Senate (1858): and antislavery wing, 64–67, 70; campaign, 42, 43, 62, 67; causes of defeat, 67, 76, 77; and Douglas, 66, 73–76, 78; responses to, 69, 77

Index

—candidacy for U.S. Presidency: campaign of 1860, 91, 92, 94, 96–102; early activities for, 79, 80; preparing for the election, 88–94; reasons for victory in Illinois, 102–3; responses to John Brown's uprising, 85

—legislative initiatives, 120, 121, 128

—and Lovejoy: and abolitionism, 29, 30; behind-the-scenes support of, 65, 70, 96; as collaborator, 7, 19, 45, 96, 109, 155; difference in campaign tactics, 45, 46, 49; encouraging supporters of, 69, 80; endorsed by, 70, 96; friendship, 125, 131, 132, 155, 157; leery of reputation of, 1, 11, 12, 15, 31; Lovejoy's early political support of, 15, 18, 48, 68, 111; Lovejoy's public support of, 97, 102, 135, 136–38, 149, 150; mutual esteem of, 27, 29, 37, 72, 112; trust between, 1, 2, 34, 44, 65, 158

—as radical: commitment to end slavery, 56, 142, 155–57; in Congress, 54, 55; statements of, 5, 6, 16, 17, 24

—and radicals, 1, 5, 6, 8, 13, 14; as colleagues, 3, 4, 7; and fugitive slave laws, 32–34; as hampered by, 3, 7, 30

—traits of character: capacity for growth, 7, 31, 48; cautious, 34, 36, 37; courageous, 31; desire for esteem, 19, 46; forgiving vs. unforgiving, 17, 83; guileless, 95; intellectual, 5, 94;kind-hearted, 154; loyal, 2; moral, 5, 6, 31; perceptive, 81; pragmatic, 4, 5, 6, 16, 87; principled, 78; procrastinator, 26; prudent, 17, 31, 55; self-reliant, 95; shrewd, 20, 40, 95; trustworthy, 56, 78;

—and Whigs: as elected official, 11, 16, 20; identification with, 25, 32, 39, 49, 55, 71; as leader, 2, 11, 12, 13, 15; uncertainty about, 17, 20

Lincoln, Mary Todd: on death of Lovejoy, 156; engagement of, 56; as First Lady, 131; as political supporter of husband, 17, 21, 78, 94, 107

Lincoln, Willie, 132

Linder, Usher, 21, 22

Logan, John, 112

Logan, Stephen T., 26

Lovejoy, Daniel (father), 20; suicide of, 57

Lovejoy, Elijah (brother): and Edward Beecher, 90; mob killing of, 21–22, 75; responses of Owen to, 12, 22, 49; speech by Codding on, 39

Lovejoy, Eunice Storrs Denham (wife), 94, 131–32, 146

Lovejoy, Joseph (brother), 21, 83–84

Lovejoy, Owen

—bills introduced by: Agricultural Department, 114, 118, 121, 128; confiscation bill, 120, 133–35, 140; criminalization of slavery, 153; D.C. emancipation, 122, 129–30; equal pay for Negro soldiers, 145; Halleck Order No. 3, 121; homestead bill, 88, 128; prohibition of return of fugitive slaves, 114, 120; recognition of Haiti and Liberia, 119, 121; tendering thanks to Capt. Wilkes, 120; universal emancipation, 153

—congressional committees chaired by: Agricultural, 114, 118, 121, 128; District of Columbia, 152; Public Lands, 88, 127, 161; Territories, 131, 162

—elections, 1854, 23; 1856, 45; 1858, 76; 1860, 102; 1862, 142

—as farmer, 88

—health/illness/death, 12, 146–48, 152, 154, 155

—and Lincoln: agreement on policies, 53, 107, 110, 148, 154; differences on policies, 29, 32–34, 60, 72, 103, 118; as friends, 112, 147–48, 154, 157–58; Lincoln's support for Lovejoy, 16, 23, 26–27, 45, 70, 96; Lovejoy's strategies supporting Lincoln, 15, 23–27, 79, 118; Lovejoy's testimonials for Lincoln, 70, 96, 137, 150; and radical/pragmatic axis, 1, 7–8, 142, 156; trust between, 1–2, 7–8, 77

—marriage, 131–32, 146

—military experience: as colonel, 133–39; as observer, 126, 148

—ministry: antislavery, 32, 79, 101, 102, 176n5; in Congress, 62, 84, 94, 127; in Princeton, Ill., 2, 3, 19, 79, 90; sermon, 57–59

—patriotism of, 125, 133

—traits of character: extremist, 18, 48; fiery, 15; honest, 154; intellectual, 156; level-headed, 28, 81, 83, 86; politically effective, 2, 12, 16, 23, 28; radical/pragmatic, 156; thief, 82; unintimidated, 46, 47, 49, 86, 93, 98, 99

—views on slavery: effects of, 71–72, 82, 85, 100, 153; horror of, 12, 51, 60, 82–83, 127; methods of resisting, 29, 31, 36, 58, 69–70, 99, 116–17; need to address openly, 89, 93; nonextension of, 11, 13–14, 25–27, 36, 45, 99, 110

Lovejoy, Owen Glendower (son), 132

Lovejoy, Sarah Moody (wife of Joseph), 83

Magdol, Edward, 1, 4, 8, 27

Martin, Elbert S., 94

Mason, James M., 120

Matson, Robert, 53

McClellan, George B., 140

Index

McClun, J. E., 48
McPherson, James M., 4, 127, 155
Medill, Joseph, 41, 76, 109, 144
Methodist Church, 37, 79, 144
Miller, Anson, 25
Miller, William Lee, 6
miscegenation. *See* amalgamation, racial
Missouri Compromise: Henry Clay and, 17, 34, 68, 75, 100; Stephen Douglas and, 35, 68, 75; Lincoln and Lovejoy on its restoration, 27, 28, 32, 33; restoration advocated, 11–14; role of Maine, 21, 167n10
Morgan Journal, 14, 40
Morrill, Justin, 128
Morrill Act, 128

Nance (indentured servant), 53
National Era, 80, 81
National Thanksgiving Praise and Prayer, 151
National Union League of America, 147
Neely, Mark, 4, 5
New York Evening Post, 92
New York Herald, 87
New York Independent, 91
New York Times, 134, 136
New York Tribune, 66, 82, 92, 130
Norton, Jesse, 24

Olin, Abram, 133
Ottawa, Ill., 46

Pacheco, Antonio, 54–55
Pacific Railroad bill, 128
Palmer, John, 35, 43, 49, 97, 101
Parker, Joel, 2, 22
Parker, Theodore, 32
Parsons, Theophilus, 116
Patriot (newspaper), 14
Peck, Rev. John Mason, 21, 22
Pennington, William, 87, 92–93
Phillips, Wendell, 129
Pierce, Franklin, 39, 69
Pinsker, Matthew, 1, 7, 166n42
Plymouth Congregational Church (Brooklyn, N.Y.), 89–91
politics and religion, 55, 57–59, 91
Porter, Albert, 136
prayer, 39, 151
property in man: American Anti-Slavery Society, 30; confiscation bills, 117, 158; John Crittenden on, 134; Lincoln and Lovejoy on, 28, 51; Lincoln's view of, 91, 53–55, 119, Lovejoy's view of, 61–62, 68, 100, 121, 129, 135; Alexander Stevens on, 108

Protestantism, evangelical. *See* evangelical Protestantism
providence, 7
Pryor, Roger, 93
public education, Lovejoy on, 17, 72, 100, 102, 130, 155
public lands, 88, 127, 161

Quincy Whig, 35, 36

race, 61, 72. *See also* African Americans
Randall, James G., 3, 5
Ray, Charles H., 25–26, 34, 42; and Decatur editors' meeting, 39, 40, 41
reconstruction, 145–46, 155
religion: in antislavery movement, 19, 32; divine power, 39, 126; influence on Lincoln's southern policy, 125; Lincoln's sense of divine assistance, 7, 112, 151, 158; Lincoln's sense of divine repentance, 151, 152, 157, 158; Lincoln's skepticism, 5, 6, 7, 150; prayer, 39, 151. *See also* Congregationalists; evangelical Protestantism; language, religious; Lovejoy, Owen: ministry; politics and religion

repentance: divine, 151, 152, 157, 158; of nation, 30, 86, 125, 144, 151–52, 158, 162
Republican Party, Lovejoy as builder of (chronological): formation, 11, 13–23, 34–38; Pittsburgh convention, 38–39; Bloomington convention, 40; Philadelphia convention, 42; nomination to Congress, 43–48; 1858 campaign, 62–77; 1860 campaign, 96, 98–102; during secession crisis, 109–11; Thirty-seventh Congress, 113–14, 116–28; 1862 campaign, 141–42. *See also* Illinois Republican Party
Republican Party National Conventions: February 1856, 38, 42; June 1856, 39, 42, 43; presidential nominating, June 1860, 96, 97
Republicans' views of slavery: conservative, 79, 110, 138–39; platform, 95; radical, 75, 79, 110, 139;
Robinson, Armstead, 143

Sandburg, Carl, 3, 157
Schneider, George, 35, 97
Schurz, Carl, 102
Scott, Dred and Harriet, 51. *See also* Dred Scott decision
secession, 98, 107–8, 109, 111, 114, 116, 125
Selby, Paul, 14, 15, 40, 41

Index

Seward, William: as candidate for 1860 presidential nomination, 79, 85, 91, 96; as Secretary of State, 112, 120, 140; supported Lincoln for president, 96–97, 109, 110

Sherman, John, 87

Sherman, Gen. William, 114

slaveholders: accusations from, 69; felt threatened, 81–82, 119, 137, 143, 155; intent to strengthen slavery, 60; intimidation by, 21, 51; Lincoln's dealings with, 117, 119, 127, 129, 140; Lovejoy on, 81, 98, 127, 135, 137; race as a weapon of, 72

Slave Power: Lincoln's responses to, 13, 69, 99; Lovejoy's responses to, 28, 55, 84, 87, 93; Maine confronts, 167n10

slave transit law, Illinois Supreme Court on, 51–52

slavery: abolitionists' position on, 22, 29–30, 32, 38, 58; and benevolent master, 84; blacks' position on, 117, 121, 144, 155–56; constitutional limitations of, 27, 62, 75, 93, 131, 134; demise of, 143; economic argument of, 4; Founders' positions on, 27, 80, 135; history of, 60, 82; Lincoln and Lovejoy's views on nonextension of, 11–12, 25–26, 31, 36, 99; protections for, 30, 91, 133; and re-enslavement, 153; as sin against God, 29–30, 69, 73, 92, 99, 151; as wrong in Lincoln's view, 28, 31, 61, 68–69, 108; as wrong in Lovejoy's view, 28, 60, 90, 93, 99. *See also* border states and slavery; Democrats' views of slavery; emancipation; property in man; Republicans' views of slavery

Slidell, John, 120

Smith, Gerrit, 114, 133

South Carolina Sea Islands, 155

southern policy, Lincoln's, 125

southern theology, 61, 84, 125, 151–52

Speed, Joshua, 37, 56, 154

Springfield, Ill. (chronological): anti-Nebraska/Republican Convention (1854), 15, 25, 40, 48, 73; Lincoln's home, 2, 11, 19, 88, 94, 107, 111–12, 132; (1855), 36; Lincoln and Lovejoy share platform (1856), 46; State Republican Nominating Convention (1858), 67; Union League Convention of (1863), 149

Springfield Register, 67

Springfield State Journal, 35, 66

Stampp, Kenneth M., 4

Stanton, Edwin, 109

Stanton, Henry, 32

Stephens, Alexander, 107–8

Stephens, George E., 144, 185n6

Stevens, Thaddeus: as chair of House Ways and Means Committee, 129; delayed compromise with South, 111; as friend of Lovejoy, 112 144, 145–46; and Negro regiment, 144; praised Lincoln, 7, 113; and reconstruction, 145–46

Stewart, Alvan, 14, 32

Stewart, James Brewer, 4

Stowe, Harriet Beecher, 90

Stuart, John T., 20

Sumner, Charles, 48, 51, 89; Lovejoy's death, 156; urging Lincoln to act, 120, 131, 146

Swett, Leonard, 24, 32, 44, 46, 94

Taney, Roger: as Chief Justice of the Supreme Court, 51, 69, 138; constitutional interpretation of slavery, 51, 59–62, 134; false religious claims by, 61–62; as voice of the Slave Power, 69

Tappan, Lewis, 32, 91

territories, 131, 162

Thanksgiving, 151

theology, southern, 61, 84, 125, 151–52

Todd, Rev. David, 114

Trefousse, Hans, 1, 4

Tremont House, 49

Trent affair, 120

Trumbull, Lyman: anti-compromise with South, 110; anti-Douglas, 46, 66; anti-Nebraska Democrat, 14, 35, 36, 38; defender of runaway slaves, 52; land-grant bill, 128; Lincoln supports, 27; supports Lincoln, 43, 66, 97, 110; supports Lovejoy, 97

Turner, Jonathan Baldwin, 128

Turner, Thomas J., 24–26, 49

Underground Railroad, Lovejoy's participation in, 2, 33, 38, 82, 99–100, 160

Union League of America, 147–48, 149, 160

Urbana, Ill., 46

U.S. Constitution, on slaves and laborers, 24, 27, 32, 33, 62, 75, 93, 131, 134. *See also* Bill of Rights; emancipation: constitutional debate over

U.S. House of Representatives

—legislation: confiscation bill, 120, 184n80; D.C. emancipation bill, 129–31; Negro recruitment bill, 144–45; Second Confiscation Act, 140–41; territories, bill prohibiting slavery in, 131

—major committees: Agricultural, 121; Commerce, 139; Judiciary, 139, Public Lands, 88, 161; Territorial, 139; Ways and Means Committee, 112

U.S. Sanitary Commission, 150

Index

U.S. Supreme Court: Dred Scott decision, 51–63; Emancipation Proclamation, 153; Second Confiscation bill, 138

Vallandigham, Clement L, 121, 130
Vaughan, John C., 34, 39

war: conduct of, 126; possibility of, 112; powers, 116–17, 136, 140, 141; slavery as cause of, 113–14, 121. *See also* battles
Washburn, Israel, 13
Washburne, Elihu, 23–26; as correspondent with Lincoln, 23, 43, 110; as leader in House of Representatives, 111, 139; and Stephen A. Douglas, 66
Washington Temperance Society, 56–57
Weld, Theodore, 31–32
Wells, Gideon, 140
Wentworth, John: at Bloomington Convention, 42, 46; as Chicago Republican strongman, 88, 94, 95, 100; as former anti-Nebraska Democrat, 49
Whigs (chronological): Lincoln's hopes for, 11–14; Lincoln's uncertainty of, 17, 19, 37; Lincoln as Congressman of, 20, 54; former, 22, 24; Illinois conservative, 32, 69, 78, 98, 142; Illinois election 1854, 16, 17; role in fusion process, 34–38, 49; role in

1855 U.S. Senate election, 25, 26, 36, 74; anti-Nebraska and Republican Conventions (1856), 40, 41, 43; election of 1856, 40–43; election of 1858, 75–77, 98–100
White, Horace, 37
Whitney, Henry, 32, 65
Whittier, John Greenleaf, 31
Wickliffe, Charles A., 126, 127, 130–31
Wide Awakes, 97–98
Wilkes, Capt. Charles, 120, 153
Willard, Julius A., 52
Williams, Archibald, 34–37, 41
Williams, T. Harry, 3
Wilson, Henry, 129, 145
Winger, Stewart, 5, 6, 57
women: political participation by, 98, 101–2; suffrage, 30
Wordsworth, William, 86
Wright, Erastus, 13
Wright, Samuel G., 84
Wycliffe, John, 86

Yancey, William L., 81
Yates, Richard: as Lincoln supporter, 95, 97; as possible Senate candidate, 25; as Union League convention advocate, 148; and Union troops, 113; as Whig member of Congress, 34

WILLIAM F. MOORE and JANE ANN MOORE are co-directors of the Lovejoy Society. They are the editors of Lovejoy's *His Brother's Blood: Speeches and Writings, 1838–64*. They manage the website www.increaserespect.com, which applies the concepts of this book.

The University of Illinois Press
is a founding member of the
Association of American University Presses.

University of Illinois Press
1325 South Oak Street
Champaign, IL 61820-6903
www.press.uillinois.edu